The Adelaide House

1836 to 1901

End papers: Map of the County of Adelaide and
surrounding districts, 1850. *(State Library of S.A.)*

The Adelaide House

1836 to 1901

The evolution of principal dwelling types

Stefan Pikusa

Wakefield Press

© Text and Illustrations: Stefan Pikusa, 1986

Published in 1986 by
Wakefield Press
282 Richmond Rd, Netley
South Australia, 5037

Wholly set up and produced in Adelaide, South Australia
Design and Production: Peter Chappell
Cover Design: Joe Benke
Indexer: Mary Pikusa
Photo-typesetting: Delmont Pty Ltd
Printing: K.B. Printing Services Pty Ltd
Binding: Advance Bookbinders Pty Ltd

National Library of Australia
Cataloguing-in-Publication entry

Pikusa, Stefan
The Adelaide House 1836 to 1901,
The evolution of principal dwelling types.

Bibliography.
includes index.
ISBN 0 949268 73 9.

1. Architecture, domestic—South Australia—Adelaide—History.
2. Dwellings—South Australia—Adelaide—History. I. Title.

728'.0994231.

Unless otherwise acknowledged all illustrations are by the author.

150

1836 SOUTH AUSTRALIA 1986

©

A South Australian Jubilee 150 Publication

STEFAN PIKUSA was born in Poland and educated in Warsaw and at the Polish Technical College, Hamburg, where he graduated with a diploma in building design. He came to Australia in 1950 and subsequently studied architecture at the University of Adelaide. In 1962 he graduated with First Class Honours and was awarded the South Australian Gas Company Prize in Architecture. After several years in architectural practice he returned to the University as a lecturer, and later, senior lecturer. His research in the field of domestic architecture has been concerned mainly with the interaction between the user and dwelling design, the adaptability of Australian houses and the functional influences in European vernacular architecture.

Stephen Pikusa is a Fellow of the Royal Australian Institute of Architects and was Dean of the Faculty of Architecture and Planning at the University of Adelaide (1980–82). He is the author of *Homes Before Houses: let users influence design* (1975) and *Designing Dwellings for Human Activity* (1979). He acted as consultant to J. N. Persse and D. M. Rose, *House Styles in Adelaide: a pictorial history* (1982), and is the author of "The Cottage: an architectural commentary" in Joseph Elliott, *Our Home in Australia: a description of cottage life in 1860* (1984). His articles have been published in professional and other journals.

Acknowledgements

My thanks go firstly to the University of Adelaide for making research time available, and to the South Australia Jubilee 150 Board for granting a subsidy for this publication. Special thanks are due to the owners and occupiers of numerous Adelaide houses who opened their doors to me and shared useful information. Without their willing co-operation my research could not have been completed.

I am grateful to all of the following people and organisations who gave of their time and knowledge: Art Gallery of S.A.; Australian Bureau of Statistics; Barr Smith Library; Corporation of the City of Adelaide, Edward T. Baulderstone; Birdwood Mill Museum; Botanic Garden and State Herbarium; Department of Environment and Planning, State Heritage Branch; Department of Lands; Department of Mines and Energy; Engineering and Water Supply Department; David Gilbert; Malcolm Reid & Co. Ltd.; Mortlock Library of South Australiana; National Library of Australia; Penfolds Wines Pty. Ltd.; Public Record Office of S.A.; Regency Park Community College, School of Plumbing; S.A. Gas Co.; Simpson Ltd.; Telecommunications Museum; George Tucker; Unley City Council; Gavin Walkley; Arnold Weidenhofer.

For giving their permission to publish original architectural drawings used in the illustrations I gratefully acknowledge: Jackman Gooden Architects for drawings by Thomas English, Daniel Garlick, George K. Soward and Rowland Rees; Woods Bagot Architects for drawings by Edward J. Woods; Helen and Peter Reilly for drawings by Henry C. Richardson; South Australian Department of Housing and Construction for drawings by George T. Light; and the South Australian Gas Company.

I am also indebted to Necia Gilbert for the use of photographs taken by the late Stephen Gilbert, to Reginald and Anne Bluff for historical photographs of 'Heywood', and to Jeff Tomlinson and Trevor Fox of the University of Adelaide for their fine photographic work.

S.P.

Contents

Preface   page. **1**

Chapter 1   **Early Shelters: 1836–1842**   **3**

  Foundations   3
  Allocation and speculation   3
  Tents, huts and bowers   4
  The Recollections of William Finlayson   6
  Kingston's Adelaide of 1842   10
  Evaluation of a sample area   12

Chapter 2   **Small Detached Cottages: 1836–1860**   **19**

  British origins   19
  Cottages in Adelaide   22
  The two room cottage   23
    von Mueller Cottage, 1849   25
    Thebarton Cottage, c.1869   26
  The three room cottage   27
    Hampton Cottage, c.1860   30
    Griffin Cottage, c.1855   31
    Gatekeeper's Cottage, 1865   32

Chapter 3   **Row Cottages and Maisonettes: 1836–1901**   **35**

  Definitions   35
  The row cottage   35
    Gray's Row, pre-1841   39
    Paxton Square Rows, 1849–52   39
    Tiver's Row, 1856   43
    Calder's Row, pre-1858   44
    Parker's Row, 1878–79   46
    Paterson's Row, 1897   47
  The maisonette   48
    City Maisonettes, 1894   50
    Kent Town Maisonettes, 1892   51

Chapter 4   **Detached Houses: 1850–1901**   **55**

A house in the suburbs   55
Public utilities   58
Building materials and methods   59
  Elliott House, 1856   66
  'The Almonds', 1850   68
  'Heywood', c.1858   70
  Para Para Lodge, 1880   73
  Botanic Garden Lodge, 1866   73
  Rounsevell House, c.1875   73
  Delano House, c.1884   78
  Lathlean House, 1877   78
  Rugless House, c.1895   79
  Lucas House, 1897   83
  Maesday House, 1906   83
  Noltenius House, 1900   85
Furnishings and household appliances, c.1901   88

Chapter 5   **Terraces and Semi-Detached Houses: 1850–1901**   **93**

The terraced house   93
  Terrace of three houses, c.1868   97
  Terrace of seven houses, c.1872   100
  'Alexandra Terrace', c.1876   102
  'Marine Residences', 1885   106
  Terrace of four houses, 1897   108
The semi-detached, double-storey house   109
  Pair of houses, Adelaide, 1891   113
  Pair of houses, Glenelg, 1883   116

Notes and Sources   **119**

List of Colour Plates and Illustrations   **127**

Index   **129**

Preface

The changing form of the Adelaide house between 1836 and 1901 is a physical expression of the city's colonial development. South Australia was founded on Utopian principles, yet the virgin bush that confronted newly arrived settlers often proved far from idyllic. Nevertheless, in a span of time almost equivalent to that of her reign, Queen Victoria's distant subjects in South Australia created an elegant Victorian city notable for its distinctive architecture. This book explores the manner in which those nineteenth century Adelaidians solved the fundamental question of housing in the developing city. It traces the evolutionary path of the colonial house and investigates some of the influences that shaped its design.

Adelaide has a long-standing reputation for being different from other Australian capitals. Readily recognised are the qualities of Adelaide's preconceived plan with the belt of parklands separating the city from its suburbs. However, other regional characteristics that distinguish the urban fabric of the city are less discernible. These more subtle differences, that emanate from the history of European settlement, or stem from the city's natural environment, are often overlooked in any general discussion of Australian architecture.

The founding immigrants to South Australia were free men and women, proud of the fact that their chosen land was never a penal colony. Indeed, it was not a colony at all but a British province where full enjoyment of civil and religious liberties was guaranteed. Thus, freedom of thought and action characterised individual endeavour from the very outset. For the first hundred years or so, South Australia depended upon agriculture and mineral discoveries for its progress and prosperity. The absence of bountiful hinterlands capable of producing the wealth necessary for rapid urban expansion meant that Adelaide experienced none of the spectacular surges of growth that swelled cities like Sydney or Melbourne. Instead, colonial Adelaide grew up more gradually, and its citizens had to rely mainly on their own resources, their dedication to puritan values and simple hard work.

During the city's formative years, both professional and amateur builders drew heavily on traditional designs and building methods imported from the British Isles. Subsequent technical innovations and adaptations arose either from necessity, or as a spontaneous response to the colonial experience. Links were always very strong between Britain and the new province, where new European inventions and a wide range of manufactured products gained ready acceptance. British influence in architectural design was perpetuated by the first generation of Adelaide architects, most of whom had emigrated from the British Isles. A number of leading architects whose work is illustrated in this book—George Kingston, Thomas English, Daniel Garlick and James Woods—all began their training overseas and maintained personal contacts with the mother country.

My interest lies not in the already well-documented mansions of colonial gentry, but rather in the dwelling houses of ordinary people. For reasons of precision the scope of this book is confined mainly to the Adelaide district and the discussion of the 'urban' house. (The houses at Burra are included because of their special significance and because no suitable plans or sources could be found for their counterparts in Adelaide.) While ordinary houses made up the great bulk of the built environment of the developing city, they have to date received only scant attention, usually confined to their visual appeal. In the pages that follow we go beyond the street facade. We enter into the private domain of Adelaide pioneers and explore their domestic environment.

Drawings of floor plans and sections through buildings are used extensively with the text. They highlight the design in three dimensions and explain the working of a particular house. In this way the drawings expose the organic nature of a house plan and demonstrate the manner in which it gradually evolves in response to the changing needs and aspirations of its owner and/or occupier. The plan is a reflection of prevailing social customs and the lifestyle of the householder who often participated actively in its design. Collectively, floor plans can also be seen as the prime generator of the urban architectural form of the city.

The book comprises five chapters divided according to house types and their period of construction. The first chapter deals with early shelters of all descriptions. In the remaining chapters, specific dwelling types are classified and discussed under different headings. The evolution of house types is traced through a series of selected case studies that are considered on a comparative basis. The emphasis is placed on aspects of design and planning, siting and land use, construction methods and domestic services. The illustrated examples are typical of house designs built in large numbers over extended periods of time. They are presented in chronological order so that design trends can be observed. Where there are widely differing standards within a classification, examples from both ends of the scale are shown. The major variants of the principal plan types are also included.

However, it is not my intention, nor would it be particularly useful, to cover all the minor derivations of plan types, or the minutiae of their stylistic decoration. Such considerations are peripheral to this study. The questions examined here are more fundamental. What were the principal dwelling types? How did a particular house plan originate? How was it used? How spacious was it and what was it built of? How was it affected by the introduction of public amenities? What new designs evolved from it? My investigations do not pretend to provide all the answers, but they go a long way towards re-opening the doors of the Adelaide colonial house for our inspection and appraisal. It is only with an imaginative appreciation of the whole design that we are better able to understand the exterior that is presented to the street, and follow the course of plan development.

The original, and previously unpublished, architectural drawings which illustrate the text provide the essential medium for tracing the evolutionary path of the Adelaide house. Interpretation of these working drawings and other original sources of information form the basis of individual case studies. This firsthand design information includes the work of some of Adelaide's first architects. The coloured reproductions are testimony to the fine quality of their drawings, originally rendered in indian ink and water–colour washes on Whatman's hot pressed cartridge paper. Drawings by the author of other plans are based either on measured surveys of extant structures or authentic descriptions of those no longer in existence.

From the settler's hut to the imposing Federation house every dwelling is an expression of the taste, preferences and constraints that determined its physical form. It is hoped that this exposition of the Adelaide house in its formative era will fill a large gap in the history of Australian domestic architecture. Like most historical endeavours it helps us to understand better the character of today's product and make decisions on future directions.

Stefan Pikusa,
Adelaide, July, 1986.

Chapter 1

Early Shelters

1836–1842

Foundations

The story of the Adelaide house begins with the first allocation of land and the basic concept of private ownership enshrined in the original proposal for the colonisation of South Australia. The scheme envisioned by Edward Gibbon Wakefield involved the sale of free-hold colonial land and the creation of a vigorous agrarian community. It was intended that the colonists would convey from the old world to the new an orderly, well organised and ready-made civilised society. Wakefield's underlying idea was not to 'rear a sapling', but to 'transplant a full-grown tree'.[1]

Although the development of agricultural land was to be the principal endeavour in the new colony, prospective settlers were offered the added inducement of cheap city property. When sales of the unknown and as yet unsurveyed land commenced in London at the beginning of 1835, the purchase of every 80 acre-section of rural land brought with it the right to purchase, at the same price, an acre of land in the proposed capital. Poor preliminary sales forced the Colonizing Commissioners to reduce the unit price from £1 to the minimum of 12s. per acre permitted by the Foundation Act while at the same time increasing the size of each rural section to 134 acres.[2] Sales of rural land subsequently resulted in options being held on 437 of the thousand or so acres of town land to be provided in Adelaide. After these town acres had been taken up the residue were to be sold at public auction.

Free-hold land, whether for private use, investment or speculation, would have been unattainable for most of the immigrants in their country of birth. Suddenly, in the new Province of South Australia, the ideal of a house on one's own piece of land became a reality and a manifestation of the great Australian dream.

The planned development of the new colony did not eventuate. In fact, the survey and development of town acres proceeded at an unprecedented rate while the bulk of rural land languished—unsurveyed, unallocated, unoccupied and, consequently, unproductive. The intrigues and contentions of early colonial administrators do not fall within the scope of this work, yet the fact remains that it was the town acres and not the all important country lands which the surveyors were to lay out first. Delays in carrying out country surveys in 1837 and 1838 resulted in pioneer settlers and their families remaining on their city acres while waiting to take up agricultural land. The continual arrival of other immigrants further boosted the urban population of the embryonic city, adding to the already intense demand for public works, housing and basic shelter. When the second Governor, Lieutenant-Colonel George Gawler, arrived in October, 1838, nearly four-fifths of the whole population were crowded into the infant capital. High prices for scarce imported foodstuffs, coupled with high labour costs, jointly aggravated the economic situation. With its heavy concentration of a largely unproductive population, the city proved fertile ground for speculation in land and building. Under these circumstances land prices soared, building boomed and the development of Adelaide became the most prominent feature during the formative years of the colony, prior to the mid-1840s.[3]

Allocation and speculation

By the beginning of March, 1837, the survey and staking of town acres was complete. Under the direction of the Surveyor-General, Colonel William Light, the 700 one-acre allotments in South Adelaide (the present city, south of the River Torrens) and the 342 similar allotments in North Adelaide were laid out in the remarkably short time of just two months. At the end of March, holders of preliminary land orders chose their 437 lots, the priority of choice being determined by ballot. The remaining unselected acres designated for private use, in streets and squares which remained unnamed until May, were sold at public auction to 'resident' and 'absentee' purchasers at an average price of just over £6 an acre.[4] Thus, the conclusion of the first Adelaide land sales marked the establishment of a 'land-owning' class in the new colonial society. And, as land soon became a great source of wealth and respectability, so the drive to own property became intense. Accounts of the 1830s and 1840s indicate that much of the politics and wealth of the Australian colonies were tied to the laws controlling the allocation of land. In this, the Province of South Australia was no exception and, in fact, it had a head start.

The first selections, followed by the auction, indicated a decisive preference for South Adelaide and, in particular, land situated nearest to North Terrace. Here best lots fetched from £8 to £10 and more, contrasting with £3 or less for excellent North Adelaide lots with extensive views. The era of the land speculator was truly ushered in by the first auction. The momentum of rising prices for town land was constantly fuelled by the influx of new settlers arriving from Britain and other Australian colonies during 1837 and 1838. It was this combination of high land prices and the rapid physical growth of Adelaide that gave South Australia a false appearance of prosperity. As the following example illustrates, local newspapers did their best to exploit the situation and stimulate the flow of capital investment from the mother country.

It was 'for the information of our readers in England' that a leader in *The Southern Australian* drew attention to the sales of 13 town acres which had taken place during July, 1838. The information was conveyed 'with pride—as one of the most convincing proofs that could be given of the judgement displayed by our late Surveyor-General in his choice of this locality for the capital town of the Province.'[5] Among the allotments sold, Town Acre 81 in Rundle Street (west) fetched £300, while the nearby Town Acres 83 and 84 sold for £200 each, and further south, Town Acre 106 located in Grenfell Street brought £175. Despite their parkland frontage in South Terrace and the proximity of the Holdfast Bay Road to Glenelg, Town Acres 698 and 699 at £100 each were the cheapest of the 13 lots sold. This example of land sales indicates the spectacular rise

in value of good town land which occurred over the first eighteen months. At the same time rural land only eight kilometres south of the city in the 'village of Marion' could be had for only seven guineas an acre.[6]

The one-acre allotments were soon sub-divided into smaller building blocks of varying sizes and re-sold or let on lease. One of the largest speculators in Adelaide land, Captain Charles Berkeley (who originally held the impressive number of 13 town acres) could well advertise 'for sale or lease—several town allotments with any extent of frontage'[7] in ten different locations in South Adelaide, including Victoria and Whitmore Squares. The terms were not disclosed. With popular demand in mind, an anonymous advertisement offered to 'labourers and others' leases of cheaper building blocks situated in Coromandel Place, Chesser and French Streets, the newly formed lanes off Grenfell Street, on the following terms: for a mimimum sized lot, measuring 20 ft wide x 40 ft deep (6 m x 12 m), the asking annual rent was £3 on a five-year lease; for £10, a larger lot, 45 ft x 150 ft (13.7 m x 45 m) could be let for either seven, fourteen or twenty-one years.[8] Similar sub-divisions occurred in the sample area of South Adelaide, discussed in detail at the end of this Chapter.

Tents, huts and bowers

When we look at the complexity and extent of Adelaide today it is easy to lose sight of the fact that only 150 years ago our early citizens faced the formidable prospect of creating a settlement in the virgin bush. Initial shelter for many of the settlers had, literally, to be hacked out of the scrub before the business of erecting more permanent structures could commence. From the day in November, 1836, when the first colonists waded ashore at Holdfast Bay, self-sufficiency was a fundamental requirement. The need for shelter was satisfied in simple ways: for some a well-equipped tent (fig. 1), and for others a reed hut, a bark and sapling bower against a tree trunk, or simply a bed of gum leaves and a blanket under the trees.

As soon as the Adelaide site was chosen ten kilometres inland, a long straggling village of tents, huts and bowers grew up by the banks of the River Torrens, where today the Adelaide Casino occupies the former railway station building.[9] Numerous contemporary diaries and other records portray the efforts of our founding pioneers to provide basic shelter for themselves and their meagre possessions. Stories of hardship in the face of summer heat and the relentless onslaught of insects are legion, yet with

Figure 1: Robert Gouger's tent and hut at Holdfast Bay, 1836. Pencil sketch by an unknown artist.
(Art Gallery of S.A.)

an almost universal voice the colonists, from their rudimentary shelters, praised their new home as 'an earthly paradise, with every prospect pleasing'.[10] William Finlayson, extracts from whose recollections follow, is no exception.

House building began in earnest when settlers took possession of their free-hold land late in March, 1837. With few exceptions the young, able-bodied men and women set to work using simple materials close at hand, building to a standard in accordance with individual ability and means. In an area where permanent structures of any kind were unknown and, therefore, where no local architectural tradition existed, it was largely up to each individual settler to cope to the best of his ability with the new and different environment. Building traditions from the old country were subject to innovation and improvisation in an atmosphere of trial and error. In general, the use of tradesmen was confined to specialised work such as thatching of roofs, fire-place construction and the luxury items of properly made doors and windows. As can be expected, tradesmen

were not only in great demand but their rates were generally beyond the means of the average immigrant. A spirit of self-sufficiency prevailed, with friendships made on board during the long sea voyage turning into building partnerships so that limited resources and scarce building skills could be pooled.

From these early days the mediterranean climate which Adelaide enjoys and the initial abundance of building land dictated a new direction in housing. In contrast to the northern European experience, it was unnecessary for solidly constructed dwellings to huddle together as a protection from the elements. Rather, a free-standing, single-storey house of minimal construction was the option exercised by at least half of the early Adelaidians whose dwelling types were first recorded on the Kingston map, discussed later in this Chapter. These first owner-built shelters marked the beginning of the much cherished Australian tradition of a privately-owned, single family dwelling which, before the end of the century, became an attainable goal for the great majority of South Australians.

5

The Recollections of William Finlayson

A significant personal record of the pioneering experience in the early days of Adelaide is preserved in the writings of William Finlayson who, with his wife Helen, disembarked from the 'John Renwick' in the summer heat of February, 1837. This newly-married young Scottish couple had set out for the infant Province of South Australia fired by missionary fervour to 'serve Christ among the heathen abroad'. However, on arrival this altruism had to be set aside in the face of the more immediate considerations of building shelter and earning a living. Extracts from Finlayson's *Recollections*[11] of the years 1837 to 1840 provide the source of this case study which highlights the early sequence of building and the gradual improvements made in the quality of the first shelters. Typically, during the first four years the Finlaysons progressed from a bower on the bank of the Torrens, to a shared hut, and then to a basic two-room cottage. Finlayson not only provides comprehensive specifications for these structures but also gives a good description of how they were constructed, who lived in them, and for how long. This adds necessary substance to the picture of early housing in general, and has enabled the accompanying illustrations to be drawn by the author in accordance with Finlayson's original descriptions.

William Finlayson arrived at the north-west corner of the present city after the ten kilometre walk from the new Port Adelaide, or Port Misery as it was aptly called by early colonists. He recollects:

> there was nothing to look at much in town but stunted peppermint trees and surveyors pegs, here and there. Outside fronting what is now the jail but nearer to North Terrace was a row of reed huts, dignified with the name of 'Buffalo Row' from the Government ship in which the inhabitants had arrived. Between that and the River Torrens, & what a miserable river, were a number of tents and nondescript huts . . .
>
> Having made a kind of survey of the place I thought I must have a place of my own as well as others so borrowing an axe I began like Elisha's party to cut down trees in the bed or on the banks of the river . . . I got four saplings cut and carried to the place I had fixed on . . . I measured as well as I can recollect a space about eight feet [2.4 metres] square—and planted a post at each corner.

At this stage Finlayson returned to Port Adelaide to fetch his wife. They returned on foot carrying two water buckets, a mattress and blankets, some ticking and other odds and ends. He continues:

> my wife took out the piece of ticking and beginning at one corner carried it round the four posts of our new home, being short of pins to fasten it—(when did woman's wit fail) she took her hair pins broke them in halves, and so fastened our airy abode,—there was enough cloth to wrap round and also to cover our new

house—so under the shelter of our thin tent we slept and thus passed our first night at home in our own house. The flat roof was subsequently covered with rough thatching but, to Finlayson's sorrow, it proved incapable of shedding the rain. He goes on to describe the scene on the banks of the Torrens:

> bowers and tents were erected near together without any attempt at regularity or order . . . no one directed or found fault with us, in building we followed our own sweet will . . .
>
> It was truly amusing to look at the various styles of architecture exhibited all around us,—as our materials were of the simplest kinds,—cloth of all kinds— interspersed with ti-tree & reeds—this was real gipsying and never was gipsy camp more picturesque than was the encampment of the immigrants of the 'John Renwick' at the end of the summer of 1837.

The one-room structure, rather grandly described as a 'living and sleeping apartment', was the Finlaysons' home for about six weeks (fig. 2). In an area of approximately six square metres the improvised 'bedstead' would have occupied half of the bower's area with other household possessions taking up most of the remaining space. Cooking and other domestic activities would have taken place in the open.

As a means of finding better quarters Finlayson agreed to help a married friend build a hut on a town acre in Currie Street. This dwelling was to be shared

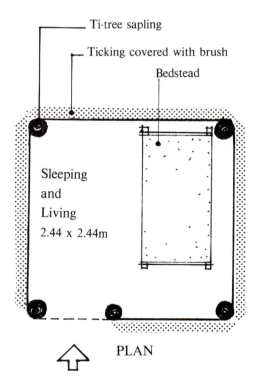

Ti-tree sapling

Ticking covered with brush

Bedstead

Sleeping and Living 2.44 x 2.44m

PLAN

Figure 2: Finlayson's tea-tree bower by the River Torrens, Adelaide, early 1837.

by the two young couples until such time as Finlayson constructed his own house with the returned help of his friend. Having identified the land by the number on the surveyor's peg—Adelaide streets were not named until the end of May—they fixed the site 'without any regard to the street, and found out long after that only one corner claimed acquaintance with Currie Street'. The particular site was chosen because it was 'freest from wood as all town lands were covered with stunted peppermint trees'. This perhaps explains why the first buildings were widely scattered on the one-acre allotments and why some encroached on adjoining land.

The Currie Street hut measured 'about 20 feet by 10 feet' (6.0 m x 3.0 m) and was equally divided into two rooms, one for each couple (fig. 3). The so-called pisé[12] walls were composed of clay and straw obtained on the site and mixed with water brought from the Torrens. This mixture was rammed hard between moveable formwork and, while it was left to dry and harden, reeds were cut for the roof. Not wishing to repeat his former mistake, Finlayson hired a thatcher to pitch the roof. 'Let us look at our new home', he writes:

> One apartment 10 feet [3.0 m] square, mud floor, walls also of mud or earth five feet [1.5 m] high, rafters of wattle, roof reeds—no ceiling, door reeds in a kind of frame, window a hole left in the wall, no glass,— separated from our neighbours by a partition also of reeds. Such was our new abode, a great advance on the tea tree bower.

This one room remained the Finlaysons' home for seven months, and saw the birth of their first son in September, 1837. In terms of space and comfort it afforded only a marginal improvement on the bower, indicating the kind of hardships which the first settlers endured.

Before the end of the year Finlayson was building again, this time on a half-acre allotment in Rundle Street where David Jones department store now stands.

> With the help of my friend afore mentioned according to agreement we began to build, this time with the front square to the street. I had Corner posts of Shea Oak squared and put down and between these we built up a mud wall, much higher than the walls in Currie St., with the roof neatly thatched with reeds, and after a time to crown all we had a chimney built, yes a real chimney of stone and mud for mortar, then it was whitewashed, with a Cedar door with a rim lock and a brass knob and little glazed windows, casements also of Cedar. Our house was the wonder and admiration of many in those primitive times.

Finlayson's pride was well justified, for any house with a lockable door, glazed casement windows and a fireplace would have been considered luxurious in Adelaide in 1837. The floor area was slightly greater than the Currie Street plan and the increased height, to around two metres, was made possible by timber

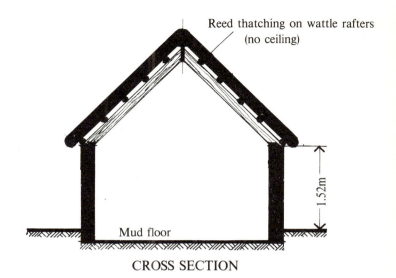

CROSS SECTION

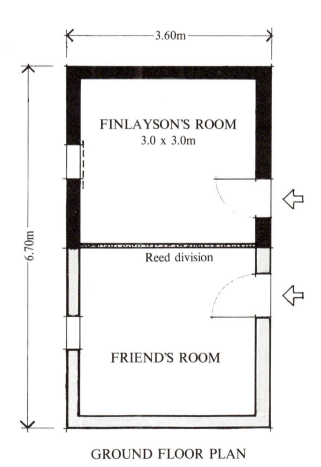

GROUND FLOOR PLAN

Figure 3: Finlayson's shared hut in Currie Street, Adelaide, 1837.

posts set at the corners to add stability to the mud walls. This type of dwelling made up a large proportion of the early Adelaide 'houses' shown on the Kingston map, discussed later in this Chapter. Contemporary paintings make an appropriate accompaniment to Finlayson's narrative. Martha S. Berkeley, in her watercolour of *North Terrace, looking E.S.E.,* (fig. 4), recorded possibly the earliest Adelaide streetscape, circa 1839, showing typical cottages taking shape in the rapidly developing north-west corner of the infant city. A glimpse of the primitive interiors typical of first shelters is captured in S.T. Gill's interior of a settler's hut, painted in the 1840s (fig. 5).

The spring of 1838 saw the Finlayson family once again living in temporary quarters—a tarpaulin tent erected near the present site of St Michael's Church, Mitcham. William Finlayson had taken a position on the South Australian Company's sheep station at Brownhill Creek where a nearby aboriginal camp afforded him the opportunity of his desired missionary work. About a year later he rented 67 acres (27 ha) adjoining the station and built—

> a little Cottage pailing outside, lath and plaster within. The size was 15 feet [4.6 m] long by 8 feet [2.4 m] wide. This was at first divided by a brick partition into sitting Kitchen &c. and bedroom. Some time after we removed the partition and had a little Kitchen added 11 x 7 [3.4 m x 2.1 m].
> . . . Next after getting our Cottage I dug a place partly underground for a Milk house or dairy and my wife in addition to nursing, cooking, making and mending for us all, took charge of this department.

Figure 4: (above) Early cottages along North Terrace, Adelaide, c.1839. Detail of watercolour by Martha Berkeley (1813–c.1899).   –   *(Art Gallery of S.A.)*

Figure 5: (opp. above) Interior of settler's hut, early 1840s. Sketch by S.T. Gill (1818–1880).
(National Library of Australia)

Figure 6: (opp. below) A pioneer cottage on the bank of a creek in the Adelaide foothills, period 1843–49. Detail of watercolour by Robert Davenport (1816–1896).
(Art Gallery of S.A.)

Robert Davenport's watercolour of an early pioneer's cottage on the bank of a creek in the Adelaide foothills, (fig. 6) painted during the 1840s, depicts features like those described above by Finlayson. Unfortunately, Finlayson's pioneering endeavours in the country were not rewarded with early material prosperity, for he continues:

> Here [in the cottage] eight of our children were born, and during those years we could not afford to put glass into the casement of our windows but at night hung up a sheet.

However, it is pleasing to note that 'Helenholme' named after Helen Finlayson, replaced this humble abode in 1852, and stands today in the street that commemorates the name of this early pioneering family.

ADELAIDE, SOUTH AUSTRALIA.

Figure 7: North-western corner of South Adelaide around 1842 by an anonymous artist.

Kingston's Adelaide of 1842

When William and Helen Finlayson moved into their second house in Rundle Street late in 1837, there were already an estimated 1,700 inhabitants[13] and 300 huts and cottages in the infant capital.[14] By 1841, the immigrant population of the Province had reached 15,500 people of all ages, of whom an estimated 7,000 resided in the city of Adelaide plus nearly 2,000 in the surrounding villages.[15] The total number of buildings in Adelaide, including houses, shops, stores and so on had risen to 1,960[16]—a remarkable achievement of the pioneering struggle over a mere five years. The result was documented graphically by George Strickland Kingston[17] on his map of Adelaide, published in 1842.[18]

Having resigned his commission as Deputy Surveyor-General in October, 1838, George Kingston was engaged as City Engineer by the Adelaide Municipal Council when he undertook the first comprehensive survey of Adelaide in 1840–41. Its primary purpose was to establish the use of land and to obtain particulars of buildings in the city for the assessment of Municipal rates. The assessment of 4d. in £1 was declared in June, 1841, but it could not be collected by the Council as the colony was in the throes of economic depression.[19] However, based on the measured survey, Kingston was able to prepare a cadastral map of the city to the scale of 'one inch to each acre' showing buildings and their main materials of construction, the extent of fences and the location of wells as they existed at the end of 1841. Also included on the map are 98 references to specific buildings located in South Adelaide and 17 in North Adelaide. For general information, the neatly set out footnotes entitled 'memoranda' summarise the principal events, population, temperatures, colonial officials and agricultural operations in South Australia.

In a descending order of worthiness the map identifies the three types of building materials used for walling, namely: brick or stone; wood; pisé or lath and plaster—the latter construction has been described already by William Finlayson in the previous section. Also shown are 'sheds' and 'unfinished or ruinous buildings' which included a variety of temporary shelters. Buildings 'with verandahs' occurred rarely at this early stage of development and appear to have been confined mainly to timber dwellings. The map also identifies locations of shallow 'wells' which, until the 1860s, supplemented water carted from the River Torrens. Roughly executed marginal sketches of six public buildings[20] which already existed in Adelaide complete the map. These were added by the publishers to show the progress being made and to promote the new colony.[21] Appropriately, 'the proprietors', George S. Kingston and Edward Stephens, dedicated the map to 'Her most gracious Majesty, Adelaide, the Queen Dowager'.

While records of building dimensions have not survived, the accuracy of the scaled drawings is borne out by measured surveys of extant structures and direct comparisons made with the Smith City Survey carried out at the end of the 1870s when the Adelaide sewage system was designed. This is despite the fact that Kingston's ability as a surveyor came to be questioned by his contemporaries.

A number of paintings and sketches of Adelaide streetscapes executed during the first ten years give a good impression of the buildings indicated on the Kingston map. Some of these show a remarkable correlation with relevant sections of the map and are worthy of further study. Of particular value is the series of streetscapes of Adelaide executed by T.S. Gill in 1845. The selected view of 'Adelaide, South Australia' (fig. 7), drawn in 1842 by an anonymous artist, gives a third dimension to the buildings indicated on the Kingston map.[22] The view looking east along North Terrace shows the typically single-storey buildings in their greatest concentration in the north-west corner of the city surrounding the original Trinity Church. On the left, the first wooden footbridge, built by Frome alongside the River Torrens crossing, links the southern and northern sections of Adelaide. The backdrop of the Adelaide Hills is rather more spectacular than life.

As might be expected, the distribution of the 2,000 odd buildings in Adelaide in 1842 was uneven and could not physically cover all of the city's one-acre allotments. Clearly, the initial choice of the allotments confirmed the overwhelming preference for South Adelaide. This was a natural choice considering the proposed location of government buildings and the commercial heart south of the Torrens valley—which separated the two sections. By 1842, fairly close settlement had taken place along the northern edge of South Adelaide, with Franklin and Pirie Streets roughly defining its southern boundaries. The southern area contained between Grote Street and South Terrace and extending east

to Hutt Street was not as closely built up but contained pockets of close settlement, mainly along secondary streets not provided in Light's original plan. Except for scattered fringe development, most of the area east of Hutt Street and south of Pirie Street remained scrub.

North of the Torrens, early development was concentrated in areas of lower North Adelaide situated nearest to the river, the area centred on Kermode Street being the most densely settled. The much larger upper North Adelaide contained less than fifty houses, with major roads defined only by surveyor's pegs.

By far the most densely built up area shown on the Kingston map is in the north-west section of South Adelaide, concentrated along the Hindley Street and Rundle Street (west) axis. At least two important factors combined to stimulate this early development—the proximity to the first source of water supply, the Torrens, and a direct link with the road to Port Adelaide, the essential artery for the new settlement.

Thus, in the initial shaping of the city, the commercial activity of Hindley Street soon extended eastward. In 1838, building sites in Rundle Street were advertised as being 'in the centre of business; they are also equally desirable as a residence being in a neighbourhood where all the respectability of the town must eventually concentrate'.[23] In the same year, North Terrace appeared as 'one of the most valuable quarters of the town', Gilles Street as 'a most respectable neighbourhood' and King William Street and Grenfell Street as 'most rising situations.'[24]

By and large the more valuable sites were built on first and the density of building reflected the land values discussed earlier in this Chapter. 1839 saw buildings of all kinds and descriptions being erected, mainly in Hindley and Rundle Streets, and the major portions of these thoroughfares becoming well defined (fig. 8). Currie and Grenfell Streets came next in order of preference with several stores being built there. The general and shopping business was almost entirely transacted in those four streets. However, the condition of these major streets remained in a 'wretched state'.[25] After the remaining tree stumps had been grubbed out the vehicles, especially heavily laden bullock drays, continually cut the surface into the 'finest dust in summer, and a regular bog in winter'.[26] Wood slab houses facing the unmade roads became almost uninhabitable during the long dry season because of the amount of dust blown inside through shrinkage cracks in the walls.

Today only a handful of buildings shown on the 1842 map of the city remain standing, the most notable being the south-eastern corner of

Government House. Built in stone by Governor Gawler under his controversial works program, it shared the distinction with the new Gaol of being more than one storey in height. Both buildings were designed by G.S. Kingston. There are also two original buildings of 1839 which have survived, situated on adjoining sites in Pennington Terrace, North Adelaide. Both are prefabricated buildings (or 'portable' as it was termed then) originally made in London by H. Manning of timber components and shipped to Adelaide. They are the Friends' Meeting House and a four-room cottage, about 7.50 m square, imported by Henry Watson and erected for his own use. After the summer of 1840 Watson decided to cover the entire house by a non-structural skin of brickwork in order to increase the insulation of the thin timber walls against the extremes of Adelaide's heat and cold. The now restored Watson house remains the earliest known South Australian, and quite likely Australian, example of 'brick veneer' construction.[27]

Evaluation of a sample area

For a more detailed study of the housing environment shown on the Kingston map we focus on a rectangular area situated in the western sector of South Adelaide (fig. 9). Bounded by West Terrace and Brown Street, Grote and Wright Streets, the sample area contains two of the longest city blocks of eight lots. It embraces a total of 32 standard town

Figure 8: (above) Rundle Street looking west across Frome Street intersection, 1845. Detail of watercolour by S.T. Gill. *(Art Gallery of S.A.)*

Figure 9: (opp.) Detail of the city area from map of *The District of Adelaide, 1839*, based on "Trigonometrical Surveys by Colonel Light". Location of the sample area used in this study is indicated on the reproduction. *(State Library of S.A.)*

acres which are shown by dotted lines on the original map, each being a 209 ft (63.6 m) square, and covering one acre (0.40 hectares) in area.[28] The two parallel blocks lie 'north' and 'south' of Gouger Street which bisects the sample area. Based on pilot studies of three different locations, the above area has been selected as most representative of early residential development in South Adelaide and comprises a good cross-section of different house types. Situated away from the closely settled north-west corner of the city and the business hub of Hindley Street, the initial development in the sample area proceeded at a more leisurely pace, reflecting more closely the housing preferences of the ordinary settler. Moreover, it retained a predominantly residential character with its working-class population remaining there until well after the turn of the century.[29]

In exercising the right of choice in March, 1837, discussed earlier, holders of preliminary land orders showed a marked preference for the north block, and

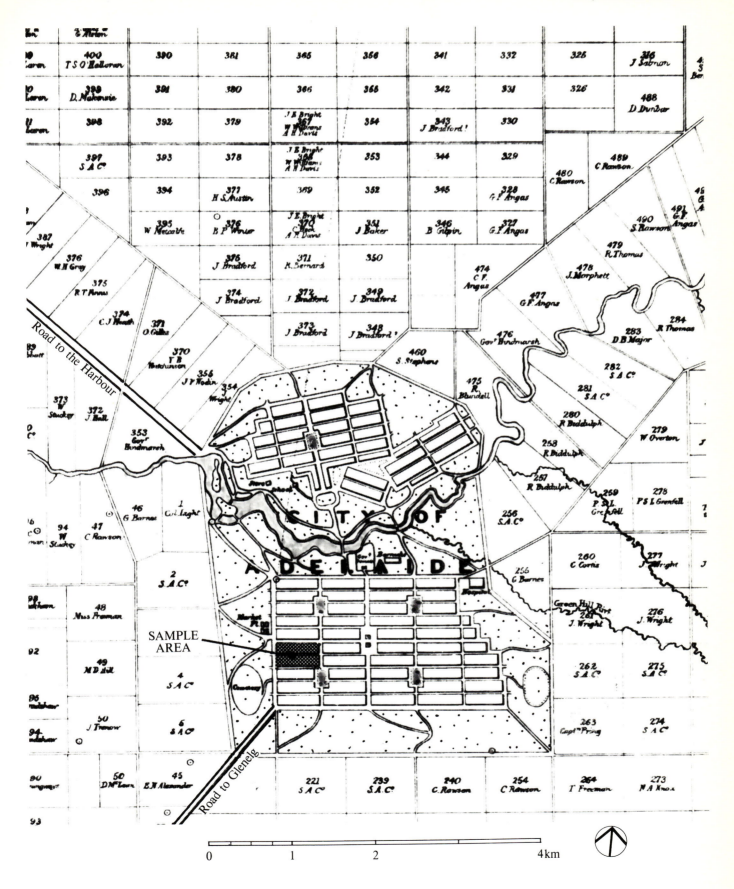

SAMPLE
AREA

Road to the Harbour

Road to Glenelg

CITY OF ADELAIDE

0   1   2   4km

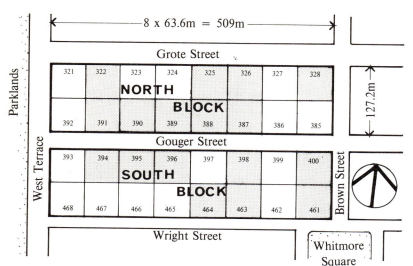

Figure 10: Sample area showing the north and south city blocks, each containing 16 town acre allotments. The town acres occupied by the beginning of 1842 are shown shaded. For details of development—see fig.11.

Figure 11: (opp.) Detail of G.S. Kingston's map of Adelaide showing development of the sample area as at 1st January, 1842. Same size reproduction.
(Public Record Office of S.A.)

in particular the Grote Street frontage—the northernmost street in the sample area and also the major east-west thoroughfare bisecting Victoria Square. A total of ten lots were taken up, including Town Acre 322 selected by the author of the map, G.S. Kingston. At the same time only three lots (on the corners) were selected in the south block. With one exception all the initial purchasers had resident status. The balance of 19 un-selected lots were sold at the first auction and the prices again confirmed the preferred locations. An average price of £9/5/- was paid for the six remaining lots north of Gouger Street, reducing to £7/8/- for the 13 lots located in the south block.[30] It is interesting to note that 12 of the 19 lots were acquired by agents on behalf of 'absentee' speculators.[31]

By the beginning of 1842, 17 of the 32 privately owned lots (53 per cent) were occupied and improved by the erection of buildings and fences, shown by solid lines on the Kingston map. They include six lots purchased originally by 'absentee' persons. The average density for the occupied lots is seven dwellings per acre (fig. 10). An interesting local build-up in the overall density of buildings can be seen near the intersection of Gouger Street with Byron Place—one of the first minor streets formed by landowners to provide north-south access between the major streets and, in this case, a direct link with the business area centred in Hindley Street. Additional focus to this locality is given by the only 'public' building, described in the 'references to South Adelaide' as a 'Music Saloon', numbered 89. Situated on the western side of Byron Place, this early stone/brick structure was classified as one of the new capital's 'principal buildings' indicating that 'already great exertions have been made in the architectural department'.[32] The only other building of note contained within the sample area was G.S. Kingston's own residence, numbered 80, situated at the western

end of Grote Street. Standing on its own fenced-in one-acre allotment the house comprises the original timber wing typically jointed on to a larger stone/brick L-shaped section constructed soon after. At this early stage of development it is exceptional to see both sections provided with verandahs along the street frontage (north side). For subsequent development of the comprehensive network of secondary streets in the sample area—see Chapter 3, (fig. 24).

On the 17 occupied allotments in the sample area (fig. 11), stood 77 separate *buildings* containing 155 'individual' *dwellings*—as far as can be determined from the original map. The dwellings are of three different types: detached, semi-detached (later called maisonettes), and rows. In addition, there are some 12 'temporary' buildings or outbuildings shown on the map and, although these have been discounted, most undoubtedly were used as temporary accommodation. The mix of dwelling types and the walling materials used in their construction are summarized as follows:

CHARACTERISTICS OF INDIVIDUAL DWELLINGS

Dwelling types	% of dwellings	Wall Materials (%)			
		pisé	brick/ stone	wood	mixed
Detached	51	48	20	15	17
Semi-detached	23	38	38	8	16
Row cottages	26	88	—	12	—
Total 100%					

It is significant to note that even at this early stage one half (51 per cent) of the dwellings were detached. A large number of these appear to be single-cell dwellings of the kind already described by William

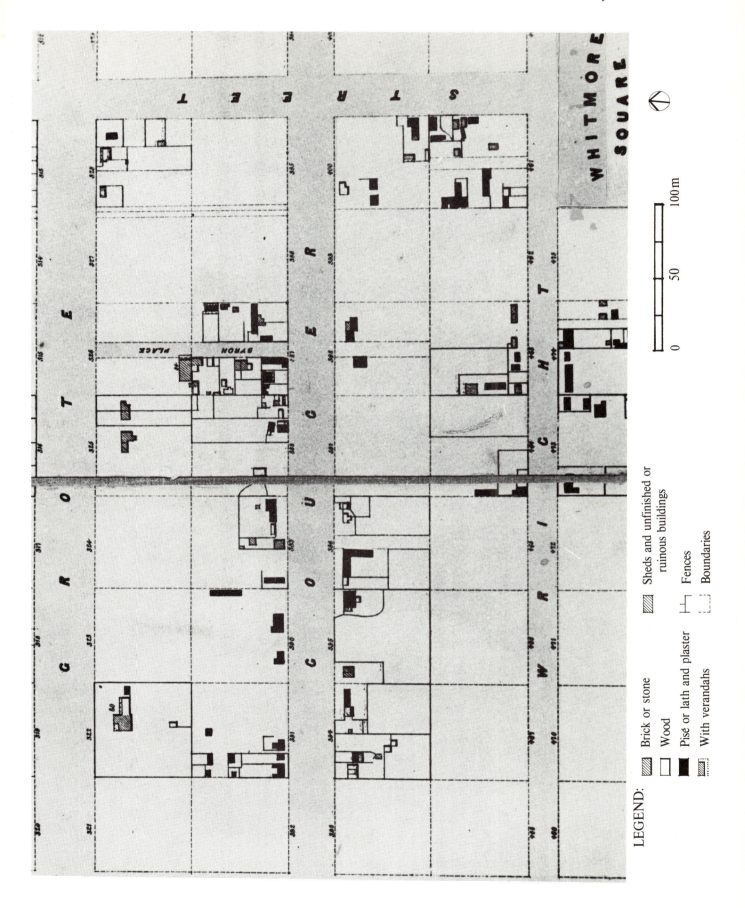

LEGEND:

Brick or stone

Wood

Pisé or lath and plaster

With verandahs

Sheds and unfinished or ruinous buildings

Fences

Boundaries

Finlayson. Their dominant wall material (48 per cent) is 'pisé or lath and plaster', while only one fifth (20 per cent) are of solid construction, either 'brick or stone'. The least popular construction was, apparently, 'wood' (15 per cent). Because only a small number of prefabricated wooden houses were imported into South Australia,[33] the majority would have been of primitive slab construction similar to the von Mueller hut discussed in Chapter 2, (fig. 17), with clay being used to seal any gaps between the timbers.

The shortcomings of this type of construction were highlighted in previous section by a contemporary writer. In the houses of 'mixed' construction (17 per cent), the solid portion located at the rear would have been the latest addition, marking the start of the general move towards solid construction in South Australia. This trend rapidly changed the face of Adelaide where, by 1860, 95 per cent of all city buildings were of stone or brick.[34]

Semi-detached dwellings—those built as pairs sharing a common wall—represent nearly a quarter (23 per cent) of all dwellings in the sample. The proportion constructed of brick/stone is the highest for any dwelling type and, especially when combined with those of 'mixed' construction, would indicate owner-occupiers rather than tenants living on leased land. While an equal number were pisé dwellings, few (only 8 per cent) were built of wood.

Attached row cottages amount to about a quarter (26 per cent) of all dwellings in the sample area and range between three and five units to a row. Their construction is confined to the cheapest materials— pisé (88 per cent) and wood (12 per cent). The great majority of these early buildings lacked durability and had disappeared before the customary seven, fourteen or twenty-one year land leases expired. Certainly only isolated buildings survived more than forty years to be recorded again in the Smith City Survey of Adelaide buildings, published in 1880. One of the few exceptions was Gray's row of four cottages (c. 1838), situated in North Terrace and discussed in Chapter 3 (fig. 26). Generally, pisé and wood buildings occur on town acres initially purchased by absentee owners. For example, on the north side of Gouger Street four adjoining Town Acres, nos. 388–391, were bought at the first auction by an absentee, John White, and except for one brick/stone house, were developed with pisé and wood buildings. The eight pisé houses on Town Acre 391 had vanished by 1880 and the town acre reverted to a vacant allotment. Nor can a trace be found of the original buildings on the remaining three town acres, all of which had been re-developed.[35]

The overall impression of the sample area of Kingston's map is conveyed by the physical characteristics of the whole buildings, rather than the individual dwelling units discussed above, as primary indicators of housing standards. Of the 77 whole buildings, nearly two-thirds were of pisé or wood construction while only slightly less than one-quarter were entirely of brick or stone. Moreover, the latter are generally smaller in size, reflecting not only a higher cost but also the longer construction period required.

Also emerging are differences in houses that are related to land tenure. Houses of owner/occupiers and those built as cheap rental accommodation or as first shelters on leased land can be distinguished by their size, the type of construction and the use of adjoining land. Generally, single family dwellings and semi-detached houses stand in fenced-in blocks, while row cottages at first shared common ground, and later had to be content with minimum-sized back yards.

Next to building, the erection of fences, usually made of local hardwood, about 1.50 m high, was a major task undertaken by pioneer towndwellers.[36] Fences defined the extent of land attached to a dwelling for the exclusive use of a household. Apart from providing some privacy for domestic activities such as washing and outdoor cooking, the enclosure contained storage of firewood, a garden plot (officially encouraged as a food source), domestic animals and play space for children. The sample area contains some 30 fenced-in allotments connected with either free-standing or semi-detached cottages. Of these, 14 have a street frontage of 7.5 m or less; ten range between 9.0 m and 12.0 m in width, and six are over 15 m wide. The overall depth of 18 of these allotments varies between 12.0 m and 21.0 m and in 12 instances it is 30.0 m or more. 'G.S. Kingston, Esq.' is the only resident with the whole of his one-acre allotment (T.A. 322) fenced in along its original boundaries.

The siting of initial buildings followed the rectilinear grid pattern of the town acres, working from the surveyors' pegs. Earlier in this Chapter, William Finlayson referred to the difficulties he experienced in finding the correct boundaries in the virgin scrub. Later, the large initial allotments were halved by private lanes (for example, Byron Place) which were used for setting out frontages of buildings, often placed right on the boundary. In a typical development the first buildings would be built close to and parallel with the street or the side boundary and then proceed towards the centre of the allotment. Encroachments on to adjoining land were commonplace, requiring subsequent adjustment of original acre boundaries.

With no prescribed set-backs from boundaries or minimum allotment size—which were not regulated until the Building Act of 1923—the siting of buildings and lot sub-division were a matter of the owners' choice or expedience.[37] However, Kingston's map suggests that adjoining owners would roughly follow established set-backs from street boundaries. Naturally enough they varied according to the street width, the size of the house and the amount of land which it commanded. For example, in Grote Street the two solid houses in the centre of the city block are set back 15 metres, standing roughly in line with Kingston's residence at the western end. However, the two houses on smaller blocks at the corner of Brown Street are built within 2.0 m of the street. All along Gouger Street, the set-backs measure either 2.0 m or 6.0 m, while nearly all houses in Wright Street are from 5.0 m to 6.0 m distant from the footpath.

George Kingston's map of Adelaide will remain a valuable record of the emerging form of a major European settlement founded in Australia at the beginning of Queen Victoria's reign. It records the truly remarkable achievement of the first five years involved in laying out a capital and the construction of two thousand buildings, mainly houses, under adverse conditions. In particular, Adelaide's wide streets, generous front set-backs and the first verandahs suggest ideas that stem from the British experience of the hot climate in India.

While many of the first buildings lacked permanence, they were varied in their design, siting and construction. Their physical characteristics, as discussed above, reflected the values and aspirations held by the founding settlers and formed the basis of later residential development in the suburbs. The Kingston map, therefore, provides the essential starting point for the study of urban housing in South Australia. From it we gain the earliest insight into the principal dwelling types, the evolution of which is traced in the following Chapters.

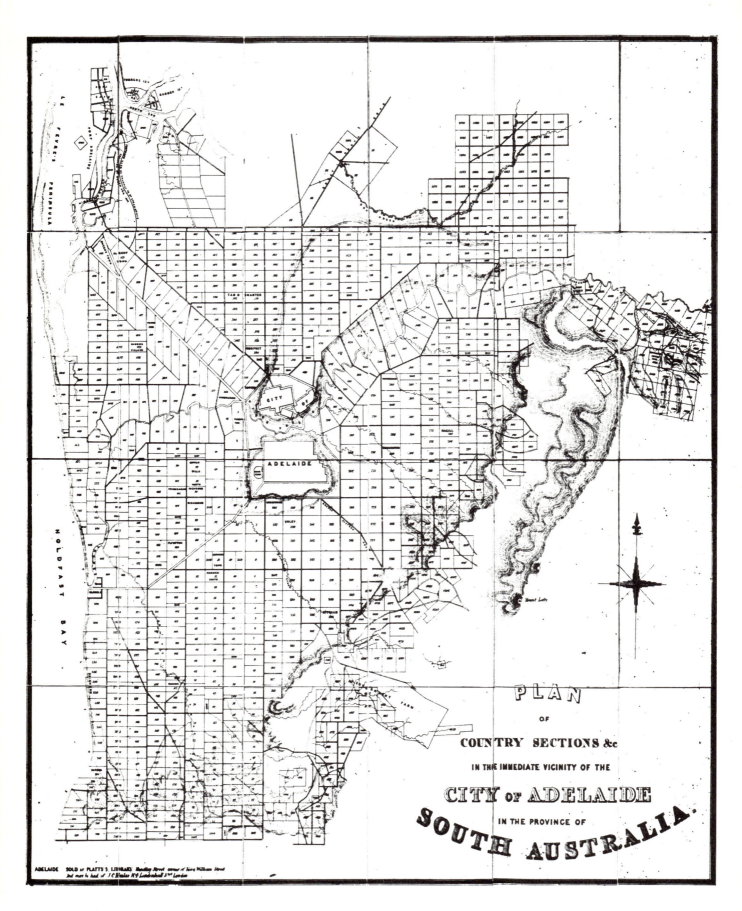

PLAN

OF

COUNTRY SECTIONS &c

IN THE IMMEDIATE VICINITY OF THE

CITY OF ADELAIDE

IN THE PROVINCE OF

SOUTH AUSTRALIA.

Chapter 2

Small Detached Cottages

1836–1860

Australia is the small house. Ownership of one in a fenced allotment is as inevitable and unquestionable a goal of the average Australian as marriage. Australia has more per head of population than other nations, and has maintained a higher standard of living in a greater number of them.

Robin Boyd, 1961.[1]

British origins

Australia's small house has its origins in the rustic cottage of the colonial settler. Enshrined in it is the fundamental concept of a single-family detached house standing on its own piece of land. As this concept soon became the Australian ideal, the popular preference for this type of house has hardly waned. As a house type, the free standing family residence—be it a humble cottage or a mansion—has remained numerically dominant in Australian housing throughout the country. And, unlike the row or terraced house, the detached house evolved concurrently as a town and country dwelling, with only minor design variations.

It is hardly surprising that the founding immigrants to South Australia sought the advantages of the Englishman's home in the form of a free-standing

dwelling house separated from the next by a garden and a fence. This was a desired goal in a country of more open space than that of their birth and where free-hold land was readily available. Moreover, ownership of a house was recognised as a mark of achievement which brought with it respectability within the emerging society of the new Province. It was not long before the ideal of 'one family—one house—one garden' was extended to include 'one person—one room'. The latter was realised as a statistical average by the end of the century.

Cottages of two and three rooms are discussed in this Chapter. The attached version of the cottage plan built in rows and those built in pairs during the Colonial period are covered under a separate heading in Chapter 3. Later development of the symmetrical-fronted cottage and the 'villa' plans, during the second half of the century is discussed in Chapter 4.

Early migrants to Australia brought with them the tradition of the small country cottage that had been long enjoyed in the British Isles. Dating from the late eighteenth century, the common cottage of the Scottish highlands and the Isles was built with walls of local stone, saddle-back roof and had fireplaces set in gable end walls. Similarly, the universally popular cottage of the west coast of Wales bears close resemblance to the early Adelaide plan. It was this type of traditional country cottage that the early colonists transplanted on to South Australian soil.

The Scottish example of the two-room 'Spital cottage' (fig. 13) compares in layout and dimensions with the early dwellings of colonial pioneers. Dating to around the mid-nineteenth century, it was located in the Grampian region, near Fettercairn. Just as we find pioneer houses built along the five creeks which cross the Adelaide plain, this, now ruined, crofter's cottage is sited close to the Burn of Dye. Its only entrance is flanked by two small windows on the

Figure 12: (opp.) Plan of country sections in the vicinity of the city of Adelaide, published in the 1850s. The map shows early development of the three growth centres forming a triangle—The City of Adelaide, situated half-way between Gulf St. Vincent and Mount Lofty Ranges; the harbour on the upper reach of Port River; and the first settlement of Glenelg at Holdfast Bay. The names appearing on country sections indicate locations of early settlements, some of which became the nuclei of later suburbs. *(State Library of S.A.)*

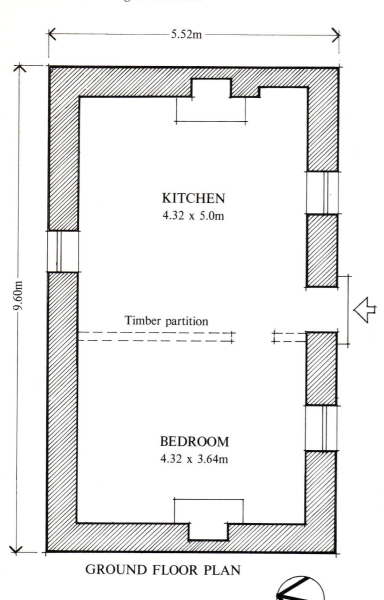

GROUND FLOOR PLAN

Detail of gable wall with fireplace

Figure 13: (above) Spital Cottage, Grampian region of Scotland, c.1850. A crofter's basic two room cottage.

Figure 14: (opp.) Municipal cottages for farm workers, near Cork, Ireland, c.1880. A simple rectangular shaped plan of four rooms which could be built either singly or attached in rows.

(National Housing Reform Council, London)

protected side facing due south. This siting, typical of northern Europe where prevailing winter winds are from the north, can be seen in the case of the von Mueller cottage (1849), which follows.

The Spital cottage, with 9.60 m frontage and gross area of 53 m², was divided into two rooms by a timber framed partition, heated by two similar-sized open fireplaces set into the end walls. While their openings were off-centre—a practice seldom followed in South Australia—the chimneys terminated in the central position at the head of the gable walls. Essential for the cold climate, the solid walls of local

stone were built 60 cm thick, reducing the usable floor area of the cottage to a mere 36 m². Slate roof would have covered this typical Highland cottage (slate replaced earlier peat roofs tied down with stone weighted ropes). Another small building located nearby provided storage space and shelter for farm animals.

The 'Municipal cottages for Irish labourers' (fig. 14) were built late in the century in the rural district of Middleton, near Cork, Ireland, under the Artizans' and Labourers' Dwellings Act, passed by the British Parliament in 1881. While the design reflects the

MUNICIPAL COTTAGES FOR IRISH LABOURERS.

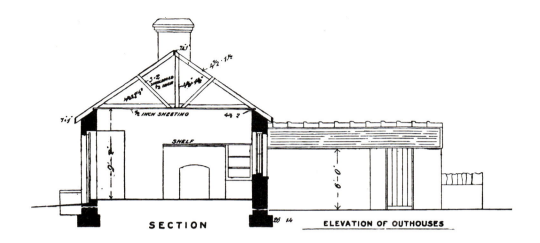

SECTION   ELEVATION OF OUTHOUSES

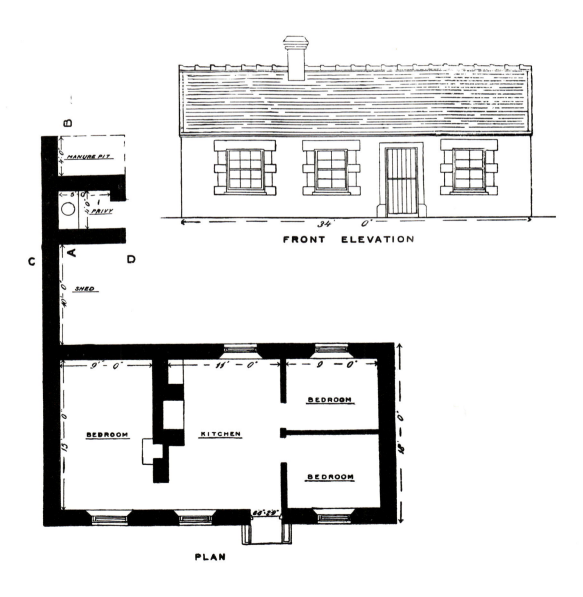

FRONT ELEVATION

PLAN

improved housing standards of the Act, it retains characteristic features of the traditional rural cottage.[2] Its plan of four rooms represents a slightly larger version of the Spital cottage. Its triple-fronted 'front elevation' extends to 10.4 m in width and the gross area of the house covers 57 m[2]. The central 'Kitchen' (4.6 m x 3.4 m), accessible directly off the street, is multi-purpose in use. The principal bedroom (4.6 m x 2.7 m) is located on one side, while two smaller, near square, bedrooms are on the other. The kitchen has a large open hearth with mantle shelf over and storage shelves fitted into an adjoining recess (see 'Section'). A smaller fireplace provided in the principal bedroom shares the common flue. Advanced for the country is the 'privy' (1.5 m x 1.2 m) built of solid construction as part of the boundary wall, and separated from the rear of the house by a 3.0 m wide semi-open 'shed'. Next to the privy the 'manure pit' provides the necessary means of disposal.

Timber roof trusses span the distance between the outer walls, and support 'board' ceilings, 2.9 m high. At each end of the building, the roof terminates flush with the gable wall, and there are no projecting eaves—a typical feature of early Australian cottages. Double hung sashes, each divided into either four or six panes, are set in the 45 cm thick walls, which are built with toothed quoins. If the principal bedroom were deleted, the remaining portion of the Middleton cottage shows a remarkable resemblance to the Thebarton cottage (1869), discussed later.

Cottages in Adelaide

Adelaide's development over the first five years of settlement resulted in not less than one-half of all dwellings being of the detached type, many already standing in fenced allotments. (See discussion of a sample area Chapter 1.) With the later growth of the suburbs, the percentage increased[3] to the point where, in recent years, nearly three-quarters of all Australian dwellings were detached single family houses lived in by eighty-five per cent of Australia's population.[4].

During the second half of the nineteenth century, the number of small cottages of less than three rooms gradually diminished to be replaced by larger houses. However, the basic cottage plan continued to be widely built as a 'starter' house. In suburban Adelaide these still appeared during the final decades of the century[5], while in rural areas their popularity was maintained well into the twentieth century.

Increasingly today, owners of large houses discover that a humble pioneer cottage formed the original nucleus of their house. Built of simple local materials or, perhaps, transported to the site as a prefabricated building, the pioneer cottage was often the now forgotten 'starter' house of early colonists. The surviving 'Collingrove' homestead, near Angaston, provides one such example. About 1850, John Howard Angas (son of George Fife Angas, founder of the South Australian Company) built a simple three-room cottage with detached kitchen, on a working farm which he established in the Barossa Valley. It became the nucleus of today's rambling house. The original walls merge with additions made by successive generations, while the low roof of the cottage was concealed when the whole house was re-roofed.

Before proceeding to discuss selected case studies of early cottages, it is useful to reflect on the general housing situation in the County of Adelaide[6]— roughly corresponding with the present outer metropolitan area (fig. 12). By 1871 [7] one half of all dwellings contained either two rooms (29 per cent— most numerous) or three rooms (22 per cent); there were only 1,000 one-room huts remaining (3 per cent); four room dwellings (20 per cent) and larger houses of five or more rooms (22 per cent) made up the rest of the housing stock. The next forty years saw the number of two room cottages dwindle to 11 per cent in 1881 and to 4 per cent in 1901. During the same period the percentage of three and four room houses (grouped together in later returns) remained fairly constant, being 41 per cent in 1901.

It must be remembered that for at least one generation there was extreme inequality in domestic comfort, a fact easily obscured by averaging the total figures. The few moneyed immigrants managed to transfer some of the comforts and elegance of England to their clearings in the bush by importing tradesmen and fine items of joinery and furniture. A large majority of early immigrants had to be content with cramped living conditions and, in many instances, hessian or sawn hardwood shutters as substitutes for glazed windows, mud floors and roughly improvised furniture. In 1851, seven persons in a family was the 'customary average'[8] for an Adelaide cottage. As more than half of the early cottages had less than three rooms, more than two persons on average occupied every available room including that used as the kitchen/sitting room during the day.

Ten years later, census figures indicate that there were, on average, 3.6 rooms per dwelling occupied by 1.2 persons per room.[9] By 1901, the number of rooms had grown to 5.0 and the occupancy rate had dropped to 0.9 person per room. It is interesting to note that the average number of rooms has seen only a marginal increase since then, but with the smaller twentieth century family, the average room occupancy has dropped to two-thirds of a person per room today.

Compared with other colonies, a remarkable improvement occurred in dwelling construction over the first twenty-five years. The 1861 census draws attention to the fact that early structures 'chiefly those built of slab, mud and other materials, are now quickly being superceded by more substantial dwellings'. A mere 1,000 (6 per cent) of early huts remained standing including 'canvas', 'slab' and 'mud' huts, as part of the total stock of 15,650 dwellings in the County of Adelaide. By 1861, 'stone and brick' construction predominated (64 per cent) and when combined with buildings built of 'concrete' made up three-quarters of all buildings. (In the city area solid buildings reached a remarkable 95 per cent.) Only a quarter (24 per cent) of the County's structures were of 'wood' or 'iron'.[10]

The two room cottage

> House with two rooms and wash-house, and a piece of garden-ground, eighty feet by thirty [24 m x 9 m][11]

Writing from Adelaide to his mother in England in November 1837, this is how one young immigrant, Peter Cooke, described the small house he shared with his sister.

The early house plan invariably consisted of two unequal rooms side by side, with no passage. The main room, slightly larger than the other, had an open fireplace (sometimes added later) in the blind end wall, and the 'front' door in the far corner. This was a multi-purpose living room-cum-bedroom where the family cooked, ate, sat and entertained. The second room, which was smaller and usually near square in shape, was the family bedroom. One window to each room was placed on either side of the main door which was at the centre point of the longer side facing the street or public space. In later houses, the larger room had a second outside door that gave access to the private yard containing a privy erected over an earth pit at the rear boundary, and other out-buildings such as the wash-house, storage shed and chicken house. In the case of a small family, this utilitarian plan allowed segregation of living and sleeping activities, with only limited degree of privacy in respect of the latter.

The rectangular shaped buildings could be simply covered by a roof pitched from the longer walls, spanning the width of a single room, and finishing either in hipped or gabled ends. The same construction method, which utilised short-length timbers economically procured from local hardwoods, continued to be used until the end of the century regardless of the size of the ground plan. The result

was a uniformly low roof profile which became a characteristic feature of the colonial house during the second half of the century.

Adelaide streetscapes, painted around 1850, indicate a majority of stone/brick houses with saddle-back roofs and gable end walls crowned with chimneys (fig. 15)[12]. Their roofs—prior to 1860—were covered with thatch and stringybark shingles; reeds from creek beds and native grasses provided thatching material, while eucalypts grown on the upper slopes of the Mount Lofty Ranges were cut for shingles. Only better-class houses could boast a roof of imported slates or flat iron sheeting with rolled side laps. A cheaper alternative was a roof covering of local slate, quarried at Willunga (south of Adelaide) since 1840. With corrugated galvanised iron sheeting becoming available in the late fifties, the use of inflammable thatch and shingles was prohibited in the city after 1858—see Chapter 4. However, the risk of fire in the built-up areas was offset by the fact that these coverings were not only cheaper, but also considered cooler than slate in hot weather (fig. 16).

The common practice of building cottages close to the footpath effectively precluded the possibility of later additions at the front. Narrow-fronted allotments made widening of the house equally impractical. Thus, the usual additions took place at the rear where one or two rooms would be constructed under either a lower-pitched skillion roof or another gable matching the front section of the house. One of the additional rooms would be the kitchen, the other a children's bedroom.

The small cottage plan took two distinct forms: the humble abode of the struggling pioneer—either a new towndweller or a squatter, and the more substantial dwelling of a better-off settler. The former, built around Adelaide mainly prior to 1850, was not far removed from the single-cell hut or cabin, providing roughly the same amount of space and few refinements. Often supplemented by temporary structures of various kinds, it had to be built quickly and cheaply using materials close at hand and little, if any, skilled labour. William Finlayson's fourth successive dwelling, which he built at Brownhill Creek late in 1839 (see Chapter 1), depicts a typical pioneer cottage. Initially of two tiny rooms, the third room (kitchen) was added afterwards. The later von Mueller cottage (1849) provides another example. Such early cottages seldom exceeded 20 m² in area, had an average 5.5 m frontage and walls that stood only 2.0 m high.

Generally speaking, the colonial settlers' cottage represents a later version of the pioneers' dwelling—see, for example, Thebarton cottage (c. 1869). It was the home of an owner-occupier, usually an

established settler, who could afford to pay for more expensive materials and quality workmanship. George Blakiston Wilson describes the circumstances and building operations to be undertaken when contemplating the building of such a residence during the late 1840s:

> The owner of one or two Sections (usually 80 acres each) will find means of passing his time both pleasantly and profitably, and, by improving his land, will soon make a comfortable and prosperous home. When he finds that the crops succeeded well, and a sufficient quantity of land is fenced and in good working order, when in fact he can see that he can manage to make a decent living, the next care will be to furnish himself with a neat and substantial house suited to his wants and to the climate. On some part of his land he will probably have stone fit for building, which can be carted from time to time, as a spare day intervenes, and unloaded near the spot chosen for his future house.
>
> In nearly all parts of the colony good building stone is readily procured; but where this is not the case, as in some of the large plains, clay for bricks is generally found. When enough stone or bricks (readily procurable) have been obtained, a couple of sawyers must be hired to cut down timber, dig a saw-pit, and then cut the wood into the sizes and lengths for rafters, beams, door-plates, or whatever else is wanted for the building.
>
> While these men are at work the farmer's own labourers will have made a lime-kiln, and burned a sufficient quantity of lime, which also is easily procured, as much as is wanted, in all parts of the colony. After this a mason or bricklayer commences building; and a substantial and at the same time a cheap house is thus obtained. The doors, window-frames and flooring, should be of deal or cedar made on the station by a carpenter on weekly wages[13].

Two room settlers' cottages, especially those built after 1850, became bigger in area and better built than before. While their basic plan and utilitarian design remained unchanged, the average floor area doubled to nearly 40 m², with the frontage increasing by three metres to 8.0 m or even wider. The ceilings, too, became loftier, adding at least 1.0 m to the overall height of the building. However, not infrequently—even in the earliest examples—ceilings exceeded 3.0 m in height. And, almost invariably, the minimum room dimension was firmly set at around 3.6 metres. In general, post-1850 cottages show a surprising consistency in their internal dimensions and basic layout, regardless of the wall materials or the standard of finishes used.

Figure 15: (opp. above) Adelaide streetscape of 1851, looking east from (probably) Light Square. The verandah-less cottages of varying sizes line the street boundaries with gable walls crowned by central chimneys predominating. Detail of oil on canvas by J.A. Gilfillan (1793–c1866). *(Art Gallery of S.A.)*

Figure 16: (opp.) 'Angmering House' situated along the Main North Road at Enfield shows extensive use of thatch as an early roof covering. The original cottage, built by John Ragless in 1840, formed part of the extended house. *(Mortlock Library of South Australiana)*

von Mueller Cottage, 1849

This small, pioneer-type cottage (fig. 17), which is listed by the National Trust of South Australia, was built early in 1849 in the Bugle Ranges, about 40 km south-east of Adelaide. Remarkably, it has survived intact and the present occupants of the adjoining farmhouse still use the original kitchen for cooking the main meal each day. In this way the cottage remains a living memorial to its builder and first occupier–a German botanist, Dr. Ferdinand J.H. von Mueller. After working for a Rundle Street chemist, von Mueller decided to try his hand at farming and took up eight hectares of rolling land near Mount Barker, an important early agricultural district. With the help of a friend, he built this tiny cottage and shared it for some months with his sister as housekeeper.[14]

Today, as one steps through the low, 1.65 m, door of the cottage into the middle of the nineteenth century, the words used earlier by William Finlayson to describe his Brownhill Creek home assume a reality (Chapter 1). One is immediately struck by the similarity of layout and construction, despite the fact that the two slab cottages were built ten years apart by two young immigrants of different European backgrounds. 'von Mueller's hut', as it became known locally, is constructed almost entirely from red gum timber which abounded in the district. The durability of these tall eucalypts was recognised by early pioneers. After splitting the large trunks into flat boards called 'slabs', approximately 20 cm wide by 4 cm thick, they were set vertically into a trench 'like a fence' (Finlayson's description) to form the outside walls some 2.0 m high. Gaps between the slabs were filled liberally with a mixture of clay and water, called 'pug', and then lime washed. After 135 years, the undulating surface of the walls has been built up by successive coatings to a maximum of 15 cm in overall thickness. Sometimes, the internal timbers were first sheathed with calico and then whitewashed, or finished with lath and plaster, as was the case in Finlayson's house. Today, the largest number of surviving slab houses can still be seen at Penola, one of the earliest settlements in the south-east, established near Mount Burr forest.

The main room (2.8 m square), which has been used as a kitchen/sitting room, is dominated by the open fireplace, 1.2 m wide and 45 cm deep, with cooking pots resting on an iron trivet over the stone hearth. Characteristic of timber houses, the fireplace and chimney project externally in the gable wall. Sawn red gum planks, butted together and laid directly on the ground, form the original floor. Typical of the pioneer cottage, the floor finishes flush with the ground level outside. Smoke-blackened, hand-split planks line the 2.0 m high ceiling. While the thick roof covering of thatch has since been covered with corrugated galvanised iron, the building still remains without a verandah. A large trestle table and a set of wooden benches standing under the 60 cm square window (now glazed) provide the main furnishings of the room. Originally, the tiny second room (2.8 m x 2.0 m) served as the bedroom.

While von Mueller's cottage conforms in general to the design pattern of early pioneer houses, there are subtle differences which betray the owner's non-British background. Sited on raised ground, the building is oriented to the points of the compass with the blank (chimney) wall facing north. This follows a European practice of providing a thicker wall to the north devoid of openings, as protection against the winter weather. Openings are provided on the other three sides, including the south which is a preferred aspect in the northern hemisphere. As the house was built during the summer, von Mueller was probably more concerned with cooling night breezes and views to the south-west than the prevailing winter rains from that quarter yet to be experienced. Not being constrained by the requirements of Georgian symmetry in the arrangement of windows and doors, their position was determined by the furniture layout and, possibly, by cross-ventilation. For example, the kitchen window is over the table placed away from the door. Also, according to the European custom, the two doors open against the wall rather than into the room as customary in Britain.

Thebarton Cottage, c. 1869

Although the 'cottage at Thebarton' (fig. 18) was constructed in 1869 or early 1870, it is a good example of a settler-type cottage of the fifties. The original drawings, traced on linen, provide a rare illustration of the two-room plan and the top-of-the-range design. While the simple plan remains basically unchanged, there is a measurable improvement in the standard of construction and finishes used. Also, clearly discernible in the treatment of the main elevation are the construction technique and the inherited aesthetic tradition.

The cottage was built for the resident engineer at the new works of the Provincial Gas Company,[15] situated near the junction of Port Road and East Terrace at Thebarton. It comprised a multi-purpose 'living-room' (4.3 m x 3.6 m) and a small 'bed-room'

Figure 17: von Mueller Cottage, near Mount Barker, 1849. A typical two room pioneer cottage of the 1840s.

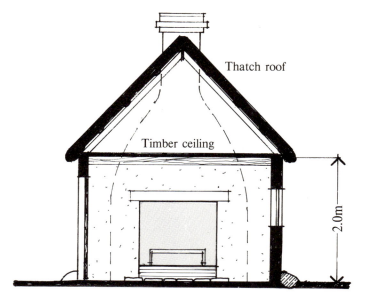

CROSS SECTION

Thatch roof

Timber ceiling

2.0m

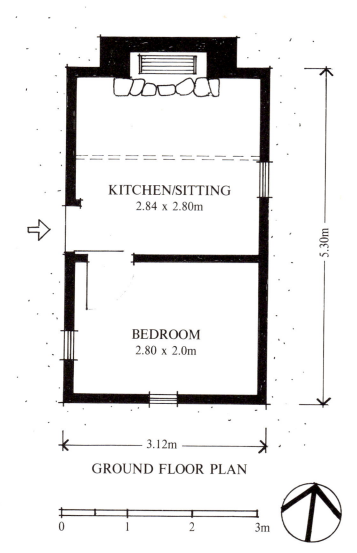

KITCHEN/SITTING
2.84 x 2.80m

BEDROOM
2.80 x 2.0m

5.30m

3.12m

GROUND FLOOR PLAN

0   1   2   3m

(3.4 m x 3.6 m) separated by a brick partition. There are no outbuildings shown on the drawing and, surprisingly for 1870, the design makes no provision for a verandah. The 'brick floor' specified in the main room anticipates heavy wear and tear in a space which is entered directly from outside, as well as extensive use of the open fireplace. Gone is the floor of compacted earth or rough gum planking: the floor level is raised 30 cm above natural ground to keep it dry in all weather and to allow air circulation under the floor boards in the bedroom, which are supported by joists of sawn hardwood. The different floor finishes used reflect the different functions of the two rooms.

The Thebarton cottage has a gross area of 37 m², but nearly a quarter is taken up by the masonry wall and fireplace projection. Typical of solid construction, the fireplace is integrated with the end wall. This traditional Scottish and Welsh practice proved especially suited to Australian cottages built on narrow blocks against side boundaries or those attached in rows. While the projection encroached on precious floor space, the recesses formed by the fireplace offered conveniently located storage space for food and cooking utensils; it was where, traditionally, the first built-in cupboards were fitted, often of the do-it-yourself variety.

In elevation, the appreciable increase in overall height of the external walls contrasts with the typically squat appearance of earlier shelters. It results from the floor level being raised above the natural ground and a significant increase in ceiling height. The 3.0 m ceiling height (see Section A–B) (fig. 18), became the norm as soon as solid walls could be carried up to a greater height. In fact, this height was often exceeded, even in low-cost Adelaide houses. Undoubtedly, overcrowding of rooms caused by the initial shortage of accommodation, combined with prolonged, hot summers, made higher ceilings necessary. This occurred long before the minimum ceiling height of 3.0 metres first became law in 1881.

The window and door openings are noticeably larger than those in earlier examples. The upright window openings in the Thebarton cottage are three times larger than the square fenestrations in von Mueller's cottage. Both comprise a pair of casement sashes of four panes each, set in a rebated frame. The casement-type window, being the cheapest to make, was commonly used in early cottages. In cottages of the forties, small sashes containing only three panes were often used. Later, with increasing local use of wood-working machinery, the sliding sash in a box frame (double hung) replaced the casement type—which was not to re-appear again until the early 1920s in the 'bungalow' cottage, minus the traditional glazing bars.

The front door, at an increased height of 1.90 m, is of the traditional four-panel design that became the norm for the rest of the century. The introduction of a glazed fan-light above the door signifies a better class of building, consistent with the taller windows. The openings have flat arches of gauged brickwork integrated with the brick quoins that form the sides of all openings and external corners. Typically, light orange coloured sand-stock brick of traditional London size[16] is used, toothed into random coursed stonework. In common with most early examples, the coursing of the brickwork is five courses to 35 cm (14 inches).

While at first glance the front 'elevation' appears to be symmetrical, the front door is positioned slightly off-centre and the flanking piers vary in width. This departure from the strict symmetry of the Georgian rule was dictated by the plan containing rooms of unequal dimensions side by side. It was not until the full-length passage was introduced that the truly symmetrical facade in the so-called symmetrical cottage finally evolved.

The three room cottage

One of Adelaide's very first houses, erected during the summer of 1837 on the south bank of the Torrens, was the 'official' residence of Governor Hindmarsh. This first 'public' building in the Province contained three inter-connected rooms and a detached kitchen with servants' quarters. Of necessity it was hastily built with rough slab walls covered with a thatched roof. Stretched calico ceilings protected the occupants from falling cockroaches.

It is understandable that the first Colonial Secretary, Robert Gouger, was not impressed and described the building with contempt as a mere 'hut', completely lacking the 'gentlemanly style and English comfort' to be expected of a Governor's residence.[17] Its shortcomings were widely discussed and even ridiculed when it became known that an external chimney was built without a fireplace. Gouger wryly observed that the embarassing omission occurred because 'the architect [Captain Hindmarsh] was a sailor, and that the workmen employed were the seamen of the (HMS) Buffalo, who, thinking they could 'rig up a house', as well as a top-mast, would not allow any interference in their arrangements'.[18] While a two-storey stone Government House replaced the first 'official' hut within four years, the three room cottage plan remained one of the main dwelling types of early colonists.

Two distinct variants of the plan evolved to suit different building sites and budgets. These were the double-fronted, L-shaped plan and the narrow, single-

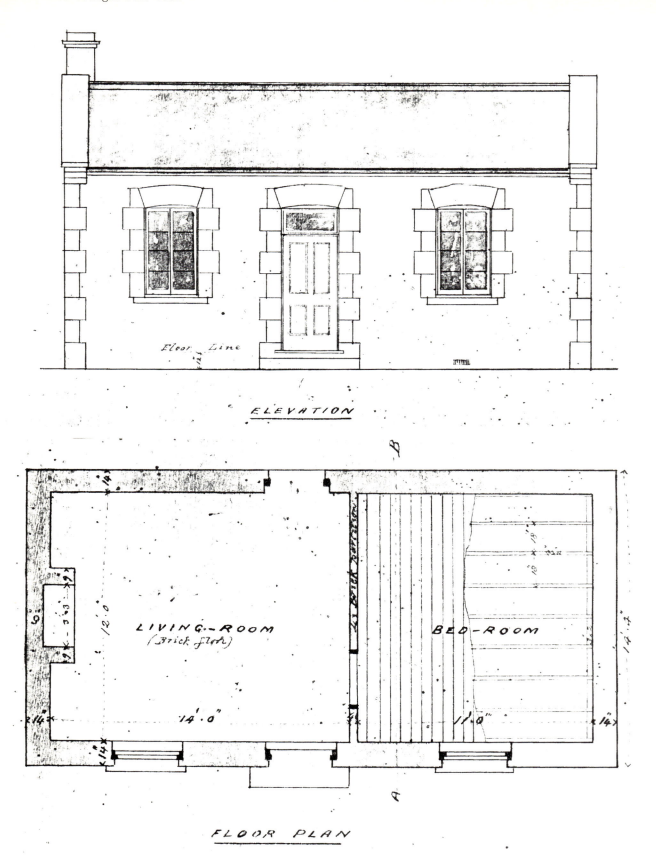

Figure 18: Thebarton Cottage, c.1869. A typical example of a stone/brick cottage of two rooms built around the mid-century. Designer unknown.
(S.A. Gas Co.)

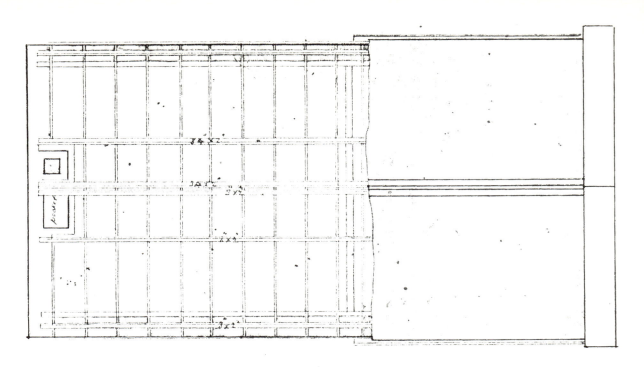

ROOF-PLAN

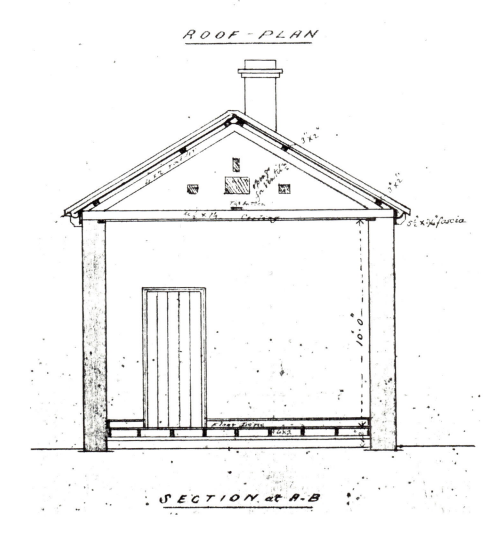

SECTION at A-B

fronted plan with rooms one behind the other. The double-fronted plan illustrated in the following examples was generally built in a detached form by owner-occupiers, while the single-fronted cottage was commonly attached in rows to provide low cost rental accommodation (see Chapter 3).

The double-fronted cottage was more spacious, more substantially constructed and had better lit rooms than the single-fronted variant. Similar in appearance from the street to the two-room cottage, it occupied a larger allotment and so was potentially more extendable. The L-shaped plan could be closed in later to form a square by the addition of a fourth room if the need for more bedrooms arose. In the three-room plan, the third room placed behind one of the front rooms served as a second bedroom or a kitchen. On wider allotments a short, and initially rather narrow, passage was introduced between the front rooms. It not only provided an entrance but also separated the two front rooms from the rest of the house, making them self-contained in their respective functions—that of the 'parlour' and the 'best' bedroom. The third room served either as kitchen, a second bedroom, or both.

Hampton Cottage, c. 1860

The L-shaped, three room cottage at Hampton (fig. 19), built in about 1860, is a good example of this type of plan without a passage, and of early habitation in the mid-north mining town of Burra. This basic plan is included here as an illustration of similar cottages built about the same time in Adelaide, where no known examples survive. It is estimated that the cottage was built soon after the initial sale of allotments in Hampton by Thomas William Powell in 1858. The cottage was occupied for a hundred years during which time a fourth room and an outside kitchen were added to the original plan. When surveyed in 1984 it was found in an abandoned and ruinous state.

The village of Hampton (present North Burra) was one of the miners' settlements which sprang up on private land outside the boundaries of Kooringa, the company town first established at the new copper mine. The original development of Hampton coincided with the new phase of growth and expansion of Burra settlements during the 1850s, when miners returned from the goldfields, and lasted until well into the 1860s. In numbers of dwellings, Hampton was probably the most substantial and longest lived of the mining villages, reaching its peak

during the 1860s when there were about 30 miners' cottages built on the subdivision of 56 allotments. District Council records of house valuations and rates assessment books suggest that houses in Hampton were smaller than those in other settlements of the town, the majority of dwellings being simple detached cottages of two or three rooms.[19] The village appears to have survived the closure of the mine with residents diversifying into agricultural and pastoral pursuits. However, by the turn of the century it succumbed to a long slow decline, which finally concluded when the last two cottages, including the one described here, were vacated some twenty years ago.

As shown, the original plan of the cottage comprised three interconnected rooms: two front rooms of equal dimensions were presumably the living room and bedroom, and a small third room with a corner fireplace served as a dining room and initially as a kitchen. The detached kitchen, partly

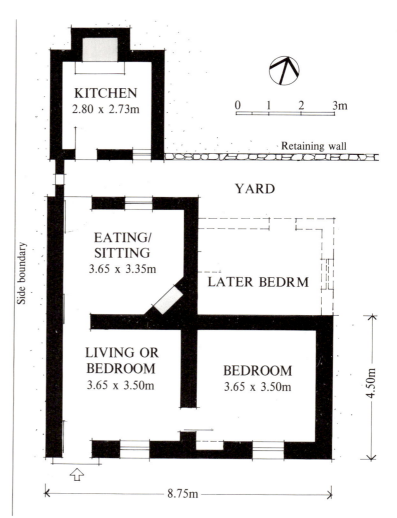

Figure 19: Hampton Cottage, Burra North, c.1860. Double-fronted three room cottage without passage.

GROUND FLOOR PLAN

EAST ELEVATION

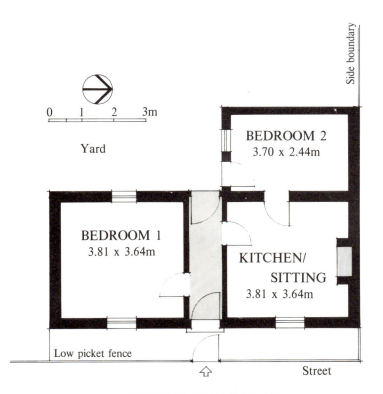

Figure 20: Griffin Cottage, South Adelaide, c.1855.
Double-fronted, three room cottage with a short passage.
(Photograph: T. Fox., 1986)

dug into the ground at the rear, together with a second bedroom were probably added later. The outside entrances and the door between the living room and kitchen are positioned at the outside corners, channelling the circulation along the outside wall. This is a departure from the usual entry. The surviving doors of simple ledged and braced construction are only 70 cm wide and 165 cm high—rather squat for today's users but probably adequate for the Burra miners who are said to have been usually less than 152 cm in height. The front rooms have a pair of well-made casement windows with rebated stiles and small glass panes. Their location in the front wall is dictated by the position of the entrance door and the cupboard recess in the main bedroom. The small open fireplace with a semi-circular head is set, unusually, in the corner of the kitchen and was probably so placed to save space in this small room. A similar arrangement was used in the three room cottages built earlier in Paxton Square—although there a larger fireplace for cooking was provided in the living room. This comparision suggests that the detached kitchen was built at an early date and that the third room (with a fireplace) was used by the family as a dining/sitting room.

The cottage has a frontage of 8.75 m and a gross area of 56 m^2 which compare closely with its Adelaide counterpart, the Griffin cottage, discussed below. However, the usable area of the Hampton cottage is reduced by 30 per cent due to the excessive thickness of its walls built of locally quarried stone. Externally, they are 57 cm thick and the dividing walls 43 cm, including a 5 cm coat of plaster. The extent of the remaining plaster suggests that the ceiling height in the two front rooms was around 2.60 m. Timber shingles, 15 cm wide x 1 cm thick covered the front gable roof and the lean-to over the rear section. There is also evidence of a white washed calico ceiling stretched under the lean-to rafters. There is no evidence of any verandahs.

Griffin Cottage, c.1855

Griffin's cottage (fig. 20) is typical of the double-fronted L-shaped plan. It was built probably around 1855 on a corner allotment (12.5 m wide x 12.0 m deep) fronting two minor streets in the south-west corner of the city of Adelaide. By 1890, it was jointly owned by Martin Griffin, saddler, and Mary Ritchie, wife of Gavin Ritchie, a Goodwood builder.[20] The superior workmanship of the cottage suggests that it might have been the builder's own house. Apart from the addition of a back verandah, now enclosed with corrugated iron and used as a kitchen and a small bedroom, the original structure remains virtually intact.

Despite its spacious corner allotment, the siting of this cottage follows the early town practice of building close to the footpath. The front set-back, which measures only 1.0 m, is enclosed by the low picket fence and gate leading to the front door, while the side wall stands right on the street boundary. The plan of 54 m^2 has a narrow passage (1.05 m wide), which gives access to the equal-sized front rooms (3.8 m x 3.6 m). The corner room containing the large fireplace was used as the kitchen/sitting room. It was not uncommon for these rooms also to contain a bed. The remaining two rooms would have been used as bedrooms, although the location of the door of the front one (adjacent to the front door) suggests that this room could have been intended as a parlour.

Externally, the design of Griffin's cottage closely resembles the two-room Thebarton cottage, detailed previously. The frontage of 9.6 m is about a metre wider and differs also in the frontal symmetry and the type of window used. The symmetry of the facade design stems from the introduction of the central passage flanked by rooms of equal width. The front windows comprise double-hung vertically sliding sashes, each divided into six glass panes, and are larger in area and more advanced in design than the casement window. The flat ceilings in the main rooms are also of comparable height (3.0 m). The outside walls of the front section, including the wall on the boundary, are built of stone, 35 cm thick with five course brick quoins. Internal partitions and outside walls enclosing the second bedroom under the lean-to are of brick. The saddle-back slate roof extends between brick-capped end walls.

Gatekeeper's Cottage, 1865

The building contract for this unusual T-shaped, three room cottage (figs. 21 & 22) was signed in December, 1865.[21] Designed by the Colonial Architect's Department, it was built as a gatekeeper's lodge at the North Terrace entrance to the then Lunatic Asylum, situated in the eastern section of the present Botanic Gardens. With the Asylum long gone from the site, the cottage has been in continuous use as a staff residence at the Garden.

On the original drawings, 'G. T. Light' witnessed the signature of the builder 'William Tims'. George Thomas Light (no relation to Colonel William Light) was at the time a Draftsman working in the Department, and was appointed Architect in 1874.[22] It seems likely that he had a hand in the design of the cottage. Light's continuing association with the building is confirmed by his signature, 'G.T. Light Architect' appearing again on the drawings for the additions of 1875.

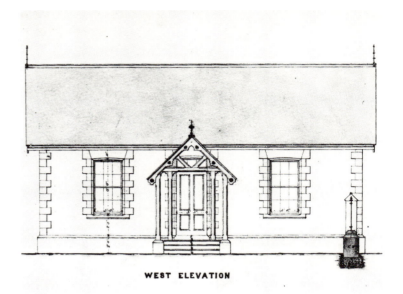

WEST ELEVATION

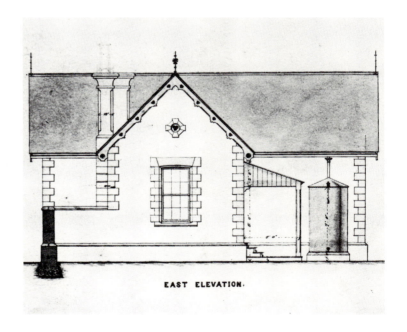

EAST ELEVATION.

Figure 21: Gatekeeper's Cottage, Adelaide, 1865. G.T. Light, Colonial Architect's Department. Double-fronted, three room cottage with an extended passage.

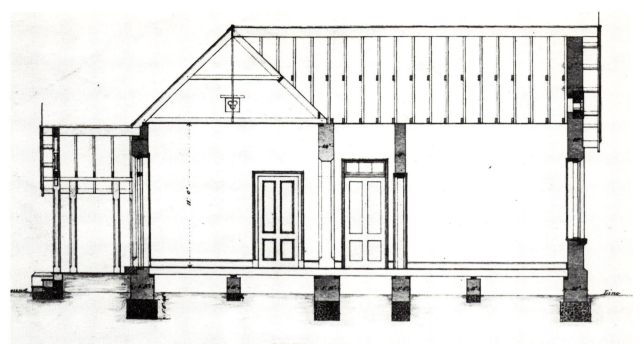

SECTION THROUGH A-B ON PLAN.

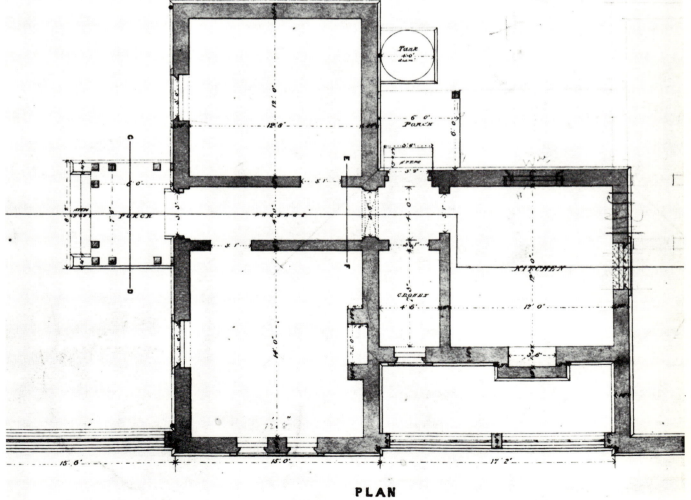

PLAN

The execution of this small building by a public works designer, and its prominent location may justify the elaborate treatment given to the elevations and the above-average standard of workmanship. Not being restricted by the site, the design reflects with good accuracy the prevailing trends and housing standards in Adelaide around the mid-1860s. In this respect, it is revealing to compare the two examples of roughly contemporary residences that were offered with different jobs: a gatekeeper, who was a Civil servant, and a resident engineer at the works of the Provincial Gas Company—an employee of a new private enterprise (see previous fig. 18). The undeniable conclusion is that the gatekeeper was housed far better than the engineer.

The gatekeeper's accommodation comprised a parlour and a bedroom at the front (facing west) and a third room, labelled 'kitchen', with a pantry labelled 'closet' attached at the rear. Although these three rooms are not exceptionally large, the inclusion of the passage and pantry increased the overall area of the cottage to 74 m².

Compared with earlier L-shaped examples, this plan is less ambiguous in the allocation of functions to individual rooms: here, the location and relative size, the built-in appointments and the position of doors all convey the intended uses. Generally, the functions assigned to the rooms are becoming more defined, with greater separation of various domestic activities. The all-purpose living room of the two-room settler cottage is replaced by the parlour. In this plan it is the biggest room—60 centimetres longer than the bedroom. It has two windows enjoying the best outlook, and its focal point is the central fireplace which is no longer used for cooking.

The door to the parlour is closest to the entrance. The second 'best' room is the bedroom, with the door moved further down the passage for greater privacy. In earlier plans the doors to the two front rooms were vis-a-vis. This was possibly done in an attempt to increase air movement from the front door when it was left open in hot weather. There was little to distinguish one door from the other, and unless the bedroom door was closed there was little protection from the unwanted glance of a casual visitor.

The archway—positioned in line with the rear wall of the main rooms—divides the house into two zones: 'formal' at the front, and 'private' at the back. The archway, usually curtained, was initially a structural element of the cross-wall. As house plans grew larger it became characteristically a decorative element in the long tunnel-type passage, as well as a visual barrier separating the two front rooms from the rest of the house.

The attached 'kitchen', 3.6 metres square, is large enough to cater for eating and general family activities, especially during winter months when the fire would have been stoked up continuously. The large 'closet' provided ample storage for foodstuffs, including garden-grown vegetables, and is a forerunner of the pantry that became a customary requirement of late Victorian houses.

A raised rainwater 'tank' stands at the back door of the cottage (East Elevation). Provided under the building contract, and made of corrugated zinc-anealed iron, the tank collected the run-off from the rear section of the slate roof. Since the late fifties, corrugated iron tanks came into general use. Typically, the lodge was extended after ten years by the addition of a rectangular wing to the north wall of the kitchen, containing two 'bedrooms', each provided with a fireplace.

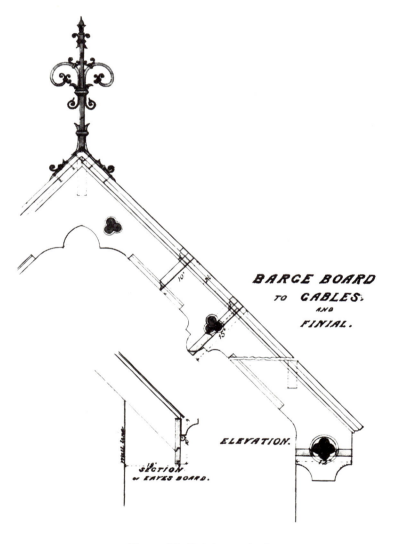

Figure 22: Gatekeeper's Cottage, Roof details.

Chapter 3

Row Cottages and Maisonettes

1836–1901

Definitions

The cottage plan, discussed as a detached house in Chapters 2 and 4, also evolved in the form of two closely related types of low-cost housing: the single-storey row cottage and the semi-detached pair, later called 'maisonettes'.[1] The term 'cottage' was used generally by colonists to describe a small house, regardless of its type or its location, either in a township or in the country.

Apart from the common name, row cottages and maisonettes shared with detached houses two fundamental characteristics: a piece of land reserved for the exclusive use of the occupants of each dwelling, and individual access from a street or 'public' lane.

In order to distinguish between different sizes and classes of houses built in South Australia, the term 'terrace' is used to describe generally larger, attached houses of multi-storey design. Similarly, a 'semi-detached house' defines a larger, double-storey version of the maisonette. These types are discussed separately in Chapter 5.

The row cottage

Adelaide's first shelters included rows of repetitive dwellings, each containing two or three small rooms arranged in single file—see, for example, Gray's row, discussed below. Common party walls, and roof reduced building costs and enabled labour to be shared with friends or neighbours. Because the typical dwelling in a row had only two outside walls it was better protected from the elements and so cooler in summer. While later multi-storey terraces and semi-detached houses provided alternatives for the more affluent, common row cottages continued to be built throughout the colonial period as a cheap form of rental house for the working-class population. For most of this period no building by-law had any real effect on the design or siting of these dwellings.

For twenty odd years timber buildings covered in thatch or shingles crowded together in the built-up parts of the city. The only rule in force, since 1841, stipulated that no building could encroach on to the footpath, verandahs being excepted. An Act restricting the use of inflammable materials for external coverings and ceilings became law in the city of Adelaide in 1858, yet the first by-laws prescribing fire-isolating party walls and the minimum ceiling height of 3.0 m for habitable rooms were not introduced in Adelaide until 1881. Building approvals granted during the 1890s suggest that the minimum width of 9.0 m, prescribed for 'private' streets by the Municipal Corporations Act (1880), had no apparent effect on the design of access lanes to the 'back' houses. See, for example, Paterson's row (1898), discussed later in this Chapter.

With no statutory constraints to affect the form of housing, important matters such as the amount of ground space allocated to each dwelling, its floor area and facilities, were at the whim of the colonial developer. In an enterprise where profit on investment was the motivating factor, substandard accommodation and overcrowded living conditions for large families on low income were the inevitable result.

The evaluation of a sample residential area at the end of 1841 (Chapter 1), shows that one-quarter of all dwellings were row houses. Without exception they were built of the cheapest materials of the day—'pisé' and timber covered with 'lath and plaster'.[2] As early as 1837, the Colonial Secretary, Robert Gouger, expounded that 'rows of cottages for labourers and artisans are much wanted'.[3] To would-be speculators he advocated the 'minor' streets of Adelaide as appropriate locations for such cottages. The pattern of development that followed clearly shows that Gouger's advice was heeded.

Adelaide's rows seldom exceeded six houses. A typical row of between three and six dwellings suited small investors and owners who could both live in the building and derive income from rent. Rows were dispersed widely throughout the city. Outside the parklands, row cottages formed part of the early villages, which subsequently became suburban centres of the greater metropolitan area.

In order to utilise the cheapest available land, they became part of a less desirable mixed development or were to be found in locations which ceased to be highly regarded as residential areas. However, the highest concentration of small cottages was to be found inside the city blocks. As the century progressed, a pattern of urban development based on different land values emerged, and gave colonial Adelaide something of the diversity usually associated with older Victorian cities. Better class houses, intermixed with commercial premises, lined the main streets. Behind these buildings, small houses, usually of single-storey construction, combined with less desirable places of business to fill the large remaining portions of the original one-acre allotments.

As shown on the Smith City Survey,[4] these inner areas became a network of minor streets and access

lanes as individual owners sub-divided their land in a typically piecemeal fashion. It was this secondary network that provided not only the address for innumerable households, but also the necessary service access to the properties with frontages to the main street. An example of the evolution of 'minor' streets and lanes during the period 1842–1880 is shown by the development of the sample area (fig. 23). The earlier development of the area which remained primarily residential in character until the turn of the century, was discussed in Chapter 1.

Two variants of the plan used in row houses are the early double-fronted (two rooms side by side), and the later single-fronted (one room wide) design.

Before mid-century, a typical Adelaide row cottage was double-fronted, consisting of just two small rooms with a 7.0 m wide average frontage. It represented the traditional form of British housing transplanted to South Australia with little adaption. At first there was ample room on the one-acre city allotments to accommodate double-fronted cottages, with rows sited parallel to the street or a side boundary. However, as land prices and building densities increased, the single-fronted plan evolved as a more economic proposition for an investor/speculator. Other factors which made the double-fronted cottage un-economic were the cost of road making and the assessment of city rates which, since 1849, took into account the frontage of each dwelling.

Figure 23: Development of minor streets and lanes in the sample area, 1837–1880. (For earlier details see Chapter 1, figs.10 and 11).

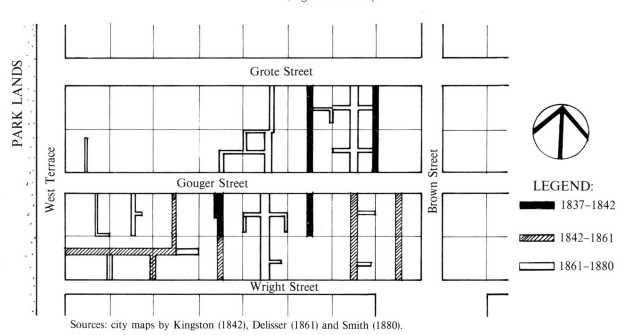

LEGEND:

■ 1837–1842

▨ 1842–1861

▢ 1861–1880

Sources: city maps by Kingston (1842), Delisser (1861) and Smith (1880).

The design of the single-fronted cottage was an outcome of continuing speculation in town lands and the growing demand for rental accommodation within easy walking distance from work. It was prompted by the doubling of Adelaide's population in the period 1845–50, and again between 1860–80. The elongated plan, running down the block, had a narrow frontage, ranging from 3.5 m to 5.5 m in width, that permitted more houses to be crammed on to a given piece of land. However, this was not achieved without a detrimental effect on the quality of the accommodation. With one room placed behind another it was difficult to admit adequate light and ventilation to the middle bedroom. This room could have only a small skylight which usually did not open. There was, of course, also a limit to the number of rooms that could be added on at the rear of the house. And, with many frontages under 4.0 m wide, there was no space left for a passage, the front room being entered directly from outside.

Not infrequently, the basic single-fronted plan was also built as a detached house standing on allotments about 6.0 m wide. Neighbouring houses would not be joined by common party walls. Instead a combined gap less than one metre wide would separate their side walls and leave their gutters almost touching. This gap was not wide enough to provide a minimum of light and ventilation to the middle rooms. Consequently, the windows which were placed along the side walls were only a slight improvement on the skylight over the middle room in a row house.

Prior to 1842, Adelaide's longest row house was the Barnard Buildings which stood on Town Acre 95 in Grenfell Street (east)—later the site of the fruit and vegetable market. The 60 m long row comprised 13 dwellings (each about 4.6 m wide x 6.0 m deep).[5] This pisé building was sited parallel with the side boundary of the acre and formed part of the early built-up area which developed east of Hindmarsh Square. It was demolished before 1880.

Arguably, the longest row house which appears on the Smith City Survey of 1880 is the David Street row of 17 single-fronted dwellings, completed in the late 1870s (fig. 24). Both the street, which ran off Regent Street (re-named Frome Street), and the 'stone and brick dwellings'[6] have disappeared from the map of Adelaide leaving no known photographic

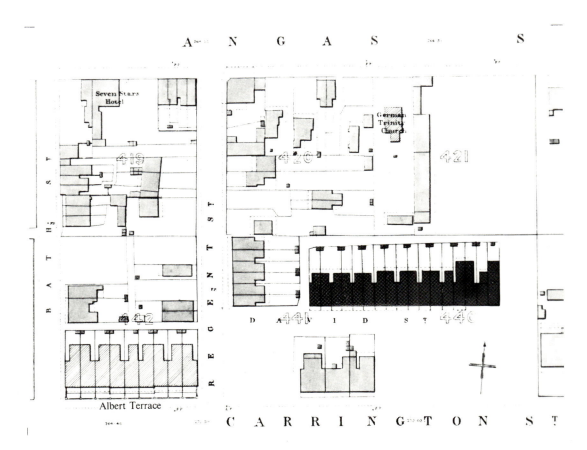

Figure 24: David Street Row of 17 single-fronted dwellings. Built in stages, this exceptionally long row of attached cottages was completed in the late 1870s. *(Smith City Survey, 1880, Sheet no. 30)*

NORTH ELEVATION

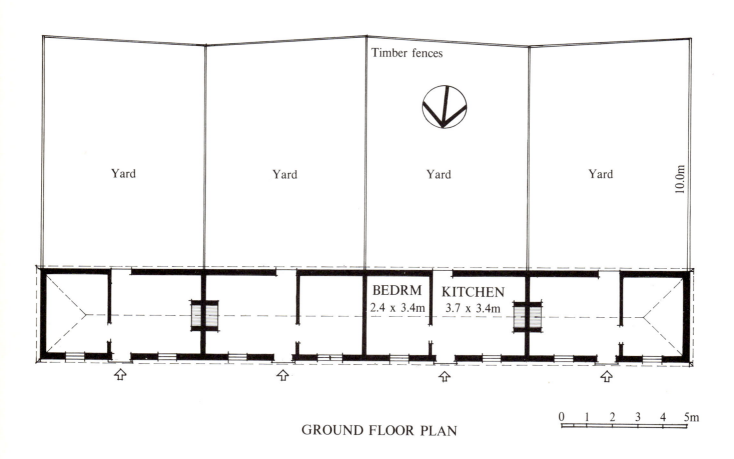

Timber fences

Yard   Yard   Yard   Yard

10.0m

BEDRM
2.4 x 3.4m

KITCHEN
3.7 x 3.4m

GROUND FLOOR PLAN

0 1 2 3 4 5m

Figure 25: Gray's Row, South Adelaide, pre-1841. A typical early row of four double-fronted cottages each comprising only two small rooms. The photograph, taken after 1880, shows a corrugated iron roof concealing the original thatch.
(Mortlock Library of South Australiana)

record. This unusually extensive row house stretched for 75 metres along the rear boundaries of Town Acres 440 and 441 in Carrington Street. The individual cottages, each with its own backyard accessed from a rear lane, were similar in size with frontages ranging from 4.2 m to 4.5 m wide, and covering a ground area of about 55 m^2. To make optimum use of land, front walls were built on the street boundary with a 1.5 m wide continuous verandah encroaching over the 7.0 m wide David Street.

Gray's Row, pre-1841

This row of four dwellings, which stood on Town Acre 3 at the east corner of Gray Street and North Terrace, is typical of early double-fronted design (fig. 25). Remarkably, they survived intact for more than forty years without any additions being made to the original buildings, thought to have been erected as early as 1838 by W.H. Gray. As well as giving access from the western end of Hindley Street to the Torrens, this early street, which bears Gray's name, extended south all the way to Grote Street by 1842. It bisected the town acres which, with considerable business foresight, Gray purchased to create this early north-south thoroughfare.

Kingston's map shows that the cottages were of 'pisé' or wood covered with 'lath and plaster', and had no verandahs—which in this case were never added. The building is one room deep, covered with a hipped roof that originally was probably thatched. The set-back from the North Terrace boundary is greater than usual, suggesting that later a more substantial front section might have been contemplated.

There were four similar dwellings of two rooms with a fenced-in back yard, 10 m deep. Each dwelling had a frontage of 6.5 m and a gross area of about 25 m^2.[7] The basic plan, comprising kitchen/sitting room with open fireplace and a small bedroom, follows that of a pioneer cottage, previously described by William Finlayson (Chapter 1).

Paxton Square Rows, 1849–52

For further evaluation of the double-fronted row cottage it is necessary to turn to the mid-north town of Burra (present name), 160 km from Adelaide, founded by the South Australian Mining Association following the opening of a rich copper mine in 1845. Burra's early cottages included in this Chapter fill the gap from 1842 to about mid-century.

Paxton Square represents not only the earliest example of company housing in Australia, but also possibly the largest single housing scheme erected in the Province of South Australia during its first fifty years. Although single-storey in height, the overall scale of the scheme is impressive. Each row of eleven cottages presents a continuous facade 105 metres long, which is considerably longer than any of Adelaide's single-storey rows or multi-storey terraces. Because of their stone construction, the type of ownership and a fortuitous sequence of events, this original group of buildings has remained largely intact. Since 1982, individual cottages have been gradually restored and converted to self-contained tourist accommodation.

The total of 33 cottages in the scheme were built in 1849–52 to accommodate Cornish miners and Welsh and German smelters who with their families came to work at the mine. Before the rush to the goldfields started in 1851, the population of the township was nearly 5,000, equal to one-third of the population of Adelaide (fig. 26). Typical of the period, Burra's early houses were of three or four rooms,[8] either free-standing or attached in short rows.

Paxton Square (fig. 27) was the largest single scheme built specifically for rental. However, most of the mine workers arriving at Burra were uncertain of the expected life of the mine and disliked leasehold. They preferred to live in temporary shelters, including dugouts excavated in the soft banks of the Burra Burra Creek on which the township was established. Rents at Paxton Square were set at three shillings per week out of an average weekly earnings at the mine of £1/5/-.[9] Generally, the miners were reluctant to move from their rent-free accommodation, and it was not until the Association would not employ miners who lived in the dugouts that all the cottages were occupied. George S. Kingston,[10] who from the outset was associated with the township of Kooringa, designed the three identical rows grouped around a common. It was named 'Paxton Square'[11] after William Paxton, a fellow director of the Mining Association who promoted the housing scheme. The first row of eleven dwellings along Bridge Terrace facing the Burra Burra Creek, was completed in 1849 by the builder, William Henderson.

The same plan was used to construct the subsequent rows along Kingston and Paxton Terraces. Kingston's design offered a unique combination of two and three-room plans with a single four-room dwelling included in each row. It occupied the central position, flanked by three three-room and two two-room dwellings on either side. The mix offered a wide range of accommodation for different sized families with the three-room, L-shaped plan predominating. Each dwelling presented a double-front to the street of roughly equal width and the continuous, straight facade of the row concealed the symmetry of the layout. Each dwelling had its own backyard, about 20 m deep, enclosed by a paling fence. The greater depth of 4.4 m given to the front rooms increased their functional flexibility and the capacity to accommodate larger families. The omission of passages from all the dwellings made optimum use of internal space—undoubtedly an important design criterion. However, with generous floor areas and ceiling height in the main rooms, combined with masonry construction, Paxton Square compared favourably with many an owner-built house in Burra or in the Adelaide district.

The smallest, two-room dwelling (fig. 28) with 10.0 m frontage and gross area of 53 m^2, presents an enlarged version of the earlier Gray cottages, discussed above. The larger room (4.8 m x 4.4 m) in the plan was entered directly off the street and contained the only open fireplace, where meals were prepared. This room also doubled as bedroom for those members of the family who could not fit into the adjoining, square bedroom.

Just over one-half of all the dwellings were three room, L-shaped cottages, each with a 9.3 m frontage and a gross area of 66 m^2. It is noteworthy that this area is 10 m^2 larger than the privately-built miner's cottage at the nearby village of Hampton (Chapter 2).

The plan (fig. 28) comprised two front rooms under the main gable roof similar to the two-room plan, except that the bedroom was only 3.60 m wide, with an adjoining third room, 3.60 m square, under the lean-to roof. This room had a corner fireplace and a second outside door to the yard. Its smaller hearth, combined with evidence that cooking was done in the main room, suggests that the back room was not intended for cooking. However, this layout is flexible enough to allow the rear room to be used either as a second bedroom or as a kitchen.

The one four-room cottage (87 m^2 in gross area) catered for the largest of the miners' families. It was a natural extension of the three-room plan with the fourth room (kitchen) behind the main living room completing the square. The two bedrooms gained more privacy with separate doors provided to each room.

Random rubble stones, built 45 cm thick were used for the external walls of the cottages. The original main gable roofs were covered with split wooden shingles while simple skillions extended over the lean-tos of the three and four room dwellings. All main rooms had generous 3.20 m high ceilings of whitewashed hessian, later changed to lath and plaster, at least in the living rooms. Originally, most floors were probably of compacted earth. Later,

Figure 26: (below) The township of Kooringa (present Burra) c. 1850, as painted by W.A. Cawthorne. In the foreground are Paxton Square and the miners' dug-out dwellings along the Burra Burra Creek.
(Mitchell Library, State Library of N.S.W.)

Figure 27: (opp.) G.S. Kingston, architect. Paxton Square Rows, Kooringa, 1849–52. Site plan showing three similar rows of eleven dwellings each, arranged around a common square. *(Measured drawings, 1985)*

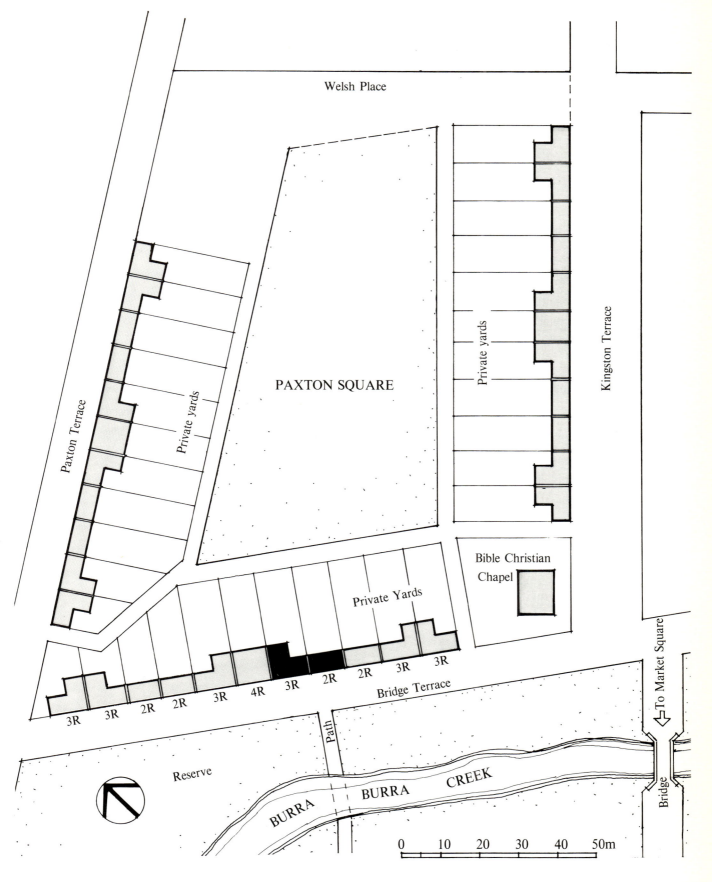

Welsh Place

PAXTON SQUARE

Paxton Terrace

Private yards

Private yards

Kingston Terrace

Bible Christian Chapel

Private Yards

3R 3R 2R 2R 3R 4R 3R 2R 2R 3R 3R

Bridge Terrace

Path

To Market Square

Reserve

BURRA BURRA CREEK

Bridge

0 10 20 30 40 50m

A STREET VIEW

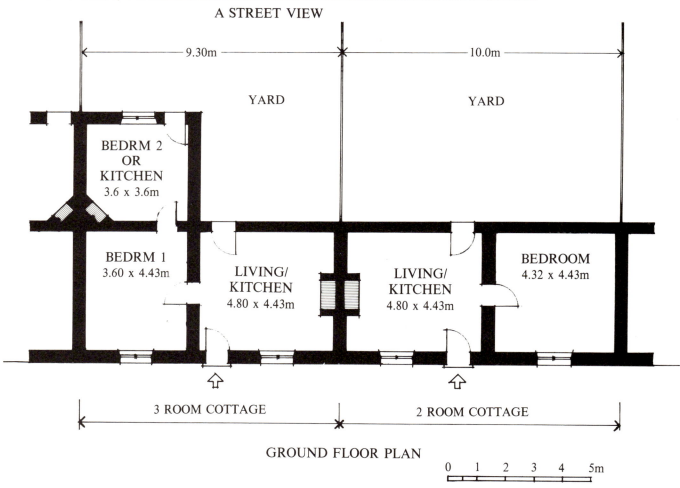

GROUND FLOOR PLAN

Figure 28: Paxton Square Rows. Two room and three room cottages. The photograph, taken in 1933, shows typical street view of the rows still without verandahs.
(Mortlock Library of South Australiana)

bricks or rough concrete were laid in the all-purpose 'living' rooms and timber floors in the bedrooms. Typically, front windows consisted of a pair of casement sashes, opening out, each with eight small panes of glass.

A significant feature of Kingston's design for this housing scheme was the large open space in the middle of the site surrounded on three sides by the buildings. Linked to surrounding streets by two walkways, it was to be a place for miners' meetings. But, in reality, the concept of the common or village green did not materialise. Probably due to lack of money, the square was never paved or landscaped. And there was another practical problem: the backs of the cottages rather than the fronts (as in an English village) faced the common space with the line of back fences punctuated by privies bounding the immediate enclosure. It is not surprising, therefore, that the area degenerated over the years. With fences and privies gone, this vast open space still remains a piece of no-man's land.

While, for good practical reasons, the idea of a common never eventuated, Kingston's attempt to create a comprehensive residential development must be commended. Admittedly, as the land was owned by the Mining Association and not a private speculator, this made Kingston's proposal more feasible at Burra than it would have been in Adelaide, where the English idea of sharing the use of residential land was never taken up. It was half a century after the experiment at Burra that the city garden movement brought similar schemes to fruition in the suburbs of London. By then, the objectionable outside privy had become an internal W.C., and consequent upgrading of the rear aspect of the houses made the enclosed common space more valuable than before.

During their first hundred years, the cottages housed a changing population of the township, and underwent certain changes and improvements.[12] In 1873 the split wooden shingles, which lasted for over 20 years, were covered with corrugated iron. But it was not until the late 1930s that verandahs were added to the street frontages. Galvanised iron lean-tos and small rain-water tanks were provided a few years later at the rear of the cottages.

During the 1880s reticulated water was laid on and five taps were installed in the common to serve all the cottages. Only in 1946 were taps installed in each back yard to supplement the five taps that had previously served the whole area. There was no running water, when, in 1877, the Burra mine closed down and the thirty-three cottages still housed 'a teaming population of 161 people', an average of five people to each dwelling, or nearly two persons to each room. With 'ashpits, cesspools, pigsties and

closets in close proximity to the cottages' epidemics of typhoid and scarlatina were common among the children of Paxton Square.[13]

By 1912, the population of Burra had fallen dramatically and when the cottages were auctioned by the South Australian Mining Association in that year they were nearly all empty. Subsequently, the Lewis Trust took over their management and they were rented to house the 'poor and the needy of Burra'.[14] During the depression years of the 1930s the cottages were fully occupied again. In 1969, Paxton Square was proclaimed a Historic Reserve under the Historic Preservation Act of 1965.

Tiver's Row, 1856

As privately-built housing for the miners at Redruth, Tiver's Row provides an interesting comparison with the Paxton Square cottages owned and rented by the mining company. Named after the Cornish town, Redruth became the first 'little Cornwall' in South Australia, where, following the public sale of land in 1849, Burra's miners were free to build their own houses. This new settlement, with its streets named after Cornish mining villages, lay just north of Kooringa, the mining company town established four years earlier.

The surviving 47.2 m long row, built in 1856, contained six similar double-fronted cottages of four interconnected rooms with no passage (fig. 29). Following the traditional pattern of Cornish villages, the front wall was set on the footpath and the building was without a verandah. Its siting and internal layout offered utmost economy in the use of land and utilisation of floor space. In the late fifties another row of three cottages of similar design was built in the next block on the opposite side of Truro Street; both rows have survived and have been continuously occupied to the present day.

Although the plan resembles the largest of the cottages in Paxton Square, the Redruth cottages were built on a smaller scale, having individual frontages of 7.64 m and a gross area of 59 m². Without apparent site limitation, the size of the dwellings must have been determined either by the cost of building or traditional Cornish space standards.

There are two distinct day rooms: at the front the 'formal' parlour is the largest room in the house (3.8 m x 3.4 m) with the informal kitchen/eating room (3.8 m x 2.9 m) behind it. The main bedroom entered off the parlour is 3.4 m square; the separate second bedroom (3.4 m x 2.9 m) is entered through the kitchen. Typically, doors of the rooms needing privacy are hung so that they screen the interior of the room when open. The status of the parlour as the 'best' room is enhanced by the large fireplace—

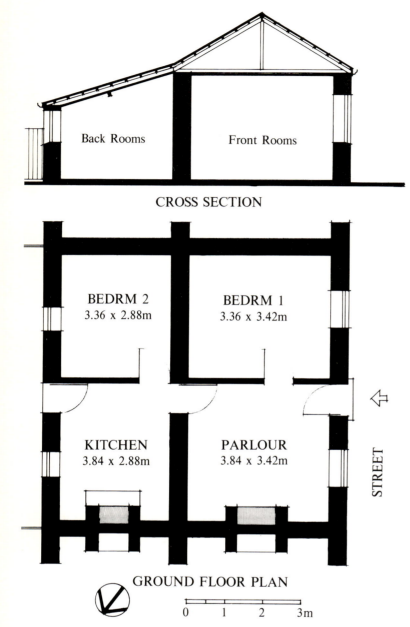

CROSS SECTION

BEDRM 2
3.36 x 2.88m

BEDRM 1
3.36 x 3.42m

KITCHEN
3.84 x 2.88m

PARLOUR
3.84 x 3.42m

STREET

GROUND FLOOR PLAN

0   1   2   3m

Figure 29: Tiver's Row, Redruth (present North Burra), 1856. Double-fronted row cottage of four interconnected rooms, built without verandahs.

used primarily for heating rather than cooking. There is a distinction made between the front pair and the rear pair of rooms shown in the Cross Section. While the front rooms have a flat ceiling, 2.90 m high under the main gable roof, the two narrower rear rooms are covered by a flat skillion roof with a sloping ceiling of 2.50 m average height. Also, window sizes used in the front rooms are considerably larger than those used at the rear. It is interesting that windows are positioned in the 48 cm thick stone walls to suit the interior rather than to conform to a preconceived external design.

Some extensions have been made over the years at the rear of individual cottages, yet the street fronts remain virtually intact and, despite the high summer temperatures in the mid-north, no street verandahs have been added to date.

The Redruth cottages also illustrate a typical four-room plan without passage which evolved in stages from a two-room settler's cottage, discussed in Chapter 2.

Calder's Row, pre-1858

This extremely small, single-fronted cottage illustrates the kind of rental accommodation that was available in Adelaide during the 1850s. Situated at the end of a row of three cottages owned by a Mrs. Scandrett in Synagogue Place (off Rundle Street east), Adelaide, it was occupied in 1858 by William Calder, his wife and two young children. Calder's contemporary Journal[15] includes a sketch plan, labelled 'our first house—Synagogue Place', on which the reconstructed plan is based (fig. 30) His description gives a comprehensive picture of a lived-in plan, indicating the functions of the rooms and their sparse furnishings. The rent of seven shillings per week reflects the high rates charged by private landlords in Adelaide during the late fifties. As William Calder earned about £5 a week on the staff of the *South Australian Register*, he would have found it easier to pay this rent than the average tradesman whose wage was half of Calder's.

Typical of early development, the cottages stood on a minimal allotment, 10 m wide by 20 m deep, sub-divided into three. Calder's cottage had a street frontage of about 3.5 m wide, and an enclosed private 'back yard' 10 m deep. Half of the site was covered by buildings. The gross area of the cottage was only 30 m^2, which was no larger than the average free-standing settler's cottage of two rooms.[16] Moreover, the usable floor area (excluding wall thicknesses) was about 15 m^2 smaller than that provided by the contemporary detached houses with three rooms, discussed in Chapter 2. Even with the minimal amount of furniture described by Calder, the reconstructed plan of his cottage clearly indicates the cramped living conditions within.

Calder's brick cottage comprised two main rooms and an attached kitchen reached from the outside. The 'parlour', which would have measured about 3.6 m square, was entered directly off the street. It had an open fireplace and one double casement window to the street; a sofa stood under the window, a large table in the centre of the room and a small table and chairs against the walls. Behind the parlour was the 'bedroom', which was slightly smaller. As the cottage was on the end of a row the bedroom

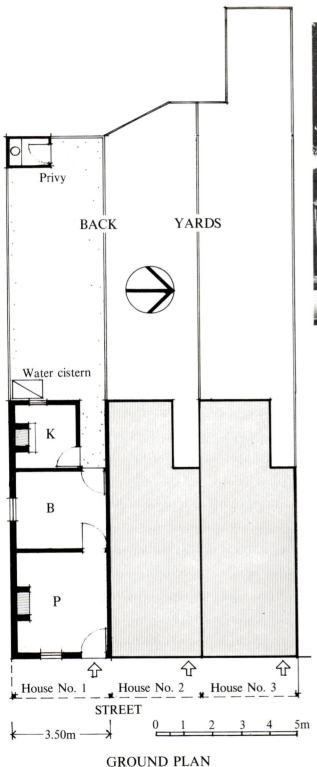

GROUND PLAN

Privy

BACK   YARDS

Water cistern

K

B

P

House No. 1   House No. 2   House No. 3

STREET

3.50m   0 1 2 3 4 5m

K: Kitchen, 2.50 x 2.90m
B: Bedroom, 3.20 x 2.80m
P: Parlour, 3.60 x 3.20m

STREET ELEVATION

Figure 30: Calder's Row of three single-fronted cottages in South Adelaide was built for cheap rental around 1850. An indication of its general appearance is given by this photograph of a similar row of brick cottages with a continuous wooden verandah, dating to the mid-1840s. *(Photograph taken early 1960s: Mortlock Library of South Australiana)*

had a small window in a side wall. But, in the middle cottage, with party walls on both sides, the half-glazed outside door would have been the only means of admitting light to this central room. In later plans, skylights were used. The bedroom contained a double bedstead, a chest of drawers, a curtain-fronted wardrobe and a chair.

The tiny 'kitchen', less than 3.0 m square, was attached at the back of the house. Its limited floor space was probably encroached by the open fireplace which had to be built inside the boundary. The only furniture Calder assigns to this room is a table and a bed labelled 'boys' bed' on his sketch. The small back yard contained a 'wood pile' stacked against the kitchen wall, and a rectangular 'water cistern' which stored the water for all domestic and garden use. The family had to rely on water being delivered by cart and economy in use was important. Calder writes: ' . . . 9d. of water lasts us for a week, if we are not washing'.[17] In 1858, this amount would have purchased a mere 20 gallons (90 litres) of water.

There is no clue given as to the laundry or ablution facilities. Generally, ablutions took place inside the house and, weather permitting, clothes were washed outside. A more detailed explanation is provided in the Elliott house (1856), discussed in Chapter 4. Calder's sketch marks the privy in its typical location at the bottom of the yard.

The first two rooms of Calder's cottage were of brick construction, with a simple gable roof probably covered with shingles. The kitchen would have been a lean-to, possibly built of timber. The photograph of a brick cottage, built in the city in the mid-1840s, shown with the reconstructed plan (fig. 30), gives an indication of the scale and general appearance of early Adelaide row cottages.

Parker's Row, 1878–79

The speculative building of low-cost attached cottages on land situated behind properties fronting major streets of Adelaide continued at an accelerated rate throughout the building boom of the seventies and early eighties. The workers' tenements built by the builder, George Murray in Parker Street (re-named Bower Street), North Adelaide, illustrate a typical development of the seventies undertaken on a somewhat larger scale (fig. 32). A total of 16 single-fronted brick cottages form two equal rows across the minor street made between adjoining Town Acres 985 and 986 in Melbourne Street.

Except for the slightly larger end dwellings, the typical row cottage contained three rooms with a frontage of 4.2 m wide and a gross area of 48 m[2].[18] As in the plans of the fifties, illustrated above, the front parlour incorporates the entrance door and the kitchen forms a rear projection under a lean-to roof. In overall size and general dimensions this scheme can be closely correlated with the David Street row, discussed earlier in this section. In both schemes, the average area per dwelling is 50 m[2]. This shows a two-thirds increase on Calder's rowhouse, built some 20 years earlier.

A notable improvement in the privacy and general appearance of the Parker Street row houses is achieved by the 4.5 m set-back from the footpath. Although, as the photograph shows (fig. 31), the strip of land in front of the houses was neglected for some time, the development of private gardens would have given the dwellings a measure of individuality. By the late 1870s, front verandahs, economically covered with curved corrugated iron, were common to all but the cheapest houses. In this case a continuous 1.6 m wide verandah (using the standard 1.8 m sheet of iron) provides useful covered space for each house, while visually unifying the whole row. Above, a series of chimney stacks protrude high above the ridge line of the common roof, as yet unbroken by the parapet walls that soon became a legal requirement.

Since the row cottages became the property of the H.J. Bower Benevolent Fund in 1933, they have been restored and modernised, and continue to provide low-cost accommodation.

Figure 31: (below) Parker's Row, North Adelaide, 1878–79, photographed in 1933.
(Public Record Office of S.A.)

Figure 32: (opp.) Parkers Row: site plan showing two similar rows of eight dwellings each.
(Smith City Survey, 1880, Sheet no.122)

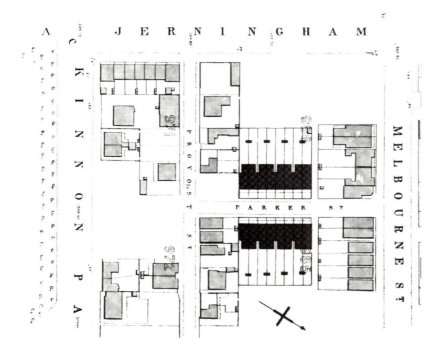

Paterson's Row, 1897

This short row of four 'one storey cottages', designed in 1897 by the architect Edward J. Woods[19] for a Dr. Alexander Paterson, was built in 1898 as part of a mixed housing development on one-half of Town Acre 675 in South Terrace, Adelaide. The surviving cottages occupy the rear portion of the rectangular site, 32 m wide by 65 m deep, (fig. 33), behind a terrace of 'two storey houses' fronting the parklands. For details of the terrace see Chapter 5 (fig. 77).

Typical of city development, the private road, which constituted the right of way along the side boundary gives public access to the cottages, as well as service to the fenced-in private back yards of the terraces and the cottages. The same road was used for the sewer run, water and gas supply. Alongside the terraces, the road is only 3.8 m wide, widening to 6.0 m in front of the cottages. Right of ways of 6.0 m or even 4.5 m wide, giving front access to a number of cottages, were still being approved in city sub-divisions during the 1890s, despite the fact that the Municipal Corporations Act of 1880 required 'private' streets to be not less than 30 feet (9.0 m) wide.

It was the combination of narrow streets or lanes and small private allotments that kept the overall density of development high and ensured an optimum return for the nineteenth century investor speculator.

Subsequent enforcement of the Act in respect of minimum road widths combined with new legislation in 1923 which prescribed site coverage and minimum allotment size of 3,960 sq. ft. (368 m²) for any private dwelling. While these measures were intended to control exploitation of land by unscrupulous developers, they combined to outlaw urban housing as such and set a pattern of uniform low-density residential development and accelerated the suburban sprawl.

Woods' design of the single-fronted cottages (fig. 34, Plate 2) follows the basic plan which had remained virtually unaltered during the last half of the century. It still contains two rooms under the main roof, with an arched passage alongside (1.2 m wide), leading to the kitchen and back verandah under the lean-to roof. The last two decades of the century saw the plan grow in overall size to 70 m², representing a 20 m² increase on the Parker cottages. A small bathroom with a 'bath' and adjoining W.C. compartment—with a door facing the yard—are now provided under the verandah. These new facilities, connected to the sewer, and the inclusion of the passage made possible by increasing the width of frontage to 5.5 m, account for half of the increase in area. The three rooms, comprising the 'front' room (3.9 m x 4.3 m), bedroom (3.9m x 4.0 m) and kitchen (4.1m x 3.6 m), are more spacious than before and the usability of the two front rooms is increased by the introduction of the passage for circulation.

During the nineties the location of a 'bathroom' and W.C. compartment, was consolidated under the rear verandah, yet a kitchen sink was not to be found in all small cottages. Unlike large terraced houses of the period (see Chapter 5), the scullery with built-in washing copper was not provided in small houses. The Paterson kitchen had no fixed sink for washing up. The 1.0 m wide fireplace opening was designed to take a solid fuel cooking range, which also provided hot water for most domestic needs. The adjoining recess contained a built-in cupboard with shelves above. Laundry was done outside with the copper and washtroughs installed in an outhouse called 'wash house' added after the completion of the house. Originally, the area of private land occupied by each cottage was about 135 m^2, or less than 40 per cent of the minimum allotment area required by the Building Act proclaimed in 1923.

The main 'Elevation of Cottages, facing West' (Plate 2), shows simple red brick walls and corrugated iron roofs with timber verandah, 1.5 m wide. In contrast with the terraces built under the same contract, discussed in Chapter 5, all external and party walls are only one brick (23 cm) thick. Still built without cavities, this typical form of construction was cost and space saving, especially in row cottage plans. Louvred ventilators in the roof are provided to ventilate the roof space, which is confined above each house by the dividing party walls terminating in parapets, projecting 30 cm above the roof covering. After 1881, parapet walls were mandatory in all attached houses.

The maisonette

As in the case of the double-storey semi-detached house, discussed in Chapter 5, the design of a single-storey maisonette represents an intentional economic compromise between a free-standing house and a row cottage. As such, the maisonette was a popular form of dwelling throughout the nineteenth century, extending into the first quarter of the twentieth century. In particular, it allowed a small owner/occupier to let part of his house separately and derive income from rent. Although for economic reasons each dwelling was invariably single-fronted, their floor areas were generally larger and the design more pretentious than row cottages. Built singly on individual allotments maisonettes often replaced a detached house in a street, the duality of design being disguised by continuous verandahs and other devices. Since the 1860s the term 'villa' was used to describe a maisonette in order to upgrade its general image.

From the turn of the century, the maisonette became synonymous with a small 'cottage' of two or three rooms. During the first two decades, this

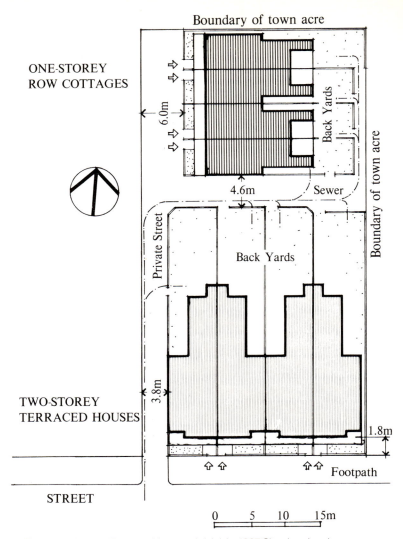

Figure 33: (above) Paterson Houses, Adelaide, 1897. Site plan showing a terrace of two storey houses with a street frontage, and a row of single-storey attached cottages occupying the rear portion of the original one acre allotment. *(Compiled from the original architect's drawings.)*

Figure 34: (opp.) Paterson's Row of four cottages, Adelaide, 1897. Edward J. Woods, Architect. (See also Plate 2)

type of dwelling was used commonly in the philanthropic housing schemes for retired workmen's cottages. In recent years, by far the largest builder of the so called 'cottage homes' for the aged, based on the maisonette concept, has been the South Australian Housing Trust.

From the earliest days of settlement, it was not uncommon for two families to live under the same roof. For example, the 'Immigration Depot'[20], Adelaide's first migrant hostel, located in the west parklands, contained 'double' cottages for rental to families on their arrival in the city. The analysis of a sample area (Chapter 1) shows that nearly a quarter of Adelaide's early houses were semi-detached. Unlike row houses, the large proportion (38 per cent) of stone

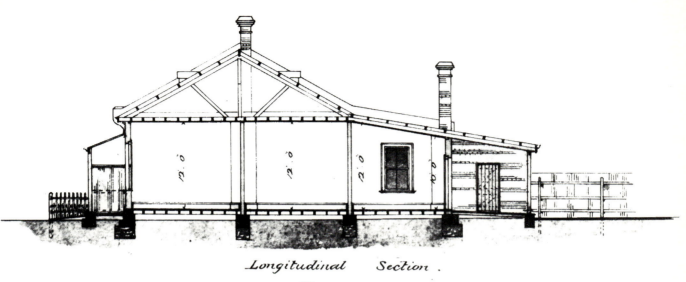

Longitudinal Section.

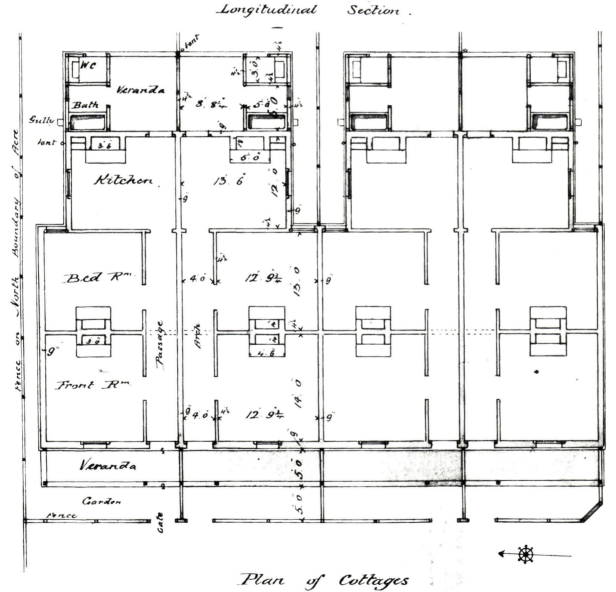

Plan of Cottages

or brick construction suggests that these early maisonettes were owner-built. A first-hand description of a very basic maisonette was given earlier by William Finlayson, (Chapter 1).

Later, when masonry houses became the norm, small cottages of similar design were often paired together in order to save the cost of a double wall, or to make full use of narrow-fronted allotments. These early pairs of semi-detached dwellings were double or single-fronted as the case may be. The double-fronted plans contained between two and four rooms, with windows to the front and the back.

Usually, side walls were blind and placed right on the boundary. With simple, single-storey construction, it was feasible to build in stages—first a cottage for the owner's use and next one for letting. While in general paired cottages were more constrained in size, their basic plans were no different from those built as detached houses.

The early version of the single-fronted plan, occupying the full width of the block, has been covered already by the description of the Calder cottage (pre-1858), included in this Chapter. However, as more rooms were added to the basic plan, the provision of windows in a side wall became essential. This was achieved by leaving a narrow space between the side wall and the boundary fence, which made the maisonettes free-standing. This separation from its neighbours increased the identity of the paired dwelling and made it more compatible with a detached, single-family house. The type of plan that evolved during the last quarter of the century is illustrated by the following case studies.

City Maisonettes, 1894

Two typical maisonettes of three rooms each formed part of an 1894 mixed housing development on part-Town Acre 482, situated in Wright Street, near the King William Street intersection. Instructed by the client, 'W. Kitcher, Esq.' the architects, Garlick, Jackman and Garlick,[21] managed to squeeze a total of six small, single-storey houses on the block, 23.6 m wide by 64 m deep. Facing Wright Street, two detached cottages of five rooms each occupied the larger blocks and, in the back row, four smaller houses were arranged as two maisonettes— see site plan (fig. 35). In January 1895, the builder, G.J. Wark, signed the 'No. 2 contract' for the 'Back Houses', being the two maisonettes.

As indicated in black on the site layout, the maisonettes front on to a 4.6 m wide private road, 'asphalte' paved, and also have service access provided at the rear by the 6.0 m wide right of way, 'Stamford Court'—an extension of the existing minor street. The right of way was used for wood deliveries

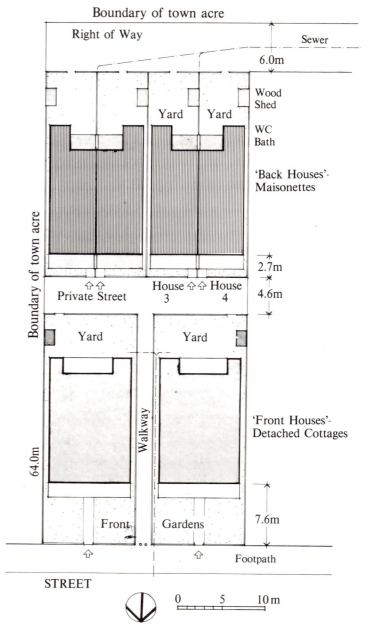

Figure 35: City Maisonettes, 1894. Site plan showing a total of six dwellings. Two single-storey detached cottages ('Front Houses') with their own gardens face the street. Behind them, four smaller dwellings ('Back Houses') are designed as two maisonettes with two plan variants. These are detailed in fig.36.
(Compiled from the original architect's drawings.)

and the sewer run to the maisonettes. An unusual feature of the site layout was the 1.8 m walkway inserted between the front cottages that gave direct foot access to the maisonettes from Wright Street. It is interesting to compare this development with Paterson's Row in South Terrace (1898), discussed earlier in this Chapter. Both schemes highlight the hierarchy of different dwelling types and their correlation with major and minor street patterns of colonial Adelaide.

The Wright Street development underlines the kind of economy in land use made possible by the maisonette plan. On the site, the two 'Back Houses' occupy the same area of land as the free-standing houses in the front row facing Wright Street. Each maisonette, with a frontage of only 5.5 m, occupies a piece of sub-divided land, 5.9 m wide by 25 m deep. The narrow strip of land on each side provides an 'outlook' for the windows of the middle rooms. In this case, overlooking of vis-a-vis windows of neighbouring dwellings is partly obscured by the 1.5 m high corrugated iron fence on the boundary. As the gutters of the adjoining houses nearly touched, the amount of natural light and ventilation admitted through the side windows was severely restricted. Nevertheless, it was this essential feature of maisonette design that distinguished it from the row cottage with its blank side walls.

The straight-fronted ground plans (fig. 36) set 3.0 m from the front boundary offered two variants. House plan 'A' (on the left hand side), with only one front 'bedroom' (3.6 m x 4.3 m), was intended for a smaller family. The short passage, only 1.2 m wide, is terminated by the full-width 'dining' room (5.0 m x 3.9 m). Next, a similar sized 'kitchen' opens on to the back verandah and the yard. House 'B' with two separate 'bedrooms' and a combined full-width 'kitchen-dining room' is comparable with the Paterson row houses (1897), discussed earlier.

While a 'sink' is included in the kitchen of the larger front houses, it is omitted from the maisonettes. The original design shows one end of the back verandah enclosed to form a bathroom with a plunge bath. On architects' drawings, the final position of the W.C. has been changed by removing it to the rear boundary where the sewer connection was readily provided. Note a large Coolgardie 'safe' shown on the back verandah. During construction the verandah was widened to 1.8 metres and enclosed completely, thus increasing the gross area of the house to 80 m^2. Frequent changes made during the 1890s to the layout of new service areas at the rear of the houses demonstrate the evolution of the plan and the effect of new plumbing regulations. As this case indicates, the designer had neither a precedent to follow nor the experience to estimate the cost of new and unfamiliar work, making variations inevitable.

The street elevation (fig. 36) is punctuated by parapet walls that divide the individual houses. Yet the continuity of the facade is enhanced by low timber picket fences and the uniform design of the front verandah with its double posts in timber and the bull-nosed roof, both characteristic elements of the 1890s. Substance is added to the appearance of the houses by the freestone fronts and the somewhat over-decorated chimney cappings.

Kent Town Maisonettes, 1892

This pair of large maisonettes of five rooms each (fig. 37) at Kent Town was designed about two years before the Wright Street project, discussed above, by the same firm of architects working for the same client. The contractor, Moss and Watts, signed the contract in December, 1892, to build the semi-detached 'villas' on an average suburban site, 15.2 m wide and 33 m deep. They represent a larger version of the maisonette plan, designed in a more personalised style.

The elongated plan, which covers 125 m^2, provides for all five main rooms under the main roof arranged in two sections separated by the archway. The front section, served by a 1.5 m wide 'Hall' alongside the party wall, contains the L-shaped 'Drawing room' (5.8 m long), with the main 'Bed' room (4.3 m x 3.6 m), plus same-sized 'Dining' room behind. The projection in the facade resulted in the awkward shape and poor lighting of the front room. The corner fireplace, which gained in popularity during the nineties, is used here as a space-saving device. Note the built-in cupboards provided in both the bedroom and the dining room. Located in the rear section are the second bedroom (3.4 m x 3.4 m) and a rather small kitchen (3.6 m x 3.4 m) which contains a 'sink' with the 'water laid on'. An inside bathroom and a walk-in pantry complete the plan.

For economy of plumbing, the bathrooms are planned together along the party wall. Each house has an attached W.C., accessible off the back verandah paved with 'asphalte'. It is interesting to note that ceiling gas outlets for lighting are marked on the plan. They are centred in each of the principal rooms and in the middle of the hall.

The front elevation (fig. 37) is made more imposing by the raised floor level being 1.3 m above the footpath and the generous 5.5 m setback. The 6.5 m wide frontages are fragmented by small-scale gable roofs and over-detailing of the short 'balcony' enclosure.

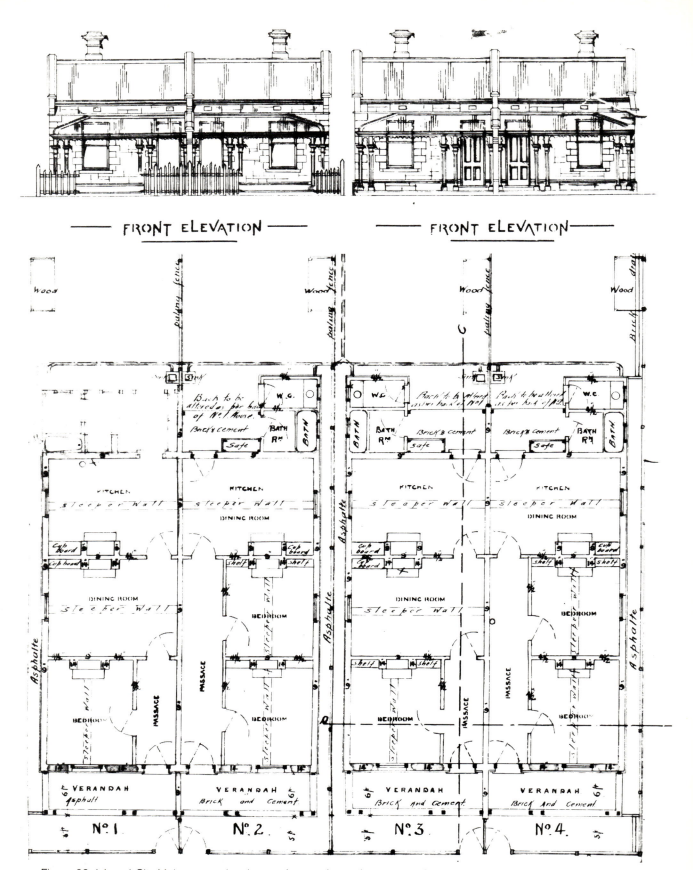

Figure 36: (above) City Maisonettes showing two house plan variants, 1894. Garlick, Jackman and Garlick, Architects.

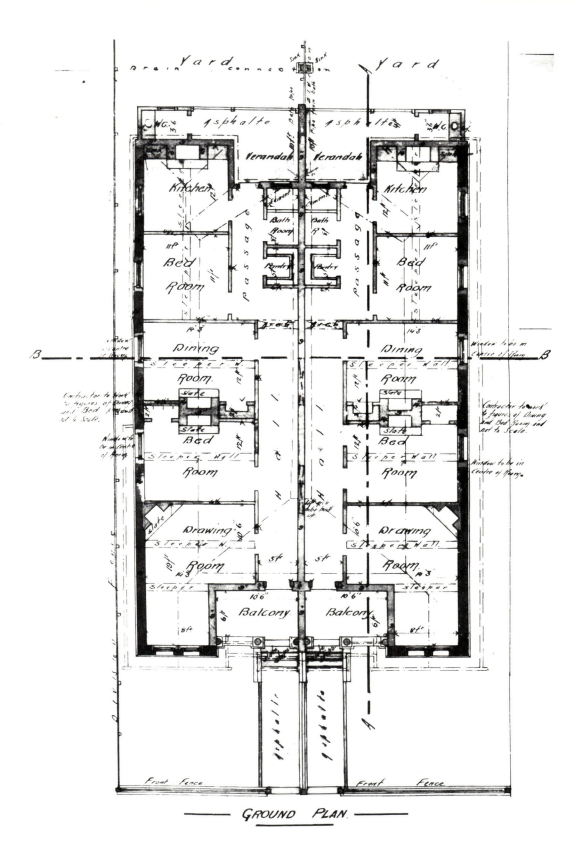

Figure 37: (above and over page) Kent Town Maisonettes
1892. Garlick, Jackman and Garlick, Architects.

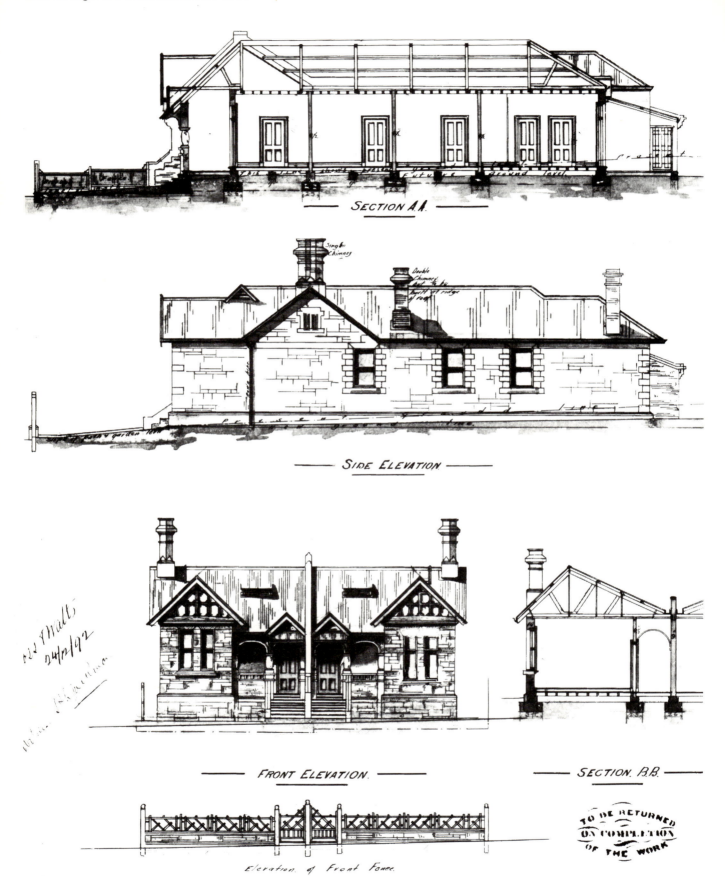

— SECTION A.A. —

— SIDE ELEVATION —

FRONT ELEVATION.

SECTION. B.B. —

Elevation of Front Fence.

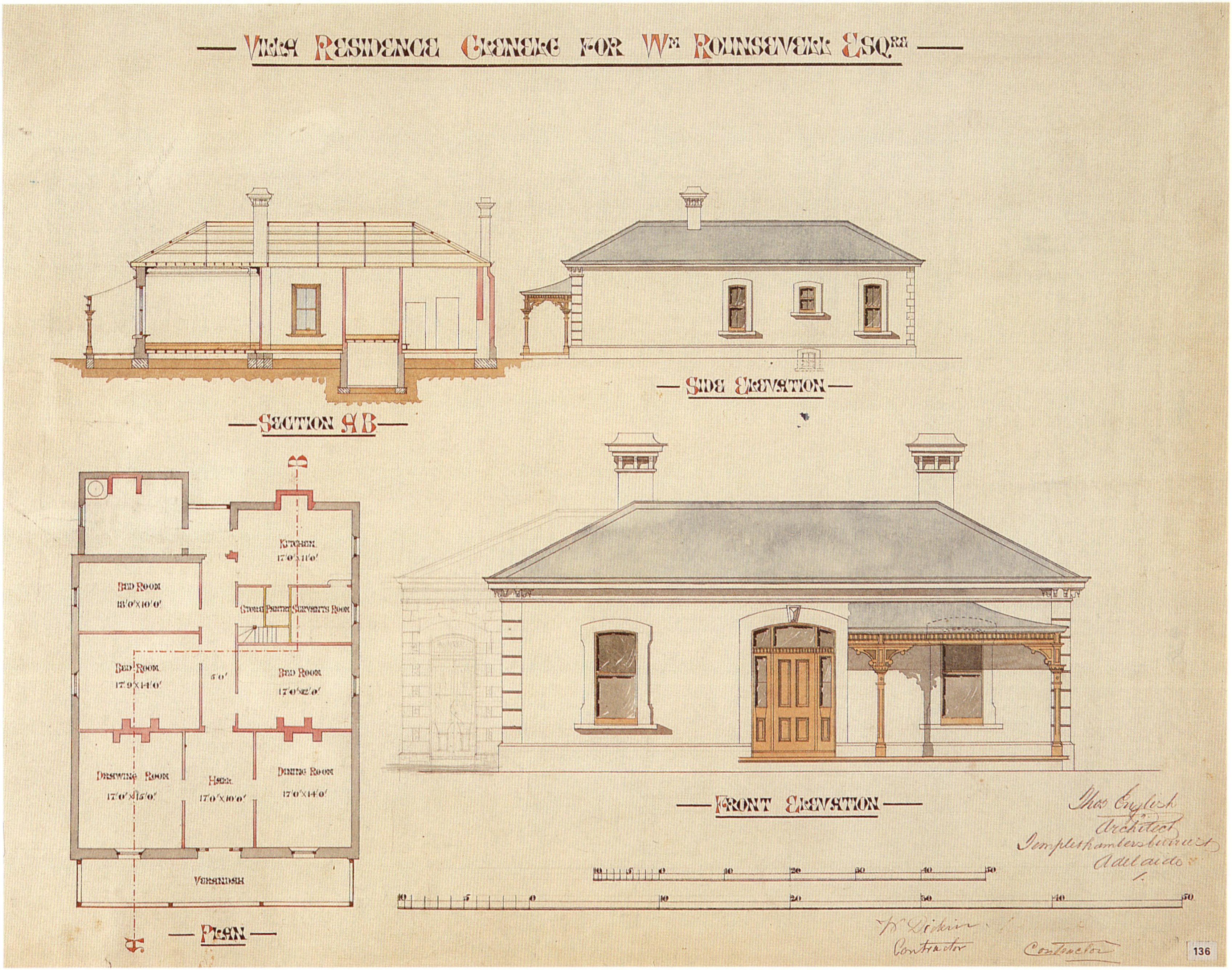

VIEW RESIDENCE GENERAL FOR Wᴹ ROUNSEVELL ESQ.

— ROUNSEVELL RESIDENCE GENERAL FOR Wᴹ ROUNSEVELL ESQ. —

— SIDE ELEVATION —

— FRONT ELEVATION —

— SECTION AB —

— PLAN —

Plate 1: Rounsevell House, Glenelg, c.1875. Thomas English, architect.

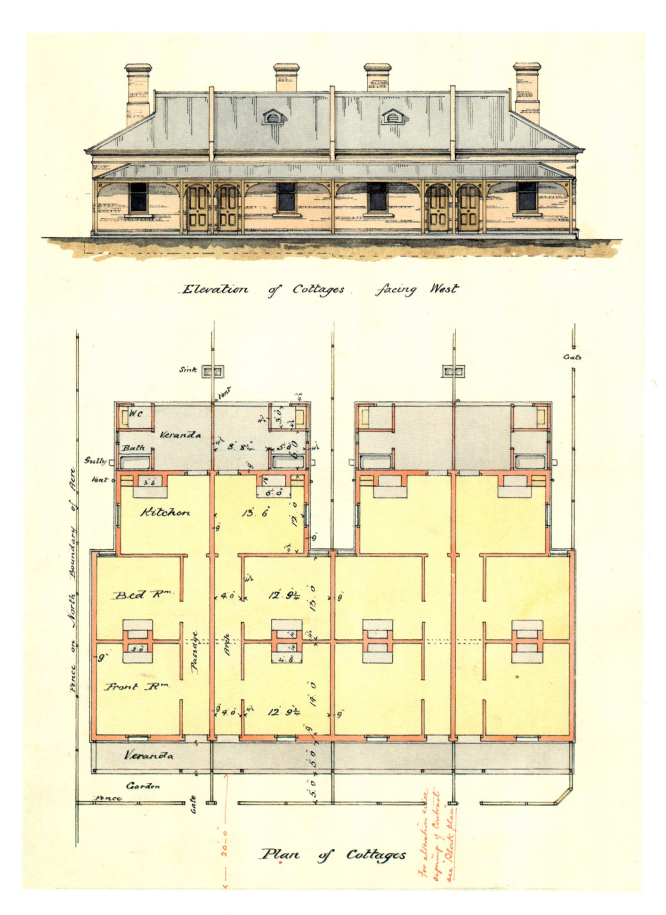

Elevation of Cottages facing West

Plan of Cottages

Plate 2: Paterson's Row of four cottages, Adelaide, 1897. Edward J. Woods, architect.

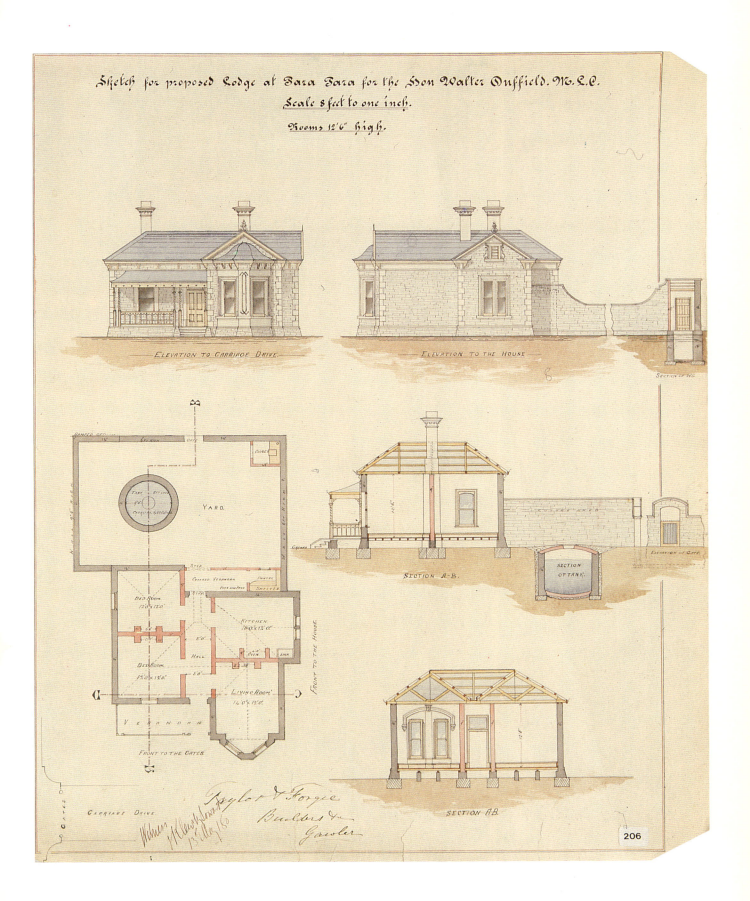

Plate 3: Para Para Lodge, south of Gawler, 1880. English and Soward, architects.

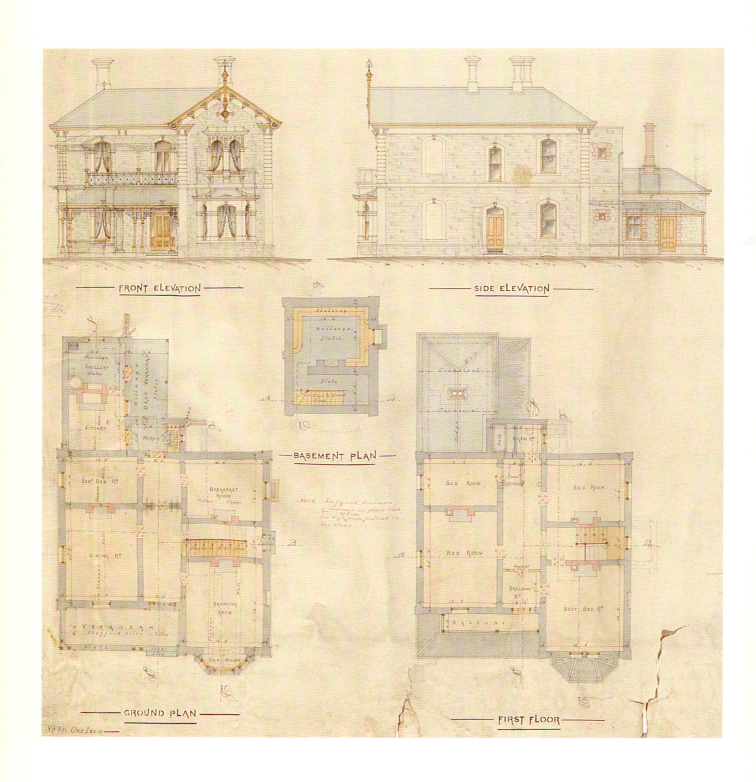

FRONT ELEVATION

SIDE ELEVATION

BASEMENT PLAN

GROUND PLAN

FIRST FLOOR

Plate 4: Lathlean House, College Town, 1877. Daniel Garlick, architect.

RESIDENCE AT COLLEGE TOWN
FOR D. LATHLEAN ESQ

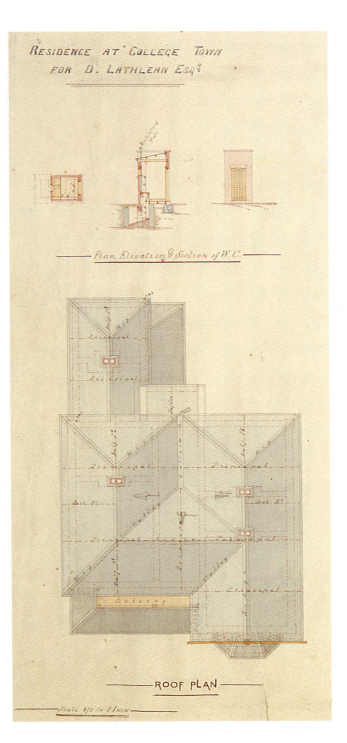

—— Plan, Elevation & Section of W.C. ——

—— ROOF PLAN ——

Scale 8ft to 1 Inch

FRONT ELEVATION

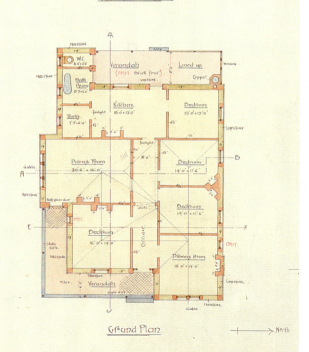

Ground Plan

→ North

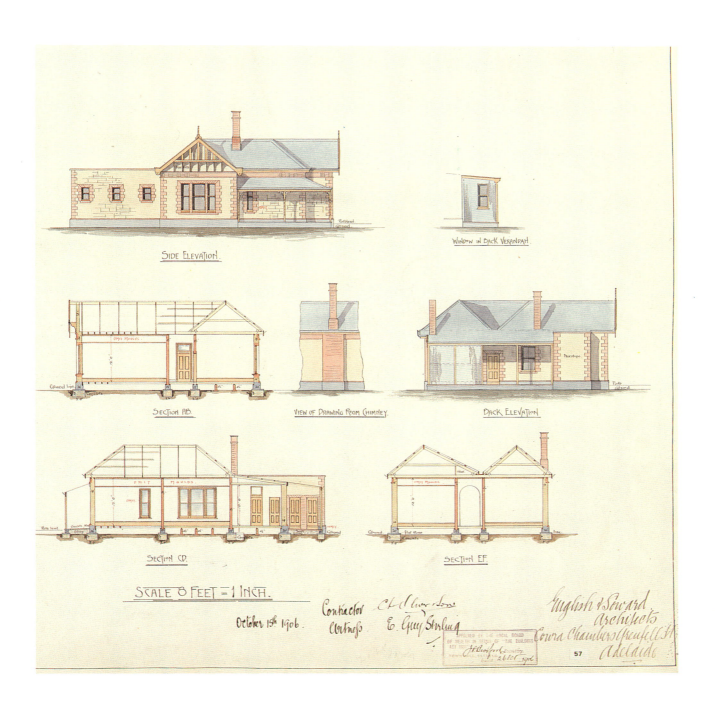

SIDE ELEVATION.

WINDOW IN BACK VERANDAH.

SECTION AB.

VIEW OF DRAWING ROOM CHIMNEY.

BACK ELEVATION.

SECTION CD.

SECTION EF.

SCALE 8 FEET = 1 INCH.

October 19th 1906.

Contractor

Witness

English & Soward
Architects
Cowra Chambers Grenfell St
Adelaide

57

Plate 5: Maesday House, Glenelg, 1906. English and Soward, architects.

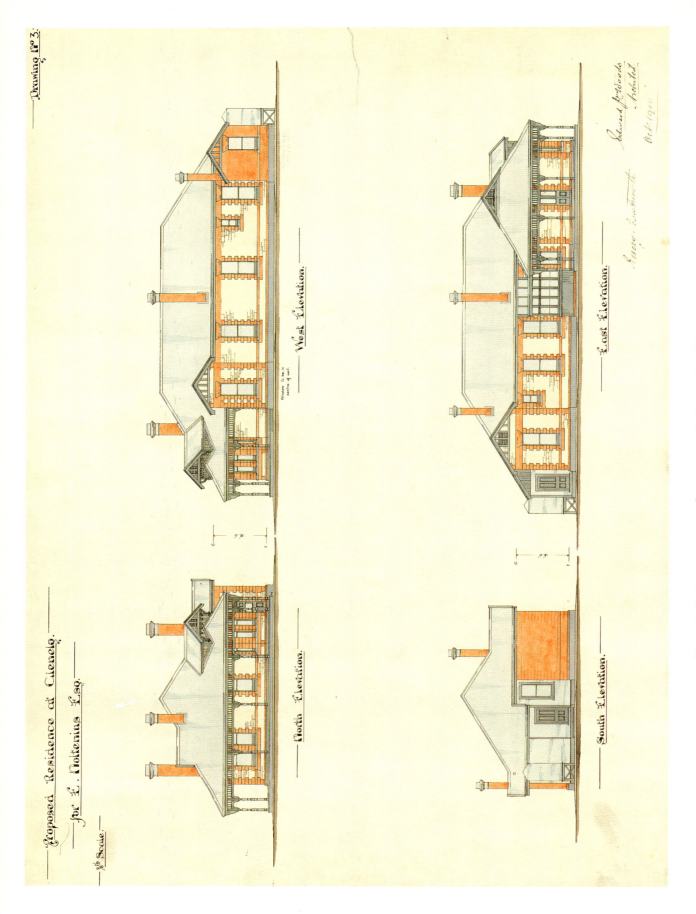

Plate 6: Noltenius House, Glenelg, 1900. Edward J. Woods, architect.

Chapter 4

Detached Houses

1850–1901

A house in the suburbs

During the second half of the nineteenth century the detached house on its own allotment became the principal type of dwelling in Adelaide. In this period it gradually became remote from the inner city and adopted an essentially suburban character.

Since the early sixties the suburban areas of Adelaide spread at a rate parallel to the increase in population (fig. 38). In forty years the population of the County of Adelaide—roughly covering today's greater metropolitan area—increased from 68,000 to 150,000, while the housing stock doubled to the 30,000 dwellings counted in the Census of 1901. The census figures included 40,000 city dwellers and over 8,000 houses which existed in the present area of the city and North Adelaide.

By 1901 the mosaic of land subdivision had spread out from the parklands and over the more elevated parts of the Adelaide plain to the north, east and south (fig. 39).[1] The main built-up areas were contained in a ring about three kilometres wide around the parklands, where the original villages had expanded and merged together. Development beyond this ring was more scattered and it was mainly confined within the broad area between the River Torrens and the foothills of the Mount Lofty Ranges—limiting continuous subdivision of land in the easterly and southerly directions.

In general, development followed the watercourses of the Torrens and the creeks—formerly called 'rivulets'—which cross the area, with the original villages as nuclei. These included along the Torrens: Thebarton and Hindmarsh (downstream) Walkerville and the German settlement of Klemzig (upstream); along Brownhill Creek: Mitcham and Unley; and along the four creeks: Burnside, Norwood, Kent Town, Magill and Campbelltown.

A considerable part of the Adelaide plain, stretching along Gulf St. Vincent from Port Adelaide to Glenelg, was low ground subject to seasonal flooding. This confined suburban expansion to the areas of Port Adelaide (Alberton and Semaphore), the city to port corridor, and the seaside resorts of Glenelg, Brighton and Henley Beach. Woodville Park was an example of a later suburb, established in 1877, which attracted substantial houses of Adelaide merchants. Its half-way location along the road and railway linking the city and its port intensified earlier development along the corridor.

Growth in land subdivisions had also occurred along the three great communication routes with the country areas established since 1840—the northern to Gawler, Burra and the River Murray, the southern to Willunga and Encounter Bay, and the easterly route over the escarpment to the agricultural district of Mount Barker.

The Torrens system of land registration, first introduced in South Australia by the Real Property Act, 1858, greatly simplified transactions in property. Under the system, devised by Sir Robert Torrens who was at the time Registrar-General of the colony, each piece of land is represented by a certificate of title registered in the Land Titles Office and guaranteed by the government. The Torrens system, which was subsequently adopted by the other Australian colonies as well as a number of overseas countries, eliminated the cost of lengthy retrospective search of documents necessary for conveyancing under the general law title. The system was designed to facilitate the sub-division of private land and, in general, stimulated transactions in real estate. By providing a simple legal mechanism for transferring the ownership of land, without any dimensional controls being applied, the Act of 1858 had a far-reaching effect on the pattern of urban development during the next forty years, and beyond.

Figure 38: A group of mid-century cottages situated close to a watercourse, probably at Kent Town or Hackney. The whitewashed masonry features gable end walls, and in two of the three houses narrow verandahs, pitched separately from the main roof, protect the openings. Oil on canvas, 1864, by James Shaw (1815–1881). Compare with Adelaide streetscape of the early 1850s, fig.15.

Following the expanding sixties, South Australia experienced a short but quite spectacular period of unprecedented development, from about 1870 to 1885. It included a ten year building boom which peaked during the middle of the so-called 'magnificent seventies' when Adelaide gained many of its major public buildings and mansions. Exports of copper, wool and wheat formed the basis of this prosperity and the scheme of 'assisted migration' greatly increased the labour force. Never before had the question of building improvements occupied so much public attention. From the early 1870s, un-occupied areas, particularly those situated in the eastern, southern and northern sections of the city began to fill up with 'handsome dwelling houses'.[2]

In general, the rate of house building increased throughout the seventies and still further into the eighties when the property boom represented a combination of attitudes and economic factors. While the level of new residential investment in Australia as a whole turned down abruptly at the start of a depression in 1889, in South Australia the decline of speculative investment in housing was less pronounced. Except for the recession years from 1893 to 1895, the volume of building expanded more or less continuously throughout the nineties.[3] The short-lived period of prosperity failed to produce a distinct 'boom style',[4] nor did the sheer volume of building compare with that in the eastern colonies. Generally speaking, Adelaide's boom style extravagance was more restrained and in domestic architecture confined to relatively few examples.

Sustained by fairly stable building costs, which remained low in relation to wages, the average house increased in size, particularly in the period from 1860 to 1890. In the County of Adelaide, small cottages of two or three rooms (discussed in Chapter 2) gradually diminished in numbers by the end of the century. Significantly, houses containing not less than five rooms more than doubled as a percentage of the housing stock. The latter, which comprised large houses and mansions, increased from 22 per cent in 1861 to 36 per cent in 1881 and reached 52 per cent in 1901.

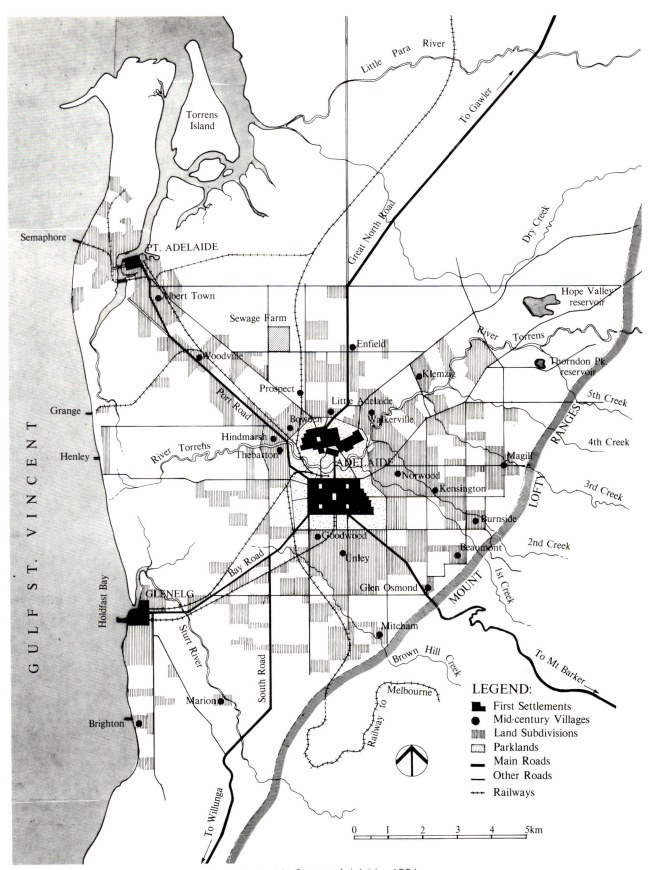

Figure 39: Greater Adelaide, 1901.

During the same forty years, average-sized houses of three and four rooms maintained a large percentage of the overall housing stock. In combination they rose from 42 per cent in 1861 to a high of 47 per cent in 1881, and still maintained 41 per cent of the housing stock by 1901 despite the lean years of the last decade. By the turn of the century the point was reached when, on average, there were five rooms per dwelling and one room for each person.

Public utilities

A number of important public works and utilities, which boosted the overall development of the capital, provided some of the amenities that make urban life comfortable and convenient. Those which had far-reaching effects on the choice of location and detailed design of the Adelaide colonial house were: public transport, reticulated water and gas supply and the central sewage system.

The initial railway system, comprising lines to Port Adelaide (opened in 1856) and to Gawler (1857), was gradually extended and so spurred on the development of some outer suburbs. Railways were built to Glenelg (1873), Semaphore (1878), Holdfast Bay (1880), Grange and Largs Bay (both 1882). However, the most important was the first stage of the Inter-colonial railway constructed to Aldgate by 1883, and its extension which completed the link between Adelaide and Melbourne four years later. Despite these additional lines, the bulk of Adelaide's growing suburbs were not serviced by railways.

While walking was the most common way of commuting within the city and across the parklands to the surrounding suburbs, horse-drawn cabs and omnibuses provided the means of public transport. However, by the seventies these could not cope with the growing population and the poor state of the roads made their use far from comfortable.

A comprehensive public transport system, radiating from the city to suburbs without the railway link began in 1878, when the Adelaide and Suburban Tramway Co. ran its first horse-drawn tram to the eastern suburb of Kensington. Over the next five years tramway tracks extended rapidly along major suburban routes, and horsetram became the principal mode of transport of the last two decades of the century.[5]

During the 1850s water was still obtained from the River Torrens, the creeks (mainly during winter), springs and shallow wells, or by collecting water shed from roofs. In the city, contractors delivered water to houses in bullock-drawn carts and charged according to distance travelled. The price of delivered water was high, at up to three shillings for 50 gallons (230 litres). Often supplies were only available in limited quantities. It is not surprising that land near a good well was especially sought after.[6]

Late in 1860, Adelaide received its first piped water supply from Thorndon Park reservoir using upstream waters of the Torrens. With the completion of the second storage reservoir at Hope Valley in 1872, a reticulated water supply was extended to all inner suburbs and also to Glenelg and Port Adelaide. Prior to the introduction of the kitchen sink and the fixed bath, the house supply was laid on to a single tap located either outside the back door, or in the scullery. From there water was carried inside by hand.

The flatness of Adelaide's site and its impervious clay soils made disposal from household cesspits and night-soil removal a growing health hazard. Consequently, water-borne sewers—the first large scale system in Australia—were authorised by the Adelaide Sewers Act of 1878. By 1881, sewage from the city (previously discharged into the Torrens) was admitted to the treatment works at Islington. By 1901, 360 kilometres of sewers were laid in metropolitan Adelaide and about two-thirds of all houses were connected.[7] Later, work commenced on the construction of town sewers for Glenelg (1903) and for Port Adelaide (1910). These suburbs had separate treatment works built that discharged the effluent into the Gulf by submarine pipelines.

The South Australian Gas Company, a privately owned company, was incorporated by Act of Parliament in 1861 to supply gas to Adelaide and surrounding villages. The first gas was produced from coal at the Brompton works in 1863, and other plants opened at Port Adelaide in 1866 and Glenelg in 1875. By mid-1866 the reticulation of gas extended to North Adelaide, Hindmarsh and Thebarton, serving more than 600 customers. The next year, the Company signed a contract to light 273 street lamps in the city, replacing earlier oil and kerosene lamps. However, it was not until 1898 that the suburban streets of Norwood, Unley, Burnside and Glenelg were lit by gas.

While all public buildings in and around the city were supplied after 1874, gas for lighting of houses was not generally used before 1885 when additional mains were laid in all suburbs to cope with growing demand and to improve pressures. The domestic use of gas increased from 1899 when the suburban price was reduced to five shillings and six pence per 1000 cubic feet (28 m³), representing a 50 per cent reduction on the rate set in 1882.[8]

The use of oil and kerosene lamps[9] remained widespread, especially in small houses, until they were finally replaced by electricity. Around 1860, 'parafine' (genteel for kerosene) was cheaper than candles and produced a 'brighter' light more suitable for reading or working in Joseph Elliott's house, a discussion of which follows.[10] Being cheap and portable, lamps and candles often remained in houses to be used after fixed gas lights were installed in the principal rooms.

Use of gas inside the colonial house was confined to room lighting. In 1892, the Gas Company erected a showroom in Grenfell Street to exhibit gas cookers but they were not widely used before 1910. Meanwhile in the washhouse the gas burner soon replaced the open fire under the bricked-in copper, yet it was not until the early 1930s that gas space heaters were introduced.

Communicating by telephone from the place of residence became possible in 1883, when the first Adelaide Central exchange opened with 27 initial subscribers. Telephone lines extended to almost all parts of the city, and business offices, doctors, and other professional people were among the first to share the benefits of the new invention. At first a subscription charge of £12 per year attracted few domestic subscribers. As an incentive to these, special rates were introduced in 1890. Private residences within a one mile (1.6 km) radius of the nearest telephone exchange paid only £6 per year, and by 1895 there were 60 domestic subscribers.[11]

While early experiments with electricity for limited street lighting were carried out at Port Adelaide in 1899, initial demands for household electric light and power were not met before 1910.

Building materials and methods

During the second half of the nineteenth century, local stone and clay bricks were the principal walling materials of domestic buildings, while corrugated galvanised iron became rapidly accepted as the universal roof covering by all except the most fastidious house owners. The 1858 legislation prohibiting the use of wood as external covering within the city consolidated the already well-established trend to solid construction. It is not surprising, therefore, that by 1881 in the County of Adelaide only one building in ten was of 'wood' or 'iron'—a considerable reduction from nearly a quarter in 1861. The remaining buildings were of 'stone', 'brick' or 'concrete'.[12]

By mid-century, it was clearly evident that Colonel Light had fulfilled the clause in his instructions which stated that the site selected for the capital should provide an adequate supply of building materials. The first settlers soon discovered that travertinous limestone and red-brown earths suitable for brickmaking existed in large and easily accessible quantities. The white or cream coloured limestone (calcrete), which proved to be a durable building stone

in Adelaide's mediterranean climate, extended over three-quarters of the present city area, the whole of North Adelaide and beyond in the northerly direction. Lying near the surface, it could be readily utilised on the spot thus saving the cost of cartage—an important consideration in the early days of the Province. This soft-textured stone broke easily into random rubble, especially useful for thick outer walls of buildings and boundary walls. Limestone was the main building stone during the first 25 years, especially in North Adelaide, Also, it was burned for lime, the main constituent in mortar and render mixes for fifty years or more. See fig. 40.

Beyond the city parklands, readily available materials such as river pebbles (gravels) and other surface-weathered stones were first employed by the pioneers who settled in the vicinity of the Adelaide creeks (see map, fig. 39), and built walls using large quantities of 'pug' made from clay mixed with water. Smaller stones, unsuitable for masonry were utilised in mass-concrete, poured between timber boards. 'Concrete', produced with either lime or imported cement, was recognised as an early walling material, as distinct from 'mud' (pisé) construction. In fact, nearly 10 per cent of all 'dwellings' standing in 1861 in the County were of 'concrete'.[13] In subsequent years their number dwindled, suggesting that this material was confined mainly to the pre-1860 houses.

Bluestone came into early use as easily accessible deposits were found in the nearby Mount Lofty Ranges. The broad term, which stems from the stone's generally blue-grey colour when fresh, covers a wide range of hard, fine-grained rocks (siltstone and shale) as quarried at Glen Osmond, Mitcham and Tapley's Hill.[14] While quarrying and dressing was facilitated by bedding joints or cleavage planes which often divide the rock into neat blocks, the stones needed sawing to obtain a straight face at right angles. These joints are frequently coated with iron oxide which produces the brown, yellow and red colours. Although adversely affecting the weathering properties of the stone, it was common practice to 'face bed' the outer stones with the natural bedding exposed in the face of the wall, thus showing the characteristic dark colourings.

The use of bluestone in housing during the growth years from 1860 to 1890, further expanded. Its greater hardness and durability than that of limestone made it especially suitable for external load-bearing walls, built solid to the standard thickness ranging between 35 cm to 45 cm (14 inches to 18 inches). Random coursework made good use of varying sized stones which required very little hammer trimming by the mason. As with limestone, joints between stones were filled flush with the stone face, and first class work—which in houses was usually confined

Figure 40: Richardson House, North Adelaide, built in 1851. Detail, oil painting on canvas, 1865, by James Shaw (1815–1881). External walls of this symmetrical-fronted house, including the boundary wall, are of local limestone edged with brickwork; the roof covering is flat iron with side rolls—an early material which preceded galvanised corrugated iron. The front elevation closely resembles that of 'The Almonds' illustrated in fig.48.
(Art Gallery of S.A.)

to the front wall—was 'tuck pointed' with thin, squared-up grooves ruled over the centre of joints and painted white.

In the period 1860 to 1890, high quality sandstone came into wide use in public buildings and in some larger houses. Dense, yet capable of being sawn or shaped, sandstone was popular for high-class work since the earliest days when fair-quality material was quarried in the Torrens valley, south of the Adelaide Bridge. It offered a lighter in colour but dearer in price alternative to bluestone. The best quality material was deeply buried and there was unavoidable waste associated with cutting the stone. The main quarries were situated at Mount Lofty, Teatree Gully and more distant Murray Bridge (80 km east of Adelaide).

The downturn in building and keen competition from mass-produced bricks in the early 1890s caused the stone industry to consolidate and diversify. Once again the softer, more readily quarried and dressed stones, particularly limestone and sandstone, came into general use in the form of the cheaper 'freestone'.[15] The regular, machine-cut blocks of light coloured stone, which could be bonded easily with brick work, became an extremely popular facing material for the front wall of domestic buildings,

otherwise constructed entirely of red bricks. The decorative freestone front remained a characteristic feature of the Adelaide house for nearly fifty years, preserving the appearance of the traditional stone facade well into the twentieth century. The familiar rock faced pattern was even reproduced in pressed metal as a front wall covering for timber-framed houses.

By mid-century the practice of combining brick quoins with irregularly shaped stonework was well established in the Adelaide region. This practical method of building up square corners and obtaining a true finish for fixing of door and window frames can be traced in history to southern England.[16] Today, the appealing combination of random texture limestone and soft orange sand-stock bricks is recognised as the hallmark of pre-1860 colonial architecture in South Australia (fig. 41).

The bricks were bonded, or toothed, into the stonework at regular intervals of either five or three brick courses, with flat brick arches spanning the openings. In general, the five-course quoins occur in the earlier examples, sometimes combining with three-course work at the windows. The first generation of settlers valued the warm texture of hand-made bricks, which usually remained unpainted. In the mid-1860s, this attitude changed as it became fashionable to cover the bricks with a smooth-trowelled coat of render, called 'stucco'. During the next two decades elaborate decorations in cement render enjoyed wide popularity. They included eaves courses adorned with projecting corbels, architraves with prominent keystones accentuating the openings, and simulated stone blocks decorated in various patterns at the external corners. Often, these different features were picked out in several paint colours (fig. 42).

Apart from other building stones, South Australia has been the foremost producer of slate and flagstone (siltstone) in Australia. In 1840, fine grained slate suitable for roofing and paving was discovered in the foothills near Willunga (55 km south of Adelaide.)[17] The Delabole quarry, named after one of the oldest British quarries in Cornwall, became the best known. Willunga roofing slate was used throughout the Province and also exported to Sydney and England. In addition to the local product, large quantities of higher quality roofing slates from the long established quarries in Wales, England, Ireland and America were imported.

Since the late 1850s, flagstone has been quarried at Mintaro (125 km north of the capital). While being too dense to be split for roof covering, this high quality siltstone found wide application as floors of kitchens, sculleries and basements. Also, the so-called Mintaro 'slate' has been specified for hearths, thresholds, steps and edgings to verandahs paved with imported ceramic tiles.

Brickmaking was one of the earliest colonial industries.[18] The first clay bricks were made on the parklands by the South Australian Company and also by private individuals until 1838 when the brickmakers were ordered away from the city. By 1860, a number of brickworks were operating near the city at Norwood, Stepney, Bowden and Hindmarsh. The increased competition and growing demand resulted in a considerable reduction in price and improvement in quality of locally made bricks. The price of 1,000 bricks dropped from 50–60 shillings in 1838 to 35–50 shillings in 1860. This made the local bricks roughly comparable in price with building stone, which sold at three shillings to three shillings and sixpence per cubic foot (0.03 m³).[19] And bricks were plentiful—the largest brickyard, Cox Brothers at Norwood, established in 1849, had a stockpile of 300,000 bricks ready for sale. Describing the success of Cox Brothers' first ten years of operation, a feature article in *The Observer* suggested that 'churches, chapels and dwelling houses beyond number have no doubt taken origin'[20] from this yard alone.

As elsewhere in Australia, the Adelaide standard brick was approximately 22.5 cm long x 10.5 cm wide x 6.5 cm high. Conforming in size with the traditional London brick meant that imported and locally made bricks were interchangeable and could be specified in the same building for different economic or aesthetic reasons. Some of the subtlety of scale and pattern of the colonial facades can be attributed to the smaller dimensions of the 'London' brick.

In order to meet the growing demand during the building boom of the seventies, many old yards were mechanised and new yards featured the latest equipment and employed recently developed techniques. At the end of the decade, double-pressed bricks were first produced in South Australia using the revolutionary semi-dry press process. This time-saving process resulted not only in harder bricks but also made it possible to utilize the vast shale deposits in the Adelaide Hills. However, the most important step in the expansion of brickmaking was the construction of the first continuous Hoffmann kiln at Blackwood in the early 1880s by The City and Suburban Steam Brickmaking Company to supply the enormous quantity of bricks required for the tunnels of the hills railway.

The success of the Hoffmann modern brickmaking process (introduced in Melbourne ten years earlier) had two important long term effects on the building industry. First, bricks could be mass produced in the Hoffmann kiln at one-quarter of the cost of burning hand-made bricks.[21] The resultant price reduction was a major factor in the revival in popularity of brickwork in the nineties (fig. 43). Second, the imported Hoffmann machines made German sized bricks measuring 23 cm long x 11 cm wide x 7.6 cm high. Gradually, this slightly longer and one-centimetre higher brick replaced the London brick, and became the Australian standard of this century.

Bricks made in England and the eastern colonies were an essential import at the beginning of settlement, and later continued to supplement the local product. Over the first twenty years, nearly 2.0 million imported bricks were used in South Australia. In the boom year of 1876 alone an exceptional 1.2 million bricks were brought in to meet the unprecedented demand. While England always remained the traditional source of supply, during the seventies a large number of bricks from Melbourne found a ready market in Adelaide. In the next decade, steady imports totalled nearly 2.0 million, increasing to 2.6 million in the nineties—despite the fact that no imports occurred during the 1893–95 building recession. It must also be noted that exports of South Australian bricks started in 1874, and in the last ten years of the century, 1.1 million were exported.[22]

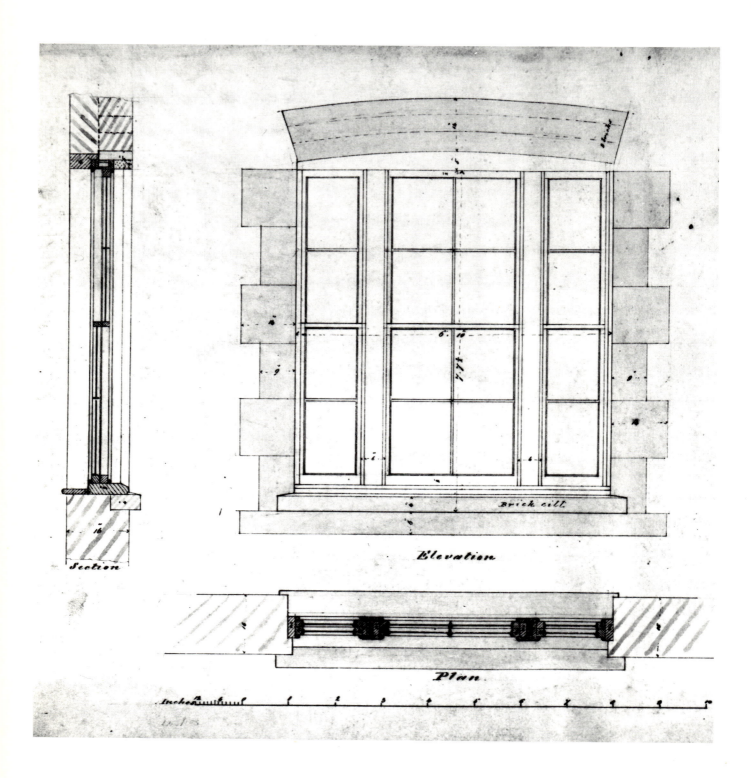

Section

Shutter

Brick cill

Elevation

Plan

Inches

DETAILS.

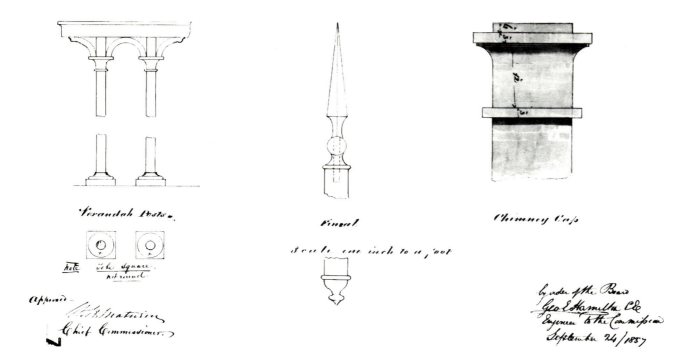

Verandah Posts.

hole *7th. square.* *not round.*

Approved –
Chief Commissioner.

Finial
Scale one inch to a foot

Chimney Cap

by order of the Board
Geo E Hamilton C.E.
Engineer to the Commission
September 24/1857

Figure 41: Architectural details, dated 24 September 1857, signed Geo. E. Hamilton, Engineer to the Water Works Commission, for a new cottage and office at Thorndon Park Reservoir. Typical of the mid-century period, they relate in particular to the Richardson House (fig.40) and 'The Almonds' (fig.48).
  a) (opp.) Details of Window. Exposed five course brick quoins, a brick arch and outer sill form the opening in 16 inch (40cm) solid stonework for the box-frame window fitted with double-hung vertically sliding sashes.
  b) (above) Selected details showing timber verandah posts, a turned finial for a gable roof and a simple capping to a brick chimney.
  (Engineering and Water Supply Department)

Good quality external walling measured 35 cm (14 inches) thick, comprising three brick widths laid in traditional 'English' bond.[23] In cheaper work, it was common to reduce the thickness by half a brick to 23 cm (9 inches) and to simplify laying by using 'Colonial' bond.[24] Even when rendered, the thinner wall was seldom waterproof in the face of driving rain. The problem of economy and good performance was not resolved until the late 1890s when the 28 cm (11 inches) brick cavity wall, an Australian invention, became adopted in house construction. The cavity wall, which fully utilised mass-produced Hoffmann bricks, comprised two parallel 'skins' separated by 5 cm airspace and tied together with twisted cast-iron bars.

This 'hollow' wall had many advantages. While using no more bricks than the solid 23 cm wall, it offered better thermal insulation, it was watertight and it was strong enough to carry two storeys. Built in running (stretcher) courses, it presented a neat appearance without headers (brick ends) showing on either side. As face brickwork returned to fashion in the late Victorian period, the cavity wall was the natural choice, especially when combined with a 'freestone' front.

The early examples of pioneer cottages, already discussed, indicate that 11 cm brickwork (half-a-brick thick) was generally used for partitions in preference to the thicker stone. The cheaper, low-grade bricks, which provided a good key for plaster, were utilised for internal work of both stone and brick houses. Only in two-storey houses of better quality did the ground floor partitions remain 23 cm thick.

When, in 1838, English ironworks commenced commercial production of the corrugated 'galvanised' iron sheet, they soon found a ready and rapidly growing market for the new product in the Australian colonies. Unlike imported bricks or roofing slate, the corrugated sheets, made in convenient lengths of 6 ft. (1.8m), 7 ft. (2.1 m) and 8 ft. (2.4m), were compact to ship and easy to handle without breakages.

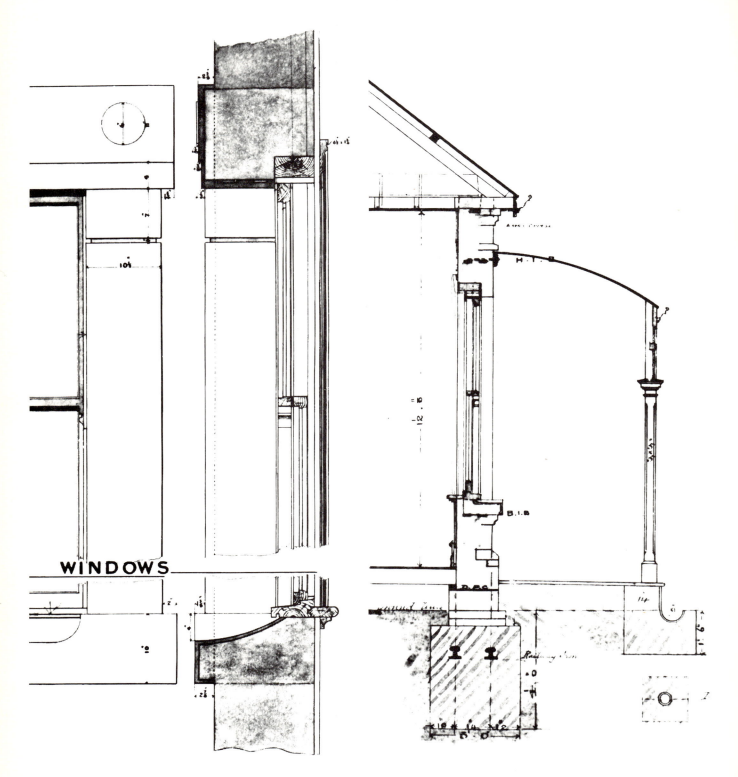

WINDOWS

Figure 42: Details of Window, 1883, for Superintendent's residence, Water Supply Works at Gawler, show the architectural treatment of the eighties. While brickwork is still used around the opening in the stone, the bricks are concealed by decorated 'stucco'.
(Engineering & Water Supply Department)

Figure 43: Details of solid brick construction, 1895, with facework built in Flemish bond. Richman House, East Terrace, Adelaide. Edward J. Woods, Architect.

During the fifties, this cheap, portable and durable building material was in great demand in the gold diggings. In these remote locations, where natural materials were often scarce or too time-consuming to use, the first 'galvo towns' mushroomed. The new sheet also provided 'rust-proof' containers and utensils which the alluvial miners needed. As the second half of the century progressed, corrugated galvanised iron became the only roofing material which could keep pace with the demand for housing in the colonies.

Duryea's photografic *Panorama of Adelaide in 1865*.[25] shows with startling clarity a number of houses and other buildings covered with the shining metal, which stands out in stark contrast with the earlier and predominant natural textures of slate and wooden shingle roofs. The latter, made from local stringy-bark eucalypt, still covers many small cottages. The occasional thatch can be seen on Duryea's and other contemporary photographs. Before long, however, these cottages would have been re-roofed with corrugated iron sheeting, usually with the earlier covering left intact.

The examples, which follow in this and the subsequent chapter, clearly show the universal acceptance of the corrugated iron roof in domestic buildings after the early 1860s. Since then, imported and local slates have been rarely used. In fact, it was not uncommon to extend an existing slate roof with corrugated iron, both materials being visible—as for example in the following case of *The Almonds* (fig. 48) It seems that any early prejudice towards iron, which might have originated from England where the material was invariably reserved for industrial buildings, was soon dispelled on technical and economic grounds.

By a historical coincidence, the processes of corrugating and galvanising were timely developments for South Australia. Corrugating a flat sheet of iron between interlocking rollers, first attempted during the 1820s, made the sheet rigid and largely self-supporting in one direction. Galvanising provided the protective coating which the earlier tinplated finish ('black' iron) lacked when used outdoors. It was in 1836, the foundation year of South Australia, that a French chemist, M. Sorel, introduced galvanisation of sheet metal by dipping in molten zinc.

A corrugated galvanised iron roof was a marked improvement on thatch or wooden shingles. With the new light-weight material fewer and smaller-sized timbers could be used for roof framing and the supporting purlins could be spaced one metre apart. Unlike shingles, galvanised iron did not warp or split, nor did it require the regular maintenance of thatch. Importantly, iron compared with slate in that it could collect freely the precious rainwater and also in its

being fire resistant. By the late 1850s local 'galvanised iron works'[26] started using the imported material to manufacture rainwater tanks and half-round gutters. These items replaced the wooden casks and hollowed tree trunks previously used by the pioneers. For verandah roofs, the corrugated sheet was curved to increase further its initial strength and to enable it to span safely the full length without side or intermediate support. Thus, the standard length of sheet determined the width of the common domestic verandah at about 1.8 metres.

The rapid change to corrugated iron roofs in the city of Adelaide was accelerated by a Building Act of 1858[27] which intended to reduce the general threat of fire. For the first time 'wood, canvas and thatch' were prohibited for use as roof or wall coverings, and 'calico, canvas and paper' for use as internal partitions or ceilings. Furthermore, the Act stipulated removal within five years of such existing buildings situated within nine metres of any adjoining building. Later, the Municipal Corporations Act of 1880 widened the scope of the 1858 Act to cover any municipality of the Province. While 'slate, tiles, metal, glass, artificial stone, or concrete' were specified as permissible roof coverings for houses and other buildings, 'metal' in the form of corrugated iron was the common answer. And it was by no means confined to the average house—for well situated, large and otherwise highly-finished houses showed, unashamedly, their iron roofs.[28] Today, this is viewed with considerable astonishment by visitors from Britain and Europe.

It is interesting to compare the prices of the two main colonial roofing materials, slate and corrugated iron, around the time of the two Acts. In 1860, corrugated galvanised iron in 1.8 m sheets sold in Adelaide at £52 per ton, while imported Welsh slates from Bangor in the more expensive 'Countess' size (50 cm x 25 cm) sold at £13/10/- per thousand.[29] These figures represent 60 shillings and 46 shillings respectively per square (9.3 m^2) of roof area. By 1880, the prices had reduced to £28 for iron and £9/10/- for slates, making the price of both materials comparable at 32 shillings per square.[30] However additional roofing timbers and the higher cost of fixing made a slate roof always more expensive than one covered with corrugated iron sheeting.

From about 1890, J.H. Weindenhofer was the South Australian agent for John Lysaght Limited of Bristol, a major English manufacturer of galvanised iron since 1857. In the year 1895, the company's exports to Australia reached 30,000 tons, and 1,240 tons of galvanised iron were sold by Weindenhofer's agencies in the Province. By 1903, Weindenhofer's sales exceeded 3,000 tons per year.[31] It was not until 1917 that John Lysaght (Australia) Pty. Ltd.

STREET ELEVATION (As drawn by Joseph Elliott, 1860)

Figure 44: (left) Street Elevation of the Elliott house as drawn by Joseph Elliott, 1860.

Figure 45: (below) Elliott House, North Adelaide, 1856. An early symmetrical plan with a short passage.

Figure 46: (opp. above) Back yard of Elliott's House, 1860. Contemporary sketch by Joseph Elliott.

Figure 47: (opp. below) Freestanding brick privy (1.52 x 1.37m inside) with lined cesspit, designed by the Water Works Commission in 1857. Although this high-standard privy was designed for the cottage and office at Thorndon Park reservoir, it serves to illustrate the design of Elliott's 'house of ease', marked 'C' on his plan of the back yard (fig.46).

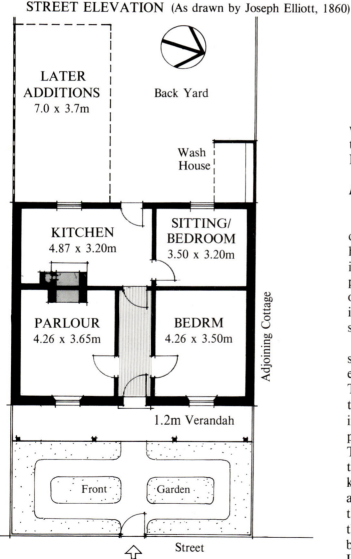

GROUND FLOOR PLAN

0 1 2 3 4 5m

was formed, and another four years passed before the first sheets were rolled in Australia at their Newcastle Works in New South Wales.

Elliott House, 1856

The four room cottage of Joseph Elliott—as depicted by the original sketch (fig. 44) contained in his manuscript of 1860[32]—represents an early stage in the evolution of the Adelaide 'symmetrical' house plan. For the first time the entrance and the functions of living, cooking and eating, previously combined in the multi-purpose living room, began to be segregated into distinct spaces.

With the increasing prosperity in the Province since 1845, the short passage emerged as one of the earliest refinements of the three- and four-cell plan. This, at first rather narrow passage giving access from the front door to the 'parlour' and the 'best' bedroom, initiated a significant change in the social and practical functioning of the early Victorian house. The formal 'parlour' is segregated from the rest of the house while, in the private zone at the rear, the kitchen becomes the focus of informal family activities. The appearance of a front 'parlour' made the pioneer cottage socially respectable. It assumed the new role of the 'best' room in the house where best furnishings and 'choice' books were on display. It was where visitors were received and entertained and where children were excluded except on rare occasions.

The short passage, which was soon extended in larger houses, became the common circulation space which at the same time served to segregate as well as link together the different domestic functions. And, in the long term, the passage made the changeability and adaptability of individual rooms possible. It formalized the entrance, which later evolved into a distinct hall, and provided separate access to the main rooms of the house. The vis-a-vis location of the doors leading to the parlour and the front bedroom made them ambiguous. This and their close proximity to the front door is typical of early plans prior to 1860. Introduction of the passage had far-reaching design consequences in that it imposed a central axis on the plan and a strict order of symmetry on the front elevation. The latter emerged as the characteristic quality of the Australian cottage, regardless of its size.

Typically, the largest room in the Elliott house was the kitchen (fig. 45). Apart from storage of food stuffs, preparation and cooking in the open fireplace, meals were taken on the kitchen table, although

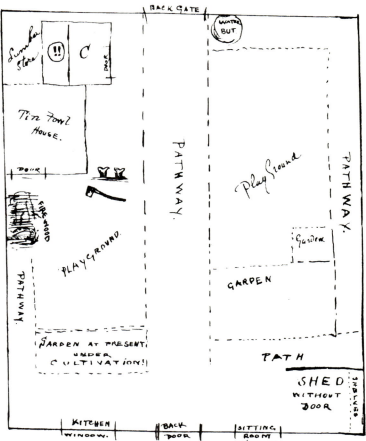

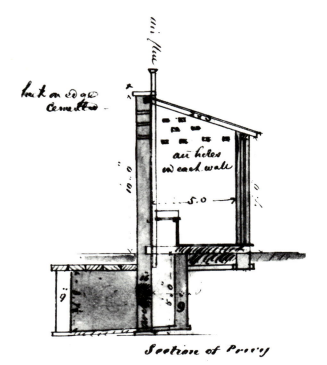

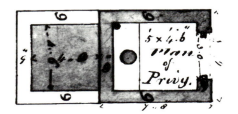

occasionally the table in the adjoining 'Sitting' room was used for dining on Sundays. Once a week the kitchen would be the place where family ablutions took place—very agreeable in cold weather. The family laundry was done in zinc tubs in an open-sided shed and washing up after meals in bowls on the kitchen table. Saturday night bath water was heated on the kitchen fire and tipped into a washing tub that had been brought in for the occasion. Other personal washing took place at the wash stand in the front bedroom.

The back yard (fig. 46) was reached through the kitchen. With rear access from a lane, the fenced-in yard (18 m x 9 m) served as a functional extension to the main plan. Being overlooked from the kitchen window it provided a safe 'play ground' for the young Elliott children and a flexible space for essential outbuildings such as the shed, fowlhouse and the privy—the 'house of ease' located in the bottom corner (fig. 47). There was space to grow a few vegetables for the kitchen and to store and cut firewood. Marked on the site plan is a simple prop-up clothes line, and near the rear gate stands the all important water supply for a household of the fifties—a large wooden cask or 'butt' filled with water carted from the River Torrens.

The near-square plan built of local stone and covered with a wooden shingle roof had a gross area of about 80 m^2, excluding outbuildings. The average size front rooms had a 'lofty' flat ceiling, 3.2 m high, with a gable roof above. The kitchen and sitting room, being narrower than the main rooms, were under a lean-to roof with lower raked ceilings. The house occupied the full width of the 9.1 m block, with both side walls built blind on the boundaries. A generous set-back of 5.0 m from the footpath allowed for a narrow verandah, 1.3 m wide, and a small front garden neatly laid out with flower beds. From the street it was enclosed by a low wooden picket fence of the kind shown on paintings of early Adelaide (fig. 4).

The cottage, which the Elliott family of five rented in 1860, was one of a pair built side by side by George Downs, a local carpenter. First, he built one cottage for his own use, and about a year later completed the second cottage of similar plan (mirror-imaged) on the adjoining land. This he let to his newly married friend, Joseph Elliott, a printer employed by the *Register* newspaper. It is interesting to compare Elliott's cottage with the rowhouse occupied by the Calders in 1858, discussed in Chapter 2 (fig. 30), because they indicate the wide range of rental accommodation available in the late 1850s. With the population of Adelaide more than doubling in the period 1846–1851 accommodation was generally scarce and house rents were high, ranging from £30 to £40 per year for a house of three or four rooms. Most new arrivals to Adelaide would find quarters, such as Elliott's, hard to obtain as one half of all houses had less than four rooms.

As this case study demonstrates, the 'symmetrical' plan with a short passage suited the small, often re-subdivided, building block. The space-saving layout proved popular with owner/occupiers, built either in the form of a free-standing house or as a semi-detached pair where one could be let. There are no known examples of row houses which incorporated the short passage plan. However, the basic four room plan survived for the rest of the century as a low-cost family house, with its average floor area increasing by about 10 m^2 during the following thirty years.[33]

'The Almonds', 1850

The introduction of the full-length central passage serving either four or six rooms under the main roof was the logical next step in the evolution of the symmetrical plan. One of the earliest extant examples is the Swann cottage (fig. 48), built in 1850 at Walkerville, one of the first villages of Adelaide. The original four room building has been incorporated into the rambling single-storey house known as 'The Almonds'. Swann's simple cottage, which represents stage one of the three main stages of construction, has been added to but otherwise hardly altered. This is undoubtedly due to its above-average size and high standard of workmanship which put it near the top of the house range of its period. The other saving factor was the cleverly designed first addition to the cottage which extended the original plan sideways, uniting the functions of its front rooms.

James Swann, a prosperous carpenter and joiner of Grenfell Street, Adelaide, built the cottage in large grounds planted with fruit trees and an almond grove that gave the cottage its name. Building for himself and his wife, Swann borrowed privately the sum of £200 with interest at the rate of eight per cent per annum.[34] However, the true cost of the house to a non-builder would have been around £250. An early painting of *The Almonds 1850* suggests that it was built without a verandah and had a gable roof.[35]

In 1856, the property was sold to William Belt, an Adelaide lawyer of five years' standing. His wife, Penelope, writing to her mother in England, gives a first-hand glimpse of the cottage in use, soon after moving in:

> W. Charles has bought a beautiful little house and a splendid garden about two miles from Adelaide . . . The entrance is through a long avenue of white trellis work covered with vines and on each side of it is a small vineyard. The front of the house is surrounded by a small but very choice flower garden . . . The house itself is shaded by a deep verandah (which is such a luxury in this climate) and the verandah is covered with all kinds of beautiful creepers . . . We have a nice little drawing room and a dining room where I generally reside with the children. There are two good bedrooms, one is ours and the servants and children occupy the other (till we can afford to build two more rooms). I have a nice storeroom well fitted up with shelves; there is a good kitchen well fitted up also and a washroom with a copper set in it and an oven. There is an outbuilding that I call a nursery where I sent the children to play . . . We might have waited and toiled on in England all our lives and never possessed such a place.[36]

The 'good kitchen', the 'nice storeroom' and the 'washroom with a copper set in it and an oven'—a rare facility to be had—were detached. They formed the 'outbuildings and the appurtenances' at the rear of the 'dwelling house' purchased by the Belts.[37] The main outbuilding was the separate kitchen located near the back door of the house, with the washroom (laundry) probably in a lean-to.

As other case studies suggest, the detached kitchen was an exception rather than a rule, especially in the case of a small house where servants were not employed. In Adelaide, the integrated kitchen—as in the Elliott house, discussed above—proved generally more convenient and versatile in servantless

'THE ALMONDS', 1970

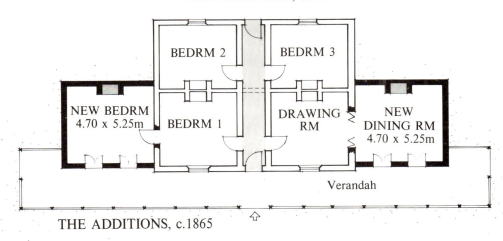

THE ADDITIONS, c.1865

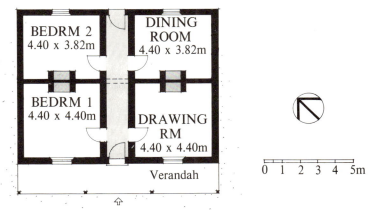

ORIGINAL SWANN COTTAGE, 1850
(Detached Kitchen, etc. not shown)

Figure 48: 'The Almonds', Walkerville, 1850–c.1865. Symmetrical cottage plan with full length passage.
(Photograph: Stephen Gilbert, 1970)

households. Australia always had a 'servant problem', especially in the towns where most families could not find nor afford domestic help. In South Australia during the 1850s less than one worker in ten was engaged in domestic service, allowing on average one servant 'to every fifth family'.[38]

In early buildings the risk of fire and the constant heat generated by the ever-burning wood fire were good reasons for building the kitchen at a distance from the main house. However, the predominance of brick and stone construction in Adelaide buildings by the end of the decade reduced the fire risk of an integrated kitchen. And, on small allotments, it saved valuable ground space as well as being cheaper to build as part of the dwelling.

What Penelope Belt called 'a beautiful little house' was, in fact, more than a little house for the mid-fifties. The cottage had a gross area of 105 m^2 (without its outbuildings) and an 11.4 m frontage, compared with the average 80 m^2 floor area and 10 m frontage for a detached cottage of four rooms. Although the central passage was only 1.2 m wide, the greater width given to the rooms on either side made them more spacious than usual; the two front rooms were 4.4 m square and those at the rear measured 4.4 m x 3.8 m each.

By the mid-1860s the growing family made the planned addition of the 'two more rooms' necessary. In an unorthodox way the four room plan was extended sideways, rather than along the passage axis at the rear. A large room, (5.3 m x 4.7 m) was attached on each side providing a new dining room and extra bedroom. A new roof of Willunga slate, with hipped ends and narrow eaves, covered the whole front section, as it does today, and the 2.0 m wide all-timber verandah extended right across, with short returns at each end. Typical of Victorian planning, access to each of the new rooms was gained through the original front rooms—two metre wide folding doors of deep coloured cedar divided the new dining room from the drawing room. When the doors were folded back a large space was created for social occasions. On the opposite side, a single door gave access to the new bedroom. Each new room had two sets of French doors leading to the verandah.

The next major addition to the house was made about 1905 by Edward Belt, who bought the property from his father's estate. This awkwardly proportioned extension next to the dining room added a huge recreation room and a separate entrance used for large scale entertaining. It is interesting to note that the new section was covered with corrugated galvanised iron as an extension to the existing slate roof.

'Heywood', c. 1858

The symmetrical cottage plan, with its straight frontage and simple roof, quickly became accepted by both town and country dwellers. The full-length central passage, giving independent access to either two or three rooms on each side, made the layout open-ended and capable of easy extension in the future. By simply adjusting the width of the passage and the number and dimensions of individual rooms, the same basic plan was adapted to suit different budgets.

With minor regional variations, the symmetrical plan continued to enjoy Australia-wide popularity well into the twentieth century. Its country version took the familiar form of the Australian homestead, characterised by the hipped roof and wide verandahs extending all around the house. In his book *Australia's Home*, Robin Boyd uses the borrowed term 'bungalow' to identify the homestead plan as one of five principal plan types of Australian houses.[39]

The first three decades saw a number of 'homesteads' built in a rural setting in the vicinity of the city. These larger than average houses occupied selected country sections and were often located in proximity to the villages. Today, those that still survive have most likely been converted to institutional use with their once extensive lands long ago sub-divided and enveloped by suburbia.

'Heywood' remains a classic example of a substantial country house designed to the symmetrical homestead plan (fig. 49) and built in about 1858 near the dormitory village of Unley. The dimensions of the original house are comparable with 'The Almonds' after the latter's first extensions were completed. William Hawke chose the site on the bank of Brownhill Creek for his residence which originally comprised six spacious rooms under the main roof. There was also a detached kitchen and a separate two-storied servants' quarters at the rear of the house. The design provided for a large basement room (5.2 m x 4.3 m) complete with fireplace, where the family could take refuge during summer heatwaves. Similar summer apartments situated below the ground floor can be found in a number of Adelaide mansions dating from the 1850s. A few years after Hawke's death the house was purchased by Simon Harvey, the founder of Adelaide's Globe Timber Mills. He lived there from 1879–86 and named it 'Dorset House'. In 1896 William Haslam, M.L.C., bought the house and changed its name to 'Heywood'.

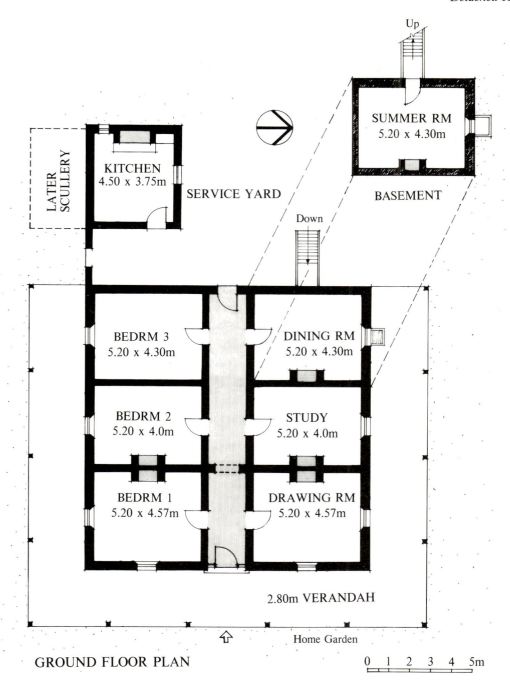

Figure 49: 'Heywood', Unley Park, c.1858. Symmetrical homestead plan with a wide verandah extending on three sides.

Although the house was altered and extended at the rear in 1883 and again in 1929, its simple and well-proportioned 14.0 m wide frontage remained intact. However, in its 125 years of existence, the house has had no less than three different verandahs. Typical of the homestead plan the generous front verandah, 2.8 m wide, returned along the two sides and French windows gave access from the bedrooms on the eastern side (fig. 50). It is reasonable to assume that the all-timber verandah covered with concave

iron sheeting, as depicted in the earliest photograph of the house taken about 1870, was the first verandah and was probably built with the original house. The photograph of the newly named 'Dorset House', dating from the early 1880s, shows the subsequent design with the verandah posts and facia decorations changed to cast iron, in keeping with the fashion of the decade (fig. 51). Heavy stucco mouldings were also added as embellishment to the original simple brick chimneys. The present verandah and new entrance porch are the result of major alterations undertaken in 1929, when cast iron was replaced with timber to resemble the original design.

THE RESIDENCE OF WILLIAM HAWKE, c.1870.
Note a buggy parked under the verandah, 2.8m wide.

'DORSET HOUSE'—THE RESIDENCE OF SIMON HARVEY, c.1880.

Figures 50 and 51: 'Heywood' Unley Park: Alterations to the exterior, c.1870–c.1880.

Excluding the detached kitchen buildings, which also contained staff quarters, the original house covered 200 m², an equivalent area to three average cottages. Bluestone, probably quarried at Mitcham, was combined with exposed brick quoins and a plinth in 50 cm thick external walls. The internal dividing walls are unusually thick at 40 cm. Appropriate to the early sixties, slate was used for the roof covering, and windows had strong hinged shutters fitted with adjustable louvres as a concession to Adelaide's climate as well as for security.

The passage, increased in width to 1.8 m, gave access to the pair of principal rooms measuring 5.2 m x 4.6 m each (almost exactly the size of the new rooms at 'The Almonds'). The ceilings, at 4.1 m high, added to the general feeling of spaciousness. The arch and its decorated pilasters, being part of the transverse wall in the passage, marked the end of the formal entrance. The plan shows the traditional vis-a-vis arrangement of the internal doors, and the back to back fireplaces accentuating the symmetry of individual rooms. An imported cast iron grate designed for burning coal still exists in one of the rooms as a reminder that imported coal from England or New South Wales was the fuel used in the colonial houses of 'great folk'.[40]

Para Para Lodge, 1880

The fine drawings (fig. 52, Plate 3) of the lodge at Para Para, north of Adelaide, for the Hon. Walter Duffield, MLC, is dated May, 1880, and signed by 'Taylor & Forgie, builders' of nearby Gawler. Although an architect's name is missing from the drawing, the date points to the English & Soward[41] partnership. Except for the kitchen projecting on one side, the four-room stone lodge illustrates the asymmetric 'villa' design which appeared in the mid-1860s.

The protruding parlour, labelled 'Living Room' (4.3 m x 3.6 m), dominates the 'front' elevation with the new gable wall adorned by a bay window and covered by a bell-cast roof. The front verandah, now shortened by the projecting parlour, becomes little more than an entrance porch. The usable floor space of the house extends to the 'covered' back verandah which contains a 'pantry' and storage shelves. The large country kitchen (4.6 m x 3.6 m), which also is a dining room, has a wide recess with flue over for the 'oven' and adjacent built-in 'sink'. Two identical bedrooms (3.6 m square) complete the simple plan of 86 m² in area.

The 1.5 m wide central passage leads to the walled-in 'yard' at the rear with a large capacity underground tank and a privy ('closet') located in the bottom corner. An architect's note on the drawing

emphasises the fact that all rooms under the main, slate-covered, roof had ceilings 12 ft. 6 in. (3.8 m) high. Typical of colonial houses regardless of their style, the ridge line is kept low by framing the roof in an M-shape with a hidden internal box gutter draining towards the rear (see Cross-Section C-D).

Botanic Garden Lodge, 1866

The North lodge at the Botanic Gardens remains one of the earliest extant examples of a small 'villa' (fig. 53). In April, 1866, the tender of the builder, Nimmo & McGee, was accepted at £305.[42] The original L-shaped house of 70 m² contained three small-sized rooms, each with its own fireplace. It is likely that the front and back verandah were included in the building contract as they appear on an 1874 map of the Garden. Until today the house has served continuously as the head gardener's residence with the plan being progressively extended at the rear since 1928. The stout bluestone walls, brick quoins and imported slate roof, which remains in sound condition, indicate the characteristic materials of the sixties.

Comparable in style with the Para Para lodge, discussed above, the asymmetrical front elevation shows a typical three-sided bay window of simple design. The traditional materials of the house were combined with the new curved roof of imported corrugated galvanised iron used for the verandahs, supported by plain timber posts.

Rounsevell House, c. 1875

This substantial house (fig. 54, Plate 1) is a late example of the symmetrical-fronted plan which, after 1875, ceased to be used for better-class houses. Perhaps it is significant that the architect, Thomas English, labelled it a 'villa residence' while following the traditional design. The signed, but undated drawings would have been prepared in the period, 1873–1877, when English was a sole practitioner.[43] The signature of the 'contractor', W. Dickin, is also recorded.

Designed as a summer residence for a well-known Adelaide undertaker, William Rounsevell, at fashionable Glenelg, it contained seven rooms including three bedrooms and a room for a live-in maid. The house presented a straight frontage of 12.8 m to the street with a wide, 2.1 m, full width verandah. The gross floor area covered 210 m². The un-named room next to the kitchen—added somewhat later—was the scullery, equipped with an open fireplace and a built-in copper for water heating. This 'wet' room served as a laundry and was also used for general ablutions.

ELEVATION TO CARRIAGE DRIVE.

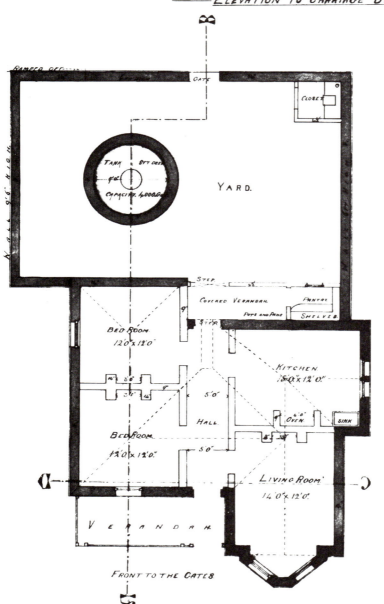

SECTION OF W.C.

Figure 52: Para Para Lodge, South of Gawler, 1880. English and Soward, architects. Asymmetric villa plan with forward projecting parlour. (See also Plate 3 and compare with an early Adelaide example, fig.53.)

Figure 53: (opp.) Botanic Garden Lodge, Adelaide, 1866. An early asymmetric-fronted villa with a simple bay window in the gable wall.

(Photograph: T. Fox, 1986)

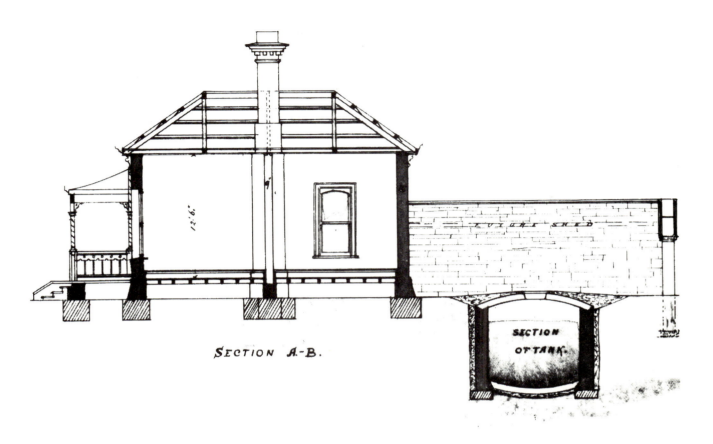

SECTION A-B.

SECTION OF TANK.

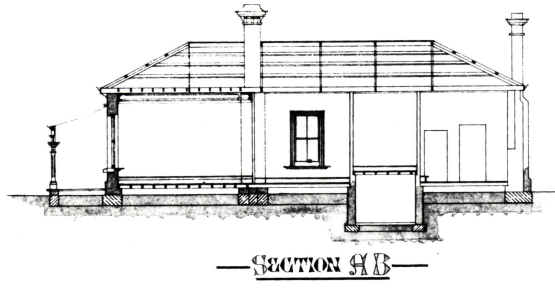

— SECTION AB —

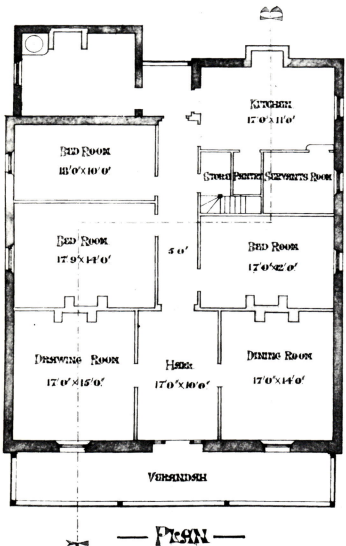

— PLAN —

Figure 54: Rounsevell House, Glenelg, designed by Thomas English, architect, between 1873 and 1877. A late example of the symmetrical-fronted plan used for better class houses. The varying width of the central passage is characteristic of the decade. (See also Plate 1.)

Figure 55: (opp.) Delano House, Norwood, c.1884. H.C. Richardson, architect. Triple-fronted villa with returned verandah which acquired the label of 'gentleman's residence'.

The notable evolution in the plan is the varying width of the central passage. Also of interest is the early appearance of a small service lobby at the end of the passage. The front section of the passage, at 3.0 m wide, forms a spacious 'Hall' which narrows to the standard 1.5 m passage beyond the archway. Flanking the hall are the drawing room (5.1 m x 4.6 m) and dining room (5.1 m x 4.3 m) serving as the main reception rooms. The slight difference in their respective widths is cleverly disguised in the widths of the outer piers, thus preserving the symmetry of the elevation about the centre line. The four-panelled front door is set between half-glazed sidelights with an enlarged fanlight above that combine to admit more daylight to the entrance hall.

The flamboyant influence of the early seventies can already be seen in the decorative treatment applied to the 'front elevation' (see Plate 1). The traditional brick quoins built with the 45 cm thick stone wall are concealed under smooth rendering which is used for the architraves with false keystones, projecting window sills and imitation corner stones.

— FRONT ELEVATION —

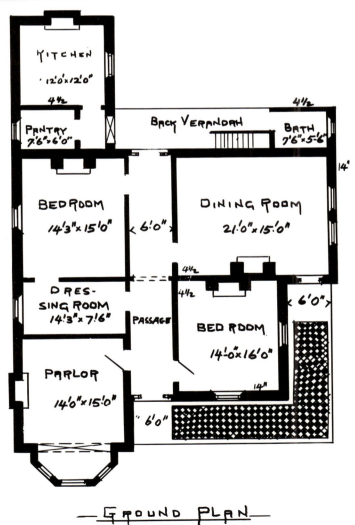

KITCHEN
·12'0"×12'0"

4½

PANTRY
7'6"×6'0"

BACK VERANDAH

BATH
7'6"×5'6"

4½

14"

BEDROOM
14'3"×15'0"

6'0"

DINING ROOM
21'0"×15'0"

DRES-
SING ROOM
14'3"×7'6"

PASSAGE

4½

4½

BED ROOM
14'0"×16'0"

6'0"

PARLOR
14'0"×15'0"

14"

6'0"

— GROUND PLAN —

The delicate corbels (brackets) under the eaves and the elaborate decorations of the verandah, including the posts, are still in wood. Ornate chimney tops stand out high above the corrugated iron roofing as a kind of status symbol. However, there is still a restraint in the decorations, and sensitive massing and good proportions remain the main qualities of the overall design.

Delano House, c. 1884

With the pioneering days truly over, the simple dignity of the symmetrical-fronted design lost its appeal, especially to affluent Adelaidians. For many the aim was to impress the passer by, not by ponderous dignity, but rather by an aggressive display that reflected the material success of the owner. The outcome was the triple-fronted villa with returned verandah, which offered almost unlimited scope in its architectural solution.

This particular plan type, which dates from about 1880, later acquired the label of 'gentleman's residence' and had evolved as the larger version of the asymmetric villa. While increasing further the asymmetry of the design, the stepped triple-front made the plan especially suited to the wide corner allotment. A significant functional innovation was the second door placed at the end of the returned verandah facing the street. Usually half-glazed, it provided direct access from the dining room to the verandah and garden.

Comparable in size and substance to the Rounsevell House, discussed above, is the Norwood triple-fronted villa of a 'collector', named William Delano. The undated linen tracing of the original drawings (fig. 55) bears the signature of 'H.C. Richardson, architect'[44]. Records of rate assessment show that it was built between 1882 and 1885. Built on an average sized block, the spacious ground plan of this villa covers 185 m², with street frontage of 13.5 m. It comprises five well-proportioned rooms, with the kitchen and pantry projecting at the rear under a lean-to roof.

The 1.8 m wide passage runs in a straight line from the front to the back door which opens on to the back verandah. Although the house was unsewered, a bathroom (2.3 m x 1.6 m) was enclosed at one end of the verandah. Its location provided easy access for hot water to be brought in from kitchen and for disposal of waste water on to the garden. The dining room (6.4 m x 4.6 m) is the largest room in the house and has an outside door. The front parlour (4.3 m x 4.6 m) extends into the deep recess of the bay window, which has developed into a major element combined with the highly decorated gable wall.

In elevation, the sandstone walls provide a subdued background to the light delicacy of the cast iron verandah columns and lace decoration of the railing executed in the same material. The mass-produced cast iron to standardised patterns combine with the elaborate stucco finishes. They include pairs or corbels, architraves, vermiculated corner stones, and neo-classical pilasters attached to the bay window. Typically, the main roof and the verandah are covered with corrugated galvanised iron, the apparent surface of the roof being somewhat reduced by the gable wall and stepped frontage.

Lathlean House, 1877

The ten-room 'Residence at College Town for D. Lathlean Esq.' (fig. 56, Plate 4) was designed by the architect, Daniel Garlick, who signed the contract drawings on 20th September, 1877, at the height of Adelaide's building boom. A two-storey villa, free-standing in spacious grounds, was the ultimate model for a family residence or 'seat' which the colonial gentry built during the last quarter of the century. With only ten rooms and a total floor area of 370 m², the Lathlean house was modest in size compared with grander houses, many of which contained fifteen rooms or more. With a 13.7 m wide frontage, it could be sited on an average suburban block.

The ground floor contained a drawing room (5.5 m x 4.9 m) with bay window and dining room (6.0 m x 4.6 m) both facing the street, and a smaller breakfast room and servant's bedroom at the rear. A generous 2.7 m verandah, paved with imported Staffordshire tiles edged with Mintaro slate led the visitor into the 2.4 m wide straight hallway with the stair to the first floor located to one side. A small porch cum pantry linked the rear entrance with the kitchen (3.6 m square) and adjoining scullery, also accessible from the back verandah. This compact arrangement of the service areas in a single-storey wing is repeated also in the contemporary terraced houses, discussed in Chapter 5. The 'wet' functions of food preparation and washing are confined to the scullery equipped with wood-fired copper and sink. Willunga 'slates' cover the floors of the scullery and back verandah.

The four bedrooms on the first floor reflect the ground floor layout, with the addition of a small dressing room at the front. A separate bathroom, with a built-in bath and a shower over, is conveniently located above the rear porch, see Section (fig. 56). A 1.2 m wide balcony over the verandah is accessible from one of the front bedrooms.

Rarely seen construction details of the separate privy are included on the architect's drawings (Plate 4). This tiny brick building typically measures 1.5 m x 1.2 m inside. Its timber framed bench seat is located over an underground permanent collection pit. This so-called cesspit had a sloping floor and external manhole for regular emptying. In rather a vain attempt to reduce the odour a 'ventilating tube' extends above the skillion roof—a forerunner of the modern main vent. This type of privy was the best that could be provided prior to the early 1880s when suburban houses started to be connected to the Adelaide sewer system. A cheaper and commonly used solution was to move a timber-framed privy as the un-lined cesspit filled up. However, the lack of drainage associated with Adelaide clay presented serious problems, especially as the density of the population increased. For this reason, Adelaide became the first sewered city in Australia. For other examples of early privies and W.C.s see, in particular, Chapter 5.

The 'front elevation' shows the best finishes and finest workmanship that money could buy. The solid stonework, 45 cm thick at ground floor, combines with rich stucco decorations which become elaborate at first floor level above the double window situated in the gable wall. A rendered eaves course runs under the gutter while an intricately fretted barge board and over-decorated finial terminate the high gable wall. The slender verandah supports are paired and made of cast iron. The iron lace is liberally used under the concave verandah and in the railings and small roof of the balcony. A passer-by would be left in no doubt as to the substance of the owner.

Rugless House, c. 1895

As the Victorian era drew to an end, the mid-century symmetrical 'cottage' and its later variant the 'villa' underwent further changes and incremental improvements. While, during the final quarter of the century the villa became more popular, especially at the upper end of the housing market, the cottage design continued to provide a slightly cheaper alternative. Usually smaller in area, the cottage plan was simpler to build with less expensive finishes and fewer decorations. For example, in 1892 a small cottage could be built for the average rate of 60 shillings per square metre while the rate for a villa was 75 shillings.[45] The Rugless cottage and the following Lucas villa demonstrate the essential similarities of their plans which existed despite the different appearance they presented to the street. As average suburban dwelling houses of the late nineties they indicate the general housing standards that prevailed in Adelaide at the turn of the century.

As mentioned earlier in this Chapter, the average house grew in size to the extent that more than one-half of all dwellings boasted at least five habitable rooms. Their designs were affected by a number of new and exciting technical innovations. Although most small houses still retained the traditional outhouse, the 'privy' became the watercloset (W.C.) connected to the sewer. There were a reticulated water supply and gas for lighting main rooms. Cast iron grates fitted to fireplaces made them more efficient and usable. New and improved household equipment for cooking and washing, as indicated on various plans, simplified daily chores, especially in the average servantless house.

In the small house the 'washroom' (laundry) still remained a flimsy outbuilding in the back yard and did not become an enclosed portion of the back verandah until the end of the Edwardian era. However, the bathroom appeared in increasing numbers in new houses of the nineties. For instance, in a group of 106 different houses approved by the Municipality of Unley during 1892, a bathroom was shown in 35 per cent of the 45 symmetrical-fronted cottages; in 50 per cent of the 30 small villas, and in 82 per cent of the 11 larger villas with return verandahs.[46]

Compared with pre-1865 plans, the planning and disposition of main rooms were influenced by changes in lifestyle. Transverse walls separating rooms no longer lined up on both sides of the passage and individual rooms were dimensioned according to their functions which had become more specific.

The kitchen was moved backwards and to one side forming an extension of the main house, while the so-called dining room evolved as the largest room. It occupied the rear corner with the door furthest down the passage providing convenient access to the kitchen. A large fireplace enhanced its frequent use by the family. The parlour, now labelled drawing room as in grand houses, retained its traditional role at the front, but with a reduced floor area. Bedrooms were more numerous and differed in size. Large windows, used in pairs in the principal rooms, made the interior lighter and more airy than previously.

The less dominant corner fireplace re-appeared in the late eighties. It had been used in earlier houses (see houses at Burra, discussed previously) as a device to save valuable floor space as well as building costs. During the last decade it was commonly used in bedrooms where the narrow hearth was fitted with a cast iron grate. However, main fireplaces in the parlour and dining room retained, for the time being, their focal position in the centre of a wall.

The straight passage, broadened to 1.5 m (5 feet) in width, maintained its rectangular form as a straight-line link between the front and back doors.

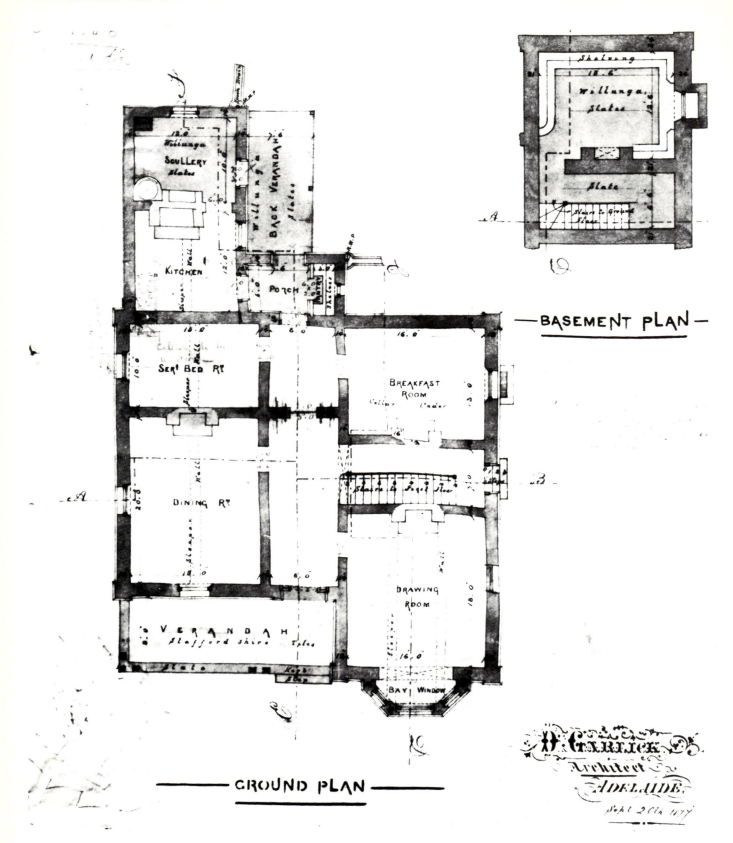

— BASEMENT PLAN —

— GROUND PLAN —

Figure 56: Lathlean House, College Town (present College Park), 1877. Daniel Garlick, architect. Two-storey version of the villa plan in large grounds—an ultimate model for a family residence built during the last quarter of the century. (See also Plate 4)

— FRONT ELEVATION —

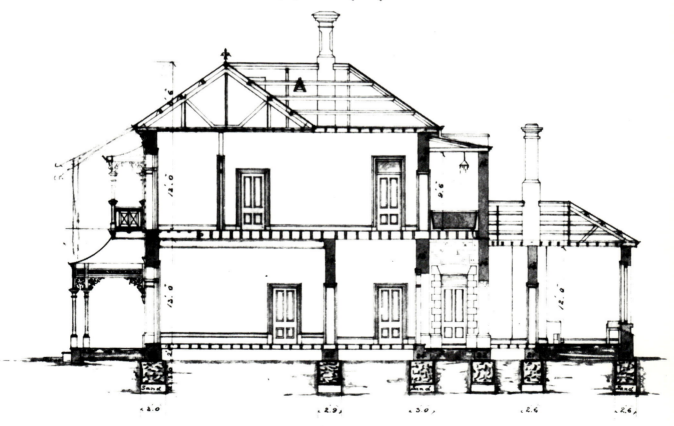

— SECTION E J —

The only variation was an attempt to change its width between the front and the rear section, which occurred briefly during the seventies. With the widening of the passage, sidelights were added to the front door to admit more natural light to the entrance than was possible with only a fanlight. The doors along the passage became staggered in plan to reduce overlooking between rooms. In particular, this arrangement ensured greater privacy to the front bedroom.

The symmetrical-fronted house of Charles Rugless (fig. 57), built in the mid 1890s—the drawings are undated—was designed by the architects English (Joseph) and Soward. Standing on an average suburban allotment, 15 m wide, the six room house with three bedrooms has a frontage of 10.8 m and a total floor area of 165 m². The economic method of construction used combines a freestone front with exposed brickwork for the remaining outside walls which are 28 cm (11 inches) thick, built with an internal cavity. The cavity wall is extended to embrace the kitchen attached at the rear. The plan includes a sizeable 'back verandah' as an extension of the passage. This area was later called the 'lobby' and, while basically a circulation space, it introduced a barrier which kept heat generated in the kitchen as well as any flies out of the house proper. Evolved from the open verandah, it provided a handy general work space and storage for garden clothes and so on. An early slop sink is located in the corner next to the kitchen. The bathroom, kept on the outside wall to simplify plumbing connections, and the adjacent pantry built in framed construction was a standard arrangement from the early 1890s until 1915. There is no evidence that fixed handbasins were used in average bathrooms before 1901.

In this example the dining room (5.5 m x 4.3 m) is considerably larger than the parlour (4.3 m x 4.0 m), the latter being called more appropriately the 'sitting room'. The traditional position of the fireplace is retained in the sitting room only, while other rooms, including the dining room, have space-saving corner fireplaces. The layout clearly indicates an 'outside W.C. to be located where directed', which was still at some distance from the rear wall of the house. The large rain water tank shown against the kitchen wall was by then standard equipment. The 'washhouse' (laundry) is undefined on the drawing and still occupies an outhouse in the back yard. The symmetrical front elevation reflects the new architectural style. Pairs of windows pierce the freestone wall under the bull-nosed verandah roof that has all timber supports. While the main roof still follows the traditional M-shaped form with low ridge line, the straight verandah roof is adorned by a small triangular gablet.

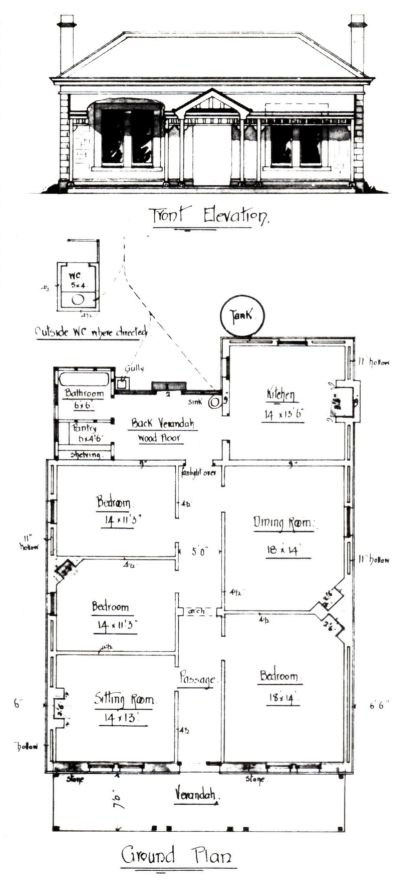

Front Elevation.

Ground Plan

FRONT ELEVATION

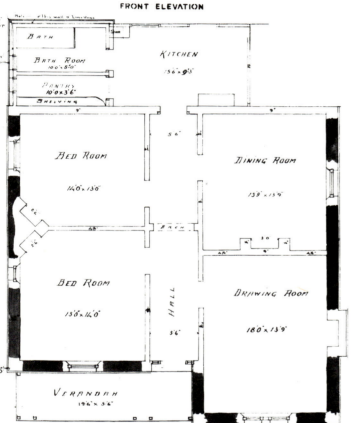

CROUND PLAN

Figure 57: (opp.) Rugless House, Glenelg, c.1895. English (Joseph) and Soward, architects. Symmetrical-fronted cottage with bathroom and pantry forming part of the enclosed back verandah. In this late colonial plan, sizes of individual rooms vary according to their functions which had become more specific.

Figure 58: (above) Lucas House, 1897. English and Soward, architects. A late example of the popular small suburban villa. The typical layout of four main rooms is comparable with the Rugless House, fig.57.

Lucas House, 1897

The main part of the Lucas House (fig. 58) is comparable with the Rugless house, discussed above. Built of solid stone at Glenelg in 1897, the five room plan is typical of the average suburban villa. A limited budget resulted in the kitchen and bathroom areas being rather smaller than usual, the omission of a back verandah, and the cheaper, timber framed construction that extended to the kitchen. Consequently, the overall area is a modest 137 m^2 which was costed at £428 by the architects, English and Soward. Also, to reduce costs, the ceiling height of 3.6 m was subsequently lowered by 30 cm. However, this still remained above the minimum permissible ceiling height of 10 feet (3.0 m), prescribed for the first time by the Building Act of 1881.

The front elevation shows stylistic changes in the design of the gable wall. The masonry is no longer carried up above the eaves level. Instead, the gable end of the roof takes the form of a projecting pediment, finished with rough-cast render set between vertical timber battens. In this case, the oversized barge board and decorative brackets attached to the pointed finial lack finesse of detail. (For an example of superior detailing see the Maesday house, which follows.) The double verandah posts are in timber, but the cast iron decorative brackets are remnants of the eighties.

Maesday House, 1906

The Maesday house (fig. 59, Plate 5), designed by the architects, English and Soward in 1906, and built at Glenelg by the contractor, Charles Oliver & Son, illustrates a turn of the century 'gentleman's villa' with the returned verandah. The 190 m^2 house, with 13.0 m frontage, contained seven habitable rooms, including four bedrooms. The wider than normal allotment of 24 m, allowed the front garden to follow the returned verandah in order to set off the extended frontage of the house.

Except for stylistic changes to the elevations, the main part of the house remains comparable in size and layout with the early villa of William Delano (c. 1884), discussed above. In fact, it is remarkable that the dimensions of the dining room and parlour in the two houses are almost identical. The later dining room (6.2 m x 4.9 m) still dominates the plan, while the drawing room (4.6 m x 4.3 m) is smaller than the main bedroom. Facing the street plain paired windows in the projecting gable wall have replaced the earlier much-decorated bay window, and minor bedrooms now have corner fireplaces. The broad, straight passage, now called 'corridor', leads directly to the kitchen which in turn opens on to the back

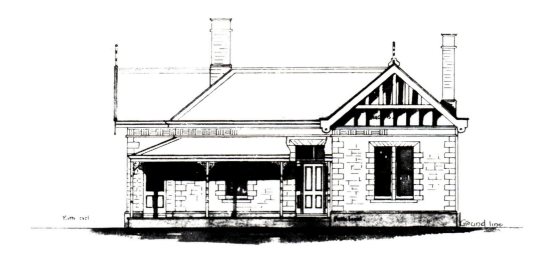

FRONT ELEVATION

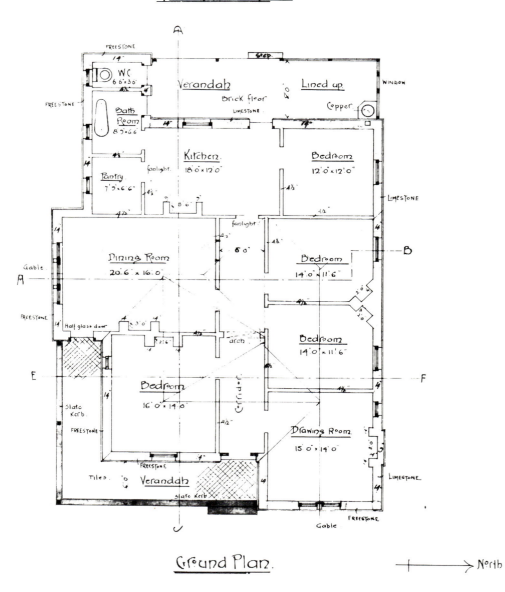

Ground Plan.

⟶ North

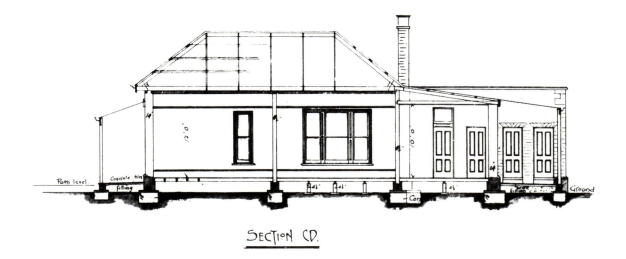

SECTION CD.

SCALE 8 FEET = 1 INCH.

Figure: 59: Maesday House, Glenelg, 1906. English and Soward, architects. This seven-room 'gentleman's villa' with returned verandah is typical of a large dwelling house of the late nineties. (See also Plate 5)

verandah. Here, the improvements over the last quarter of a century are evident. Attached to the house under the verandah roof are the W.C. compartment, the bathroom with a tin bath but no handbasin, and the partly enclosed laundry with a copper built into the corner.

Externally, the design presents a mixture of traditional methods of construction and prevailing architectural fashions. While internal partitions are in brick, two types of stone have been used in the solid outside walling. The walls not visible from the street are built in common 'limestone', while the gable walls including the stepped walls facing the front and side garden, display the best 'freestone' masonry. The beautifully executed ink and watercolour drawings indicate the fashionable pattern of the rock-face texture of the stone trimmed with brickwork. In subdued contrast are the verandah posts, used singly, with their sparse decorations. The main roof still retains its traditional form, except for the gable ends which show fine detailing using timber and roughcast panels.

Noltenius House, 1900

This last example, which is included to show the new directions in domestic architecture that emerged following the end of the building recession about 1895, is also at Glenelg. Apart from the stylistic modifications of the nineties already discussed, the planning of the front entry and the change in traditional roof construction must be mentioned. It was at the turn of the century that the front entrance moved first to the side and emphasis was given to roof shape.

Leading Adelaide architect, Edward J. Woods, departed from tradition when in 1900 he designed a double-fronted house of nine rooms for E. Noltenius (fig. 60, Plate 6). The price of the contractor, Essery & Coatsworth, to build the 260 m² residence was £1,170. The main planning innovation is the entrance porch protruding on the side, with the entrance hall at right angle to the central passage, the traditional archway separating the two. The passage, which can not be observed from the formalized entrance, becomes a private domain of the house. The main reception room has a rectangular alcove extending diagonally across a corner—a typical feature of the Edwardian drawing room. Under the straight verandah front, which is returned on either side, the fenestration of the front wall is intentionally random. It should be noted that in small houses without servants, the Noltenius' dining room became the main bedroom facing the street, while the dining room was situated at the rear, near the kitchen.

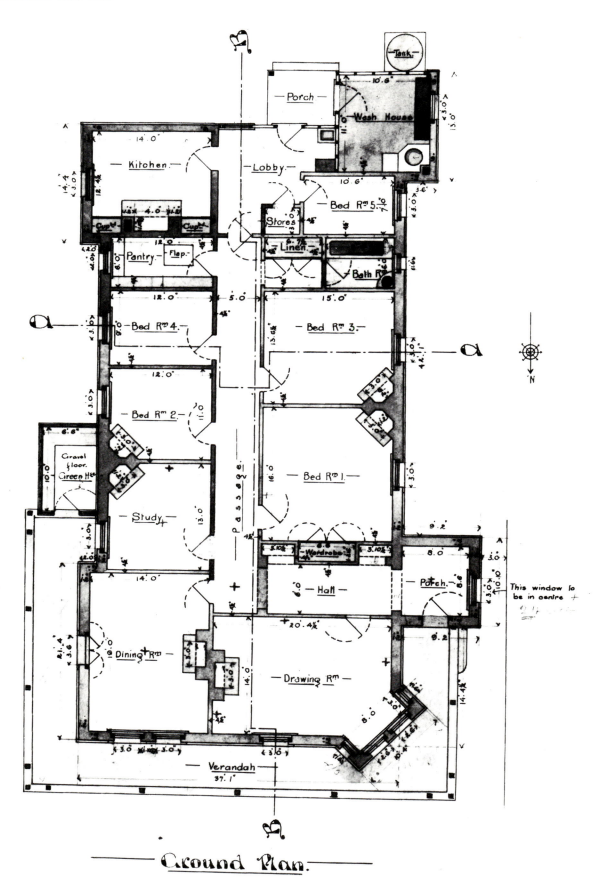

Ground Plan.

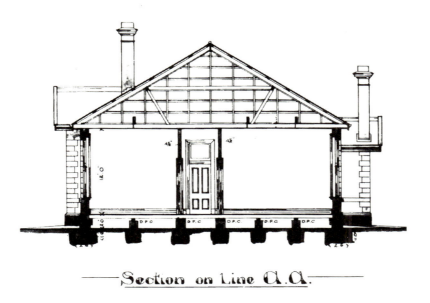

Section on Line A.A.

Figure 60: Noltenius House, Glenelg, 1900. Edward J. Woods, architect. The design of this turn of the century large, double-fronted, residence signals the demise of the Adelaide colonial house. New innovations include the side entrance, internal bathroom, attached wash house and the massive roof incorporating the verandahs. (See also Plate 6)

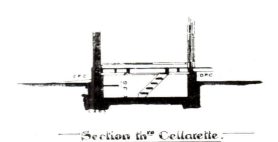

Section thro Cellarette.

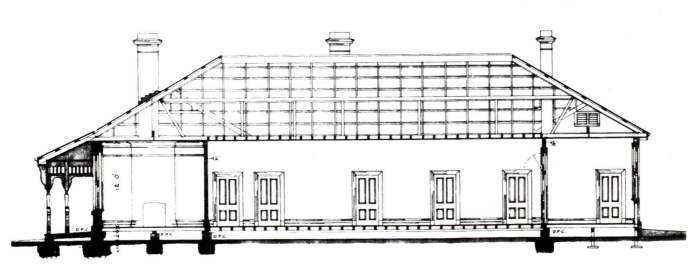

Section on Line B.B.

In this large house there are two other significant planning innovations. The bathroom is planned internally and is accessible off the passage. It contains a built-in bath and a corner handbasin. A fully enclosed 'Wash House' forms part of the plan. Entered off the back porch, it contains a triple washing trough and a built-in copper. As the house was built just before sewerage came to Glenelg, the bathroom and laundry fittings discharged into a septic tank, but a separate 'privy' had to be provided initially in the back yard, adjacent to the woodshed.

The massive roof, with its high ridge and long rafters extending beyond the wall line to form verandah roofs, is the focus of the building. As indicated on the Cross-Section 'A-A' (fig. 60), pairs of rafters span the full width of the ground floor plan, thus superseding the low colonial roof pitched with short timbers across a single room width. The vast surface of roof covering, which is corrugated iron, is only broken with the picturesque but non-functional 'gablets', angled above the drawing room. The low sweeping verandahs partly conceal the contrasting pattern of freestone and brick combination used in the external walls. Verandah posts and decorations, turned in wood and painted, introduce a new finishing touch to the elevations.

The new direction in design, as illustrated in this case study, signalled the demise of the Adelaide colonial house that had evolved during the last fifty years of the Victorian era.

Furnishings and household appliances, circa 1901

The following details of the main furnishings and appliances common to an average household at the turn of the century are included in order to enhance our general understanding of the design of Adelaide's colonial houses. It is the inventory of furniture and the specifications of household equipment that indicate the functions of the plan and highlight the use of its individual rooms. The information provided is relevant to the detached houses, already discussed in this Chapter, as well as to the other types of average sized dwellings contained in Chapters 3 and 5.

A shopping list of furnishings, considered to be the basic essentials for a family house, was compiled by a leading Adelaide furniture manufacturer, Malcolm Reid. In 1901, the cost of furnishing a '4-Roomed house', as listed, was £29/10/-.[47] Items which reflect prevailing living standards are the washstand in each bedroom, the two washing tubs in the kitchen, the kerosene lamp in the parlour and the candle stick in the best bedroom. The deal safe in the kitchen is probably of the Coolgardie variety, referred to later.

Parlour

1 Drawing room suite, beautifully upholstered in cretonne and plush, consisting of 1 couch, 2 easy chairs and 3 small chairs
1 Round table with polished top and claws, pedestal
1 Carpet square
1 Lamp
1 Wooden clock
1 Hearth rug and fender
1 Pair of curtains

Best Bedroom

1 Half-tester bedstead, full size
1 Chest of 5 drawers, cedar
1 Washstand and dressing table (Duchess pair)
1 Looking glass
6 Yards of carpet or matting
2 Cane-seated chairs
1 Candle stick
1 Water bottle and glass

Second Bedroom

1 French bedstead, mattress etc.
1 Washstand and dressing table
1 Water bottle
1 Chair
1 Looking glass on stand
4 Yards drugget

Kitchen

1 Deal table, 4'6" x 2'6"
1 Deal safe, flyproof, good size
2 strong chairs (Painted)
2 Washing tubs (different sizes)
1 Lamp and shade complete
1 scrubbing brush
Crockery, cutlery and various cooking utensils

For a larger house with a sizeable drawing room, the five-piece suite listed for the parlour above would be replaced with a 'typical 7-piece suite', fully sprung, with carved frames, and upholstered in tapestry and plush, or better. It consisted of one couch, one gentlemen's chair, one ladies chair and four small chairs. Depending on the size of the room, items additional to those listed for the parlour would include an easy chair and a bookcase or possibly a sideboard/bookcase combination.

The provision of public utilities and the availability of household appliances had a profound effect upon the functions of the Adelaide house and the lifestyle of its occupants. Today, it is hard to imagine an urban dwelling without the domestic facilities that give Australia living standards that are higher than many other countries. As already stated in this Chapter, by the year 1901 many Adelaide houses enjoyed the benefits of such public utilities as piped sewage, reticulated water and gas for lighting. An ever increasing number of professional and business people had a telephone connected to their private home. However, electricity, refrigeration and wireless

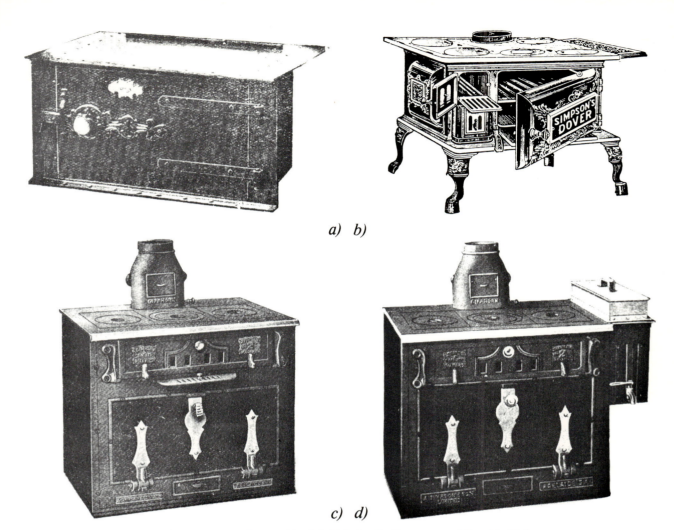

a) b)

c) d)

Figure 61: Stoves and ovens, manufactured in Adelaide by A. Simpson and Son Limited.
   a) Box-like 'colonial' oven was made in varying widths for building into existing or new fireplaces. The fire was made on top of the oven and side brackets supported rails on which kettles and cooking pots were placed. If extra heat was required inside the oven a second fire could be lit in the space provided underneath.
   b) Free-standing 'Dover' pattern cast iron stove. The design was based on an earlier model imported from England. A door opened in front to reveal a good sized oven. The wood fire was tended by lifting circular covers off the openings on the top, while the smoke discharged through a pipe supplied with the stove and usually fitted inside the chimney.
   c) 'Giffhorn' Patent Improved pattern combined cooking stove and oven in the one unit called a range. It sold from the early 1890s and was designed to burn coal, coke or wood.
   d) 'Giffhorn' kitchen range fitted with a five gallon (23 litre) side boiler to supply hot water on tap.

(Simpson's Catalogue)

(radio) had a slow introduction into the house during the first quarter of the twentieth century. With electricity came the major appliances that vanquished household drudgery.

Prior to the electrical liberation, the main kitchen appliance was the solid-fuel burning range which fitted into the recess that was a modified version of the open fireplace of pioneering days, The 'Giffhorn' improved pattern, designed and built in Adelaide by A. Simpson and Son[48] became a popular unit available in three standard sizes, varying in width from 24 to 36 inches (60–90 cm). Designed to burn wood, coal or coke, it featured a fall-down door to admit long lengths of wood and a damper at the base of the flue to control the flow of air through the fire. Legs could be detached if the unit was to be built in. The similar 'Economic' ranges were available in sizes to suit a cottage or a mansion. The ranges represented a significant advance on the earlier 'Dover' Stoves and primitive 'Colonial' ovens. A kitchen range in a house of modest means at the turn of the century would probably have had one oven, three or so 'ring' openings on the top and a five gallon (23 litres) copper water boiler with a tap (fig. 61).

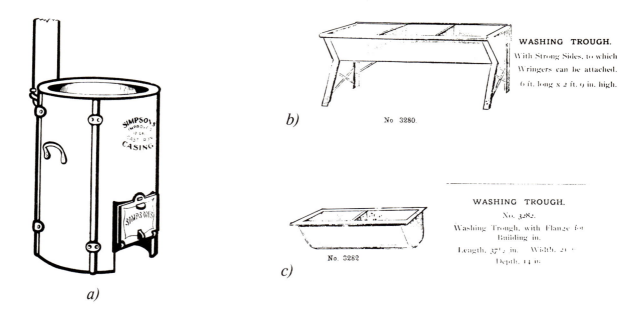

Figure 62: Laundry equipment.
a) Simpson's Improved portable washing copper. The rounded pan is set inside a cast iron casing and heated by a solid fuel fire. For built-in washing coppers a separate furnace door, grate and frame were manufactured.
b) and c) Galvanised washing troughs 'with strong sides' for attaching wringers were made with two or three compartments.
(Simpson's Catalogue, 1910 Edition)

Before refrigeration food was kept cool in either the traditional 'Coolgardie' drip safe or the more costly ice chest. The widely-used drip safe, equivalent in size to an average modern refrigerator, was framed either in timber or metal and had its sides and door covered with hessian. The interior was kept cool by evaporation of moisture soaking down from the overhead tank and dripping into a tray in which the safe stood. Because air movement improved the cooling, and also because of the constant use of water, the unit was often located on the back verandah. When manufacture of block ice started in the early 1860s, ice chests, also made as portable ice boxes, became the forerunner of the domestic refrigerator. The 1910 Simpson's catalogue contains two models with the appealing names of 'Perfection', made in metal, and 'The Klondyke' that had a wood frame with oak grained finish. Both measured, outside, 26 inches (66 cm) wide by 18 inches (75 cm) deep and were 41 inches (100 cm) high. The smaller in size 'meat safe'—a portable cupboard covered with flywire—should also be mentioned as indispensible in any colonial kitchen, particularly for storing cooked meat. A deal table, a tin washing-up dish, a toasting fork and a flat iron on its stand near the fire were also typical of the basic amenities in the colonial kitchen.

In the bathroom, the galvanised iron plunge bath remained the sole item of equipment shown on the various architects' drawings prior to 1900. Fitted with a fixed outlet, the 'Adelaide' pattern, with one end rounded and with four legs, was made in a standard length of 6 ft. (1.8 m). For un-sewered houses, the moveable 'Plunge' pattern, with both ends rounded, was made in lengths ranging from 4 ft. (1.2 m) to 6 ½ ft. (2.0 m). Galvanised iron shower roses, with fringe, began to be fitted above the bath and were rather large at 20 cm or 25 cm in diameter. Bath and shower heaters were a major innovation that appeared about 1900 (fig. 63).

Towards the end of the century coppers of various patterns, both free standing or built-in, became the norm in back yard wash-houses. 'Simpson's improved portable copper' ranged in size from 10 to 18 gallons (45 to 82 litres) and had the round copper tub set in a cylindrical cast iron casing. A small door at the bottom gave access to the fire, while a tall flue at the back kept smoke and soot away from the clothes. A handle on each side indicated the unit's portability, although this could not have been achieved with ease.[49] A galvanised iron or copper cover was an optional extra. Built-in coppers probably had one of the standardised furnace doors and frames that were widely available at the time. As houses were connected to sewers, wash-houses were usually equipped with a double or sometimes even a triple washing trough, either free standing or built-in. Mechanical wringers had been in use for at least two decades prior to the turn of the century. Mounted over washing tub or trough, they not only shed water from the clothes but allowed the hot soapy water to be returned to the copper for re-use (fig. 62).

During the seventies and eighties, washing machines of varied sophistication, and generally of American origin, made their appearance in press advertisements. Potential users were tantalised by such testimonials as 'the most useful machine ever invented',[50] or 'Washing Machine Extraordinary! Genuine efficient—should be in every house',[51] or

simply 'Dobbies celebrated American Washer 35s. to 45s'.[52] The latter appears to have been little more than an ordinary washing tub with a wringer mounted over one side. The much publicised 'Star Washing Machine',[53] price five pounds in 1880, rotated its burden through the soapy water in a star-shaped drum. Others utilised a 'dolly' type plunger as an agitator attached to a system of levers. While these manually operated machines represented some improvement over washing and wringing clothes by hand, their operation required a substantial input of time and energy in a hot, steamy atmosphere. It is little wonder that gas coppers and electric powered wringers and washers were warmly welcomed into Adelaide houses early in the twentieth century.

A "SIMPSON" BATHROOM

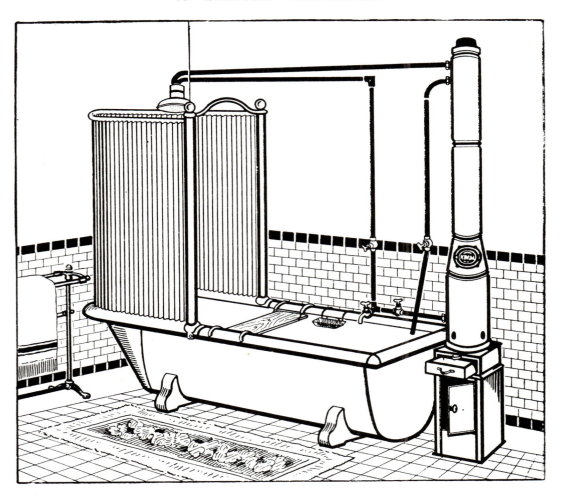

Figure 63: A 'Simpson' Bathroom, around 1900. The plunge bath is the 'Adelaide' pattern, 6 feet (1.83 m) long, made of galvanised iron with matching corrugated 'bath screen' fitted under the shower rose. The 'Economic' pattern bath heater—a post 1910 model—is equipped with an improved cast base and a sliding grate for easy operation. The simple 'chip heater', as it became known, brought instant hot water to the bathroom. Waste paper and wood chips were the common fuel—a newspaper provided an 'abundance of hot water for a Shower Bath and a small quantity of chips a Plunge Bath'.   *(Simpson's Catalogue, undated)*

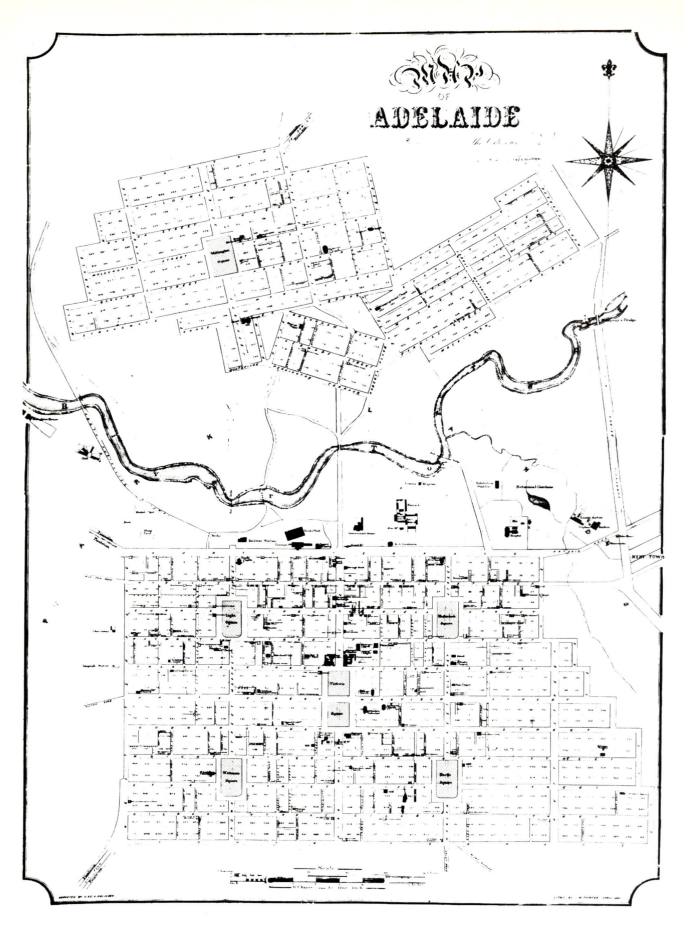

Map of ADELAIDE

Chapter 5

Terraces and Semi-Detached Houses

1850–1901

The terraced house

When growing demand for larger family houses coincided with rising land prices at about 1850, the multi-storey terraced house[1] made its appearance in Adelaide and continued to evolve at a varying rate throughout the second half of the century. After 1901, the exodus of the city population to the suburbs and the effect of constraining legislation put an end to the concept of terrace living—not to be revived until the 1970s.

It was during the 1850s that owners of well-situated land naturally endeavoured to make the most of their investment by building two, or even three-storey terraces. One of the first investors was G.M. Waterhouse, who in 1851 built a substantial two-storey terrace of six stone houses, each with a generous 5.6 m wide frontage (fig. 65), on land beside the Chalmers (Scots) Church in North Terrace, then an already fashionable residential address.[2]

The next decade saw the erection in South Adelaide of not less than six known double-storey terraces, containing from three to six family houses each.[3] Among them was an unusual design built in 1862 in Rosetta Place, off Franklin Street. It consisted of four houses, two in the middle being two

storeys high while the two end houses reached three storeys. The three-storey height was exceptional for a domestic building in Adelaide and was not to be repeated until the 'Marine Residences' (1885), discussed later, were built at Grange.

However, the multi-storey terraced house, as we know it today from surviving examples, is the product of unprecedented building activity during the period of prosperity, from 1870 to 1885, that followed the expanding sixties. Unlike the eastern capitals, Adelaide had no extensive areas of working-class terraced houses concentrated on the city's fringe, and consequently their numbers were small by comparison. Small, single-storey cottages, built singly or attached in short rows catered for Adelaide's working class population (see Chapters 1–3).

The multi-storey terraced house was a form of high-density housing which provided mainly for the more affluent middle-classes a family residence conveniently located close to the office or place of business. For those not located within easy walking distance, the availability of public transport was an important consideration. Before the introduction of horse-drawn tramways in 1878 (see Chapter 4), an omnibus service had operated between North Adelaide and the city since the early sixties. Beyond the parklands, Port Adelaide (since 1856) and Glenelg (1873) were linked by railway. The latter became the main location for terrace development.

From the earliest days the marine township of Glenelg at Holdfast Bay, the birthplace of South Australia, was a favourite summer retreat for the citizens of Adelaide, 'where the dust and fatigue of town are blown off'.[4] During the season of 1844, for example, more than twenty houses were already being rented by 'respectable families'.[5] It is hardly surprising that house building at the 'Bay' was seen as a profitable investment. Glenelg soon became the

Figure 64: (opp.) Map of Adelaide, 1861. Based on a survey by C. and E.A. Delisser, the map records the achievements of the first 25 years. It shows principal city buildings (outlined in black), the first railway line to Port Adelaide and the new bridges over the Torrens with the extension of King William Street linking North Adelaide with the heart of the city. While the six squares remain as originally planned by Colonel Light, an extensive network of secondary streets had evolved. Narrow streets and private lanes running in the north-south direction had been added to the plan as town acres were sub-divided and occupied. For comparison with the original plan, see fig.9.　　　　　　　　*(Public Record Office of S.A.)*

foremost resort for grand holiday houses of the gentry from both city and country. This development was spurred on by the building of the railways to an extent indicated by the scale of the case studies, which follow.

In 1874, a year after the Adelaide, Glenelg and Suburban Railway was opened between Victoria Square and Glenelg, more custom and importance was added to the township when it was decided to land overseas mail at the Glenelg jetty instead of Port Adelaide. In 1880, a second private railway began operating to Holdfast Bay from North Terrace in the city.

There was no set discernable pattern in the siting of terraces within a particular neighbourhood. It was only the difference in the size and quality of design, and not the address, that distinguished a worker's cottage from a double-storey terraced house. Often the two types of dwelling were built in close proximity and in some instances shared, apparently quite amicably, the same town acre. As a rule a typical terrace contained only four to eight double-storey houses. It was built singly, widely dispersed throughout the built-up areas, and became woven into the urban fabric of mixed building types that made up colonial Adelaide. Occasionally, a small terrace of attached houses would be built along the main shopping street of an inner suburb. These usually incorporated ground floor shops with dwellings above.

Practically all Adelaide terraces were built speculatively for sale or for rental investment. As the following case studies indicate, each project was an individual enterprise promoted by a private investor or, occasionally, by a small company. While no planning or building regulations existed to control piecemeal development, small investors and builders alike preferred to erect single buildings rather than to embark on more risky large-scale projects. However, it seems certain that this investment approach also recognised that close city living had a limited appeal for the average Adelaidian who, given a choice, preferred a detached cottage in the suburbs. And yet, during the seventies and eighties favourable conditions did exist for large-scale development of city housing, especially around its garden squares and along the terraces overlooking the parklands.

By 1881, the population of the City of Adelaide reached a near peak of 38,000, having more than doubled over the previous twenty years.[6] Nevertheless, the demand for city housing and the prosperity of the province were not enough to change the pattern of development established since

settlement began. It can be said that the often praised physical assets of Light's plan of Adelaide turned out to be a hindrance rather than a help in the way the city developed (fig. 64).

Firstly, the Terraces along the parklands proved to be a misnomer: E.E. Morris, in his description of Adelaide in 1888, felt obliged to explain that although 'the Terraces are popular and land along them commands a high price . . . the houses are not in a continuous row as in a London terrace.'[7] With minor exceptions, by the end of the seventies the best stretches of parkland frontages were occupied by the detached houses and mansions of colonial gentry set in spacious gardens.[8] Secondly, the development that had already occurred around the squares left much to be desired. Around the five squares, excluding Victoria Square, buildings were sparse and large parcels of land were either vacant or under-utilised. On the face of it they were ripe for further development.

Apart from their central location, the squares offered an attractive environment for city living. They contained public gardens planted with trees covering the entire space except for a narrow roadway that channelled traffic around the perimeter. Only narrow footways criss-crossed the central spaces which were not bisected by main streets as nearly all of them are today. Some were fenced in the manner of London's residential squares. It is surprising, therefore, that only few terraced houses were ever erected around these squares and that little attempt was made to revive their earlier, predominantly residential, character.

Of the four minor squares in South Adelaide, Hurtle Square had the largest number of double-storey terraces (four), followed by Whitmore (two) and Hindmarsh (one). Curiously, the impressive 'Albert Terrace' (1880) of nine large houses was built a mere hundred metres east of Hurtle Square in Carrington Street. A few years later, another terrace of four houses missed the same square's north-west corner by a mere few metres. Then, there was the case of 'Landrowna Terrace'—Adelaide's longest terrace of eleven stone houses that was built in the only non-residential square, Victoria Square. 'Landrowna', built for Thomas Tapson in 1875, occupied the entire frontage of Town Acre 375 on the corner of Angas Street. This terrace of simple and elegant design (fig. 74) contained one larger 'key'

Figure 65: Terrace of six houses, North Terrace, Adelaide, 1851. It was demolished in 1925 and replaced with an office building.
(Photograph taken about 1910: Mortlock Library of South Australiana. Site Plan: Smith City Survey, 1880, sheet no. 76)

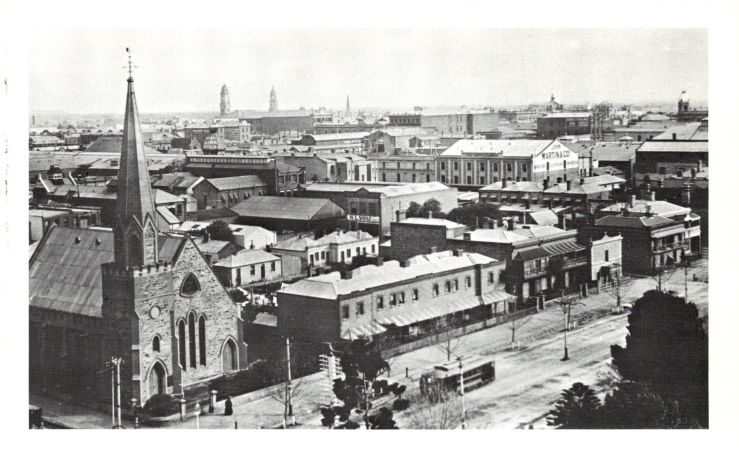

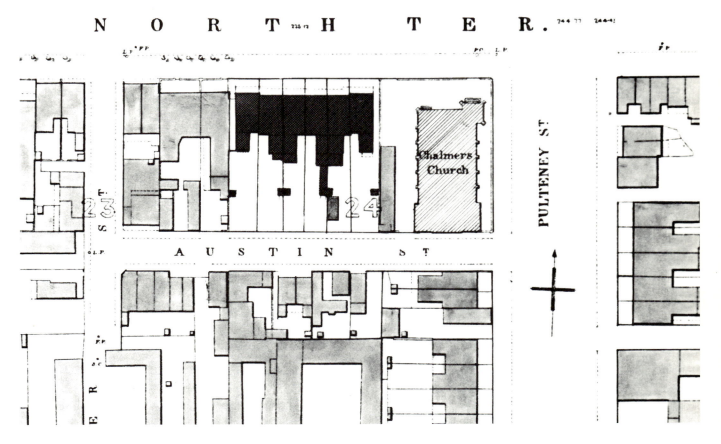

house on the corner attached to ten identical houses (each with a frontage of 5.8 m and a gross area of about 150 m^2).[9] It was demolished in 1923 to be replaced by administration offices of the Municipal Tramways Trust.

It is surprising that Wellington Square, the only square north of the Torrens, did not attract any terrace development considering the popularity of North Adelaide as a residential area. Instead, terrace building concentrated in the narrower streets east of O'Connel Street. The largest group, dating from about 1875, developed in Archer Street where five individually built terraces ranging from three to five houses each clustered around the Dover Castle Public House and the police station. As they survive today, it is possible to experience the urban scale and character the terraces created when built in a narrow street. The basic relationship between the height of buildings and the width of the public space differs in this example from the typical Adelaide streetscape of low buildings separated by wide public spaces. Archer Street suggests a preference for a more intimate urban environment than that offered by the typical Adelaide square.

The five minor Adelaide squares are characterized by their uniformity of size and generous proportions, 240 m long by 160 m wide. They must be compared with the old squares of Bath and London with which Colonel Light was presumably familiar. English residential squares are much smaller and of varying shape, and are between one-half to three-quarters the size of their Adelaide counterparts. It may be understandable that in planning Adelaide Light intentionally erred on the generous side. However, the repetition of size and final dimensions, determined by the oversized planning module of the square one-acre block, is difficult to explain except to suggest expedience in pegging-out.

The vast scale of the squares and the broadness of the main streets overwhelmed early citizens who often complained of getting lost when crossing a street. Walking, which remained the common form of commuting for the first fifty years, must have had an impact on the physical development of Adelaide, considering the distances to be covered. The sheer excess space provided by the Adelaide plan proved a serious practical obstacle to closer development for a small population with limited resources. A comprehensive housing development around a square required the acquisition of a large tract of privately-owned land and expenditure on buildings well beyond the resources of an average colonial investor.

The limited extent of terrace building could not alter the character of the squares and thereby entice further residential development. Architecturally, the

buildings were insufficient in bulk to physically define a square and to create the necessary enclosure of an urban space. Generally, location of terraces owed far less to conscious planning on the part of the investor or his architect than it did to the fortuitous ownership of land.

The terraced house plan is an exclusively urban form of housing in Australia, modelled on a London precedent. Not without justification Robin Boyd once considered it to be 'un-Australian' in type. In Adelaide, a number of well-known architects of the day played their part in the design of some of the most impressive projects. As the following case studies show, initially they followed the traditional English plan, but on a somewhat reduced scale. Addition of verandahs and provision of french doors opening on to balconies were typical concessions to Adelaide's mediterranean climate.

It was the great fire of London in 1666 that gave rise to the rapid development of the English terraced house as a town dwelling for ordinary inhabitants. Until then only the rich had built their mansions in town, while the poor lived in a conglomeration of crammed rooms, jutting out into the street over shops and workshops. In re-building London, Christopher Wren devised a new town house plan which basically remained unchanged until the 'flat', introduced from the Continent, became an accepted alternative at the end of the nineteenth century.[10]

The basic plan of the English terraced house had two floors with two rooms each.[11] It was enlarged vertically by additional floors above and a semi-basement underneath. Back extensions frequently extended the plan horizontally. The ground floor contained a small entrance hall alongside a parlour and dining room. A narrow staircase led up to the principal floor where the drawing room extended across the entire front and the main bedroom faced the rear. Other bedrooms were located on the second floor and in the attic. The kitchen and service rooms were placed out of sight in the semi-basement, with a separate front entrance off the sunken 'light area'. By the mid-1850s basements were included in most of the larger houses.

In Victorian London, a middle-class extended family with live-in servants would occupy a house of three storeys, raised on a semi-basement and topped by an attic housing the servants' bedrooms. One of the largest terraces, *Albert Houses* in Queen's Gate, South Kensington (1859–60), contained nineteen habitable rooms piled up on four levels above the basement, all within a street frontage of only 8 m.[12] At the other end of the scale, houses of artisans and labourers comprised two floors without a basement, the kitchen being located on the ground floor.

Terrace of three houses, c. 1868

The Sussex Street houses are an early example of a short terrace of 3 houses (fig. 66, Plate 7). They were designed by the architect, Thomas English[13] during the late sixties for a corner site situated in the heart of old Glenelg. The owner-speculator for the scheme, whose name appears on the architect's drawings, was 'William Parkin Esq. J.P.', and the houses are referred to somewhat loosely as 'Semi-Detached Villas'—thus raising their appeal as desirable residences. A 'David Miller', whose witnessed signature also appears on the un-dated drawings, contracted to erect the buildings.

Compared with the post-1870 examples, which follow, this terrace plan shows a number of distinctive features not to be repeated later. It may be that the plan can be considered representative of the Adelaide terrace for the period 1850 to 1865, of which there exists only scant information, mainly confined to the exterior.

The land on which this terrace stood corresponded in size to an average suburban block. The 18.2 m (60 ft.) frontage to Sussex Street was divided equally into three. However, the terrace contains two types of houses: the corner house on the right hand side is larger and better appointed while the other two smaller houses offer cheaper accommodation for sale or rental. In this case, the corner house, sometimes called the 'key' house, was custom-designed for the use of the owner. It occupies the most prominent position, has a generous entrance hall off the side street, spacious rooms and generally superior finishes. The upstairs bedrooms are more numerous and all are provided with windows in the end wall. The kitchen has a sizeable 'sink'—quite a luxury for the sixties—and a wider fireplace opening to fit a larger stove.

The two smaller houses have similar plans and share a common verandah along the street frontage. Each provides a modest standard of accommodation designed to suit a middle-class family with a live-in domestic servant. The middle house is typical of the terraced house, having a party wall on each side. It consists of seven smallish rooms (including 5 bedrooms) arranged on two floors, providing a gross area of 153 m².

At ground level, a typically narrow passage, 1.2 m wide, gives access to the main bedroom, dining room and, beyond the archway, the kitchen with an external pantry located under the back verandah. Upstairs, the drawing room is the principal room (5.5 m x 3.6 m) extending right across the street frontage, with children's bedrooms and servant's room behind. There is an open fireplace in each of the principal rooms, positioned opposite the window as in the cottage plan.

There is no bathroom provided in any of the houses. The water for personal and clothes washing was heated in the 60 cm diameter 'copper', built-in adjacent to the kitchen fireplace. Each dwelling has its own private yard, enclosed by a high stone wall. The service access is provided via a private road, for deliveries of firewood, and the regular emptying of the cess-pits located under the privies at the bottom of the yard, located as far as possible from the back door of the house.

This early design of Thomas English shows a fascinating mixture of the British tradition combined with Australian vernacular design and building practice. The deliberate location of the drawing room on the first floor reflects the middle-class London terrace, while the front bedroom and the integrated kitchen on the ground floor resemble the Adelaide cottage plan. Also interesting is the outside pantry placed under the back verandah in order to economise on the floor area of the house proper. A decidedly local element which provides the main embellishment to the otherwise plain street facade (see East Elevation, fig. 66) is the finely detailed timber verandah with a concave iron roof.

The elongated plan form has the inherent problem of providing adequate natural light and ventilation to its central rooms. In the dining room this is done by a borrowed light from the staircase—this room could not be used without supplementary light provided by candles or a kerosene lamp. Likewise, the upstairs children's bedrooms have no outside walls and have small overhead 'dormer' windows as the only means of light and ventilation. These are shown in Section 'A-B' (fig. 67).

The drawings show the cross-section through the typical 'M' type roof over the rear section of each house, and the timber trusses spanning between party walls. These double-pitched roofs discharge to box gutters which run along the top of the party walls. The fire regulations did not yet require parapets above the roof covering. The complete roof plan is shown dotted on the first floor plan.

The generous ceiling heights, 3.5 m and 3.3 m on the ground and first floors respectively, give a tall appearance to the facade further accentuated by the bellowed chimneys rising well above the ridge line. Timber eaves brackets add an individual touch to an otherwise plain design. Lack of any glazing bars in the double-hung sashes indicate the improved technology of glass making, enabling the use of large panes.

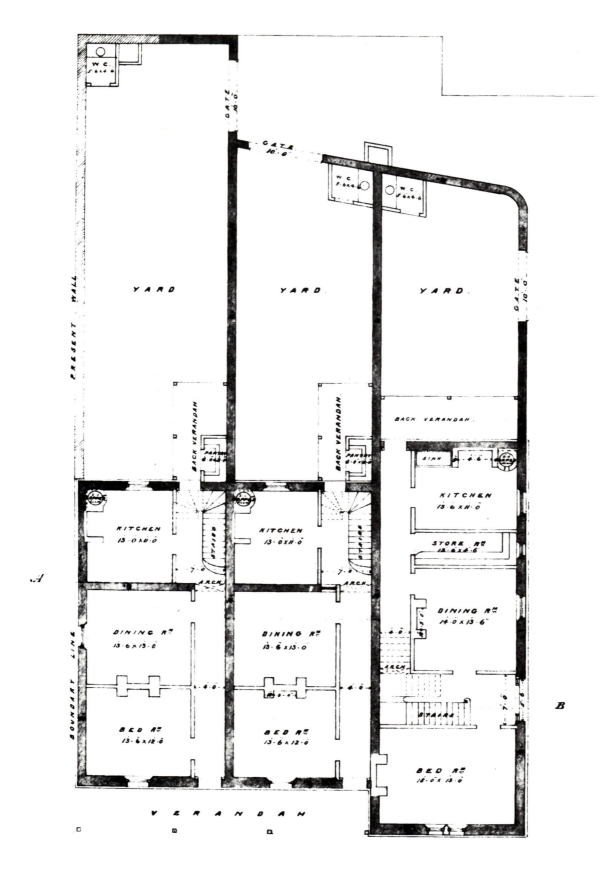

GROUND PLAN.

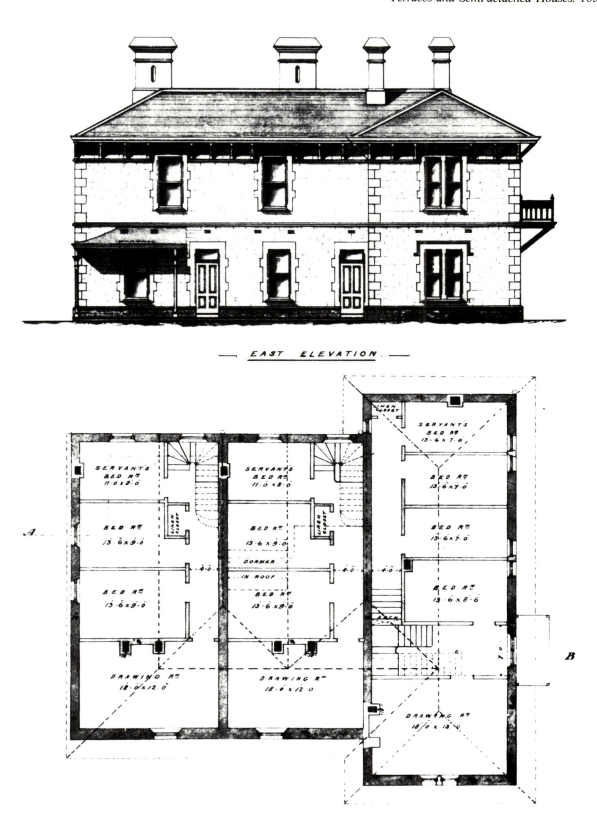

— EAST ELEVATION. —

— FIRST FLOOR PLAN —

Figure 66: Terrace of three houses, Sussex Street,
Glenelg, c.1868. Thomas English, architect. (See also
Plate 7 and fig.67)

— *SECTION A B.* —

Figure 67: Terrace of three houses, Glenelg c.1868: Section A-B.

Terrace of seven houses, c. 1872

An extensive terrace of 7 houses at Glenelg (fig. 68) was designed in the early seventies by the short-lived partnership of Thomas English and Rowland Rees, architects. And, again involved in this rather large speculative venture were Parkin and Miller as client and builder respectively. The only surviving drawing of the scheme is the ground plan of the 42 m long terrace. In all, there are 7 identical houses, each with an area of 190 m² and 6.2 m frontage to the street. Only one of the houseplans is varied—where at the end of the row a small 'shop' replaces a front 'drawing' room.

Compared with the preceding example, this design shows significant changes in the planning and intended use of the spaces. The two most important variations are the vertical separation of the living/dining rooms from all the bedrooms and the relegation of the kitchen to a separate wing attached at the rear of the house proper. In subsequent designs, the kitchen wing became a standard adjunct to the terrace plan. As these dwellings are larger by 37 m² than the Sussex Street example, the buildings cover more of the site, thus diminishing individual yard space. Other smaller changes include the width of the entrance/passage being increased to 1.5 m and the fireplaces in principal rooms being moved to the party wall.

Of special interest is the source of water supply shown on the ground plan. A circular well sunk under alternate boundary walls supplies the underground tanks of two adjoining houses. However, the proximity of the wells to the cess-pits of the privies, arranged in pairs along the service road at the rear, could present a health risk. It is worth noting that this project was proposed just prior to the first Health Act of 1873 which established a Central Board of Health.

The two principal rooms on the ground floor are those intended for daytime living/dining activities, the formal 'drawing room' (5.8 m x 4.3 m) at the front and the 'parlor' (4.9 m x 3.6 m), which in this case would have been also used for dining, situated at the rear. The spacious kitchen (4.9 m x 3.3 m) is separated from the house by an enclosed 'lobby' containing a small 'pantry'. As in the early row house plan, the kitchen being narrower than the house forms a rectangular light-well for windows at the rear and allows access to the yard beyond.

The standardised ground floor plan, as designed by English and Rees, has a lot in common with London terraced houses erected in large numbers from around 1830 onwards. For example, the layout

Figure 68: (opp.) Terrace of seven houses, Glenelg, c.1872. English and Rees, architects. Typical ground floor plan.

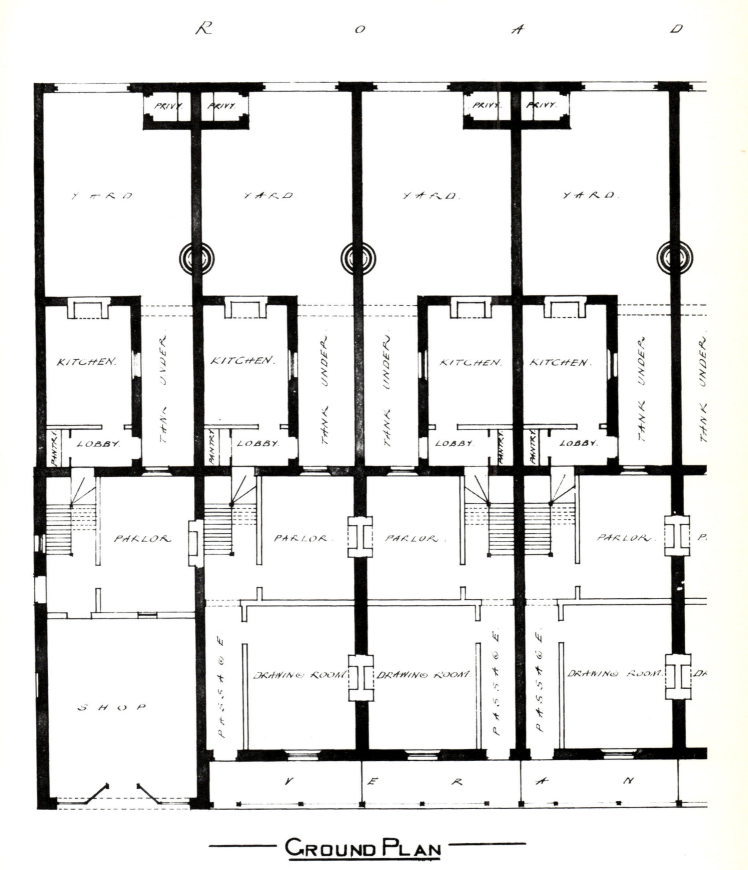

R O A D

PRIVY. PRIVY. PRIVY. PRIVY.

YARD. YARD. YARD. YARD.

KITCHEN. KITCHEN. TANK UNDER. TANK UNDER. KITCHEN. KITCHEN. TANK UNDER. TANK UNDER.

PANTRY LOBBY. PANTRY LOBBY. PANTRY LOBBY. PANTRY LOBBY.

PARLOR PARLOR. PARLOR. PARLOR. P.

SHOP PASSAGE DRAWING ROOM DRAWING ROOM. PASSAGE PASSAGE DRAWING ROOM. DR

V E R A N

GROUND PLAN

and use of rooms closely resembles the 'Second class house' built in 1833 for the 'Artizans' and 'Labourers' at Hornsey Estate, North London.[14] This architect-designed second largest house of five 'classes' built at Hornsey, had five rooms including three upstairs bedrooms. The plan is similar in every detail except for a scullery and a privy compartment incorporated in the kitchen wing—these are included in other Adelaide plans, which follow. Interestingly, only 'first' and 'second' class Hornsey houses had the back lobby, which normally can not be found in speculative London houses of that period.

'Alexandra Terrace', c. 1876

The 'Design for a terrace of houses proposed to be erected at Glenelg for Alexander Cunningham, Esq.' is believed to be the original proposal prepared in about 1876 by Thomas English, architect. The architect's sketches for the parapet of the building include the name, 'Glenelg Terrace'. The terrace of four houses, re-named 'Alexandra Terrace 1878', was built on a reduced scale and remains standing on the corner of Moseley and Elizabeth streets (figs. 69–72, Plate 8).

The sheer size of the scheme and its exuberant design reflect the great confidence of the seventies—not to be surpassed later. Moreover, this particular design is unusual for Adelaide in that it contains a semi-basement beneath a raised main floor, this being a typically British characteristic of larger terraces. There is only one other terrace of this type and size in Adelaide, the surviving 'Botanic Chambers' of seven houses in North Terrace, designed by Michael McMullen and completed in 1877 (fig. 73).

Without doubt Alexander Cunningham was aiming at the top end of the residential market when he briefed his architect. The accommodation, as shown on the drawings, is not only commodious but also includes new innovations: a 'bathroom' with a long bath on the first floor and a 'scullery' adjacent to the kitchen. Before air-conditioning, the 'summer' rooms in the basement, duplicating the drawing and dining rooms on the ground floor, would have been a major selling point in a seaside resort. While the idea was tried in early Adelaide mansions, its application to the terraced house is novel (see also 'Heywood', Chapter 4).

At this stage, it is significant to observe the change in room names used on the plans. The room called 'parlour' in the previous terraces is labelled here as 'dining room'. With its origins in the large houses of the British upper-classes, the term 'drawing room' was used in preference to 'parlour' by the new middle-class in the Province—see for example Penelope Belt's description (1856) of *The Almonds* at Walkerville (Chapter 4). Assigning exclusive functions such as dining to a particular room of the house signifies a genteel Victorian lifestyle and the involvement of domestic servants in the preparation and serving of food.

Designed for a small corner site, only 27 m (90 ft.) deep, the terrace consists of three, 6.8 m wide, 'standard' houses joined on to a corner 'key' house. While of similar area, the ground floor of the latter varies: there is an additional sitting room with its own side entrance which, on the amended drawings, became a doctor's surgery. Each of the standard houses has seven habitable rooms on the ground and first floors, covering an impressive area of 235 m², plus three 'apartments' and a 'larder' in the basement of 90 m². The ceiling height of the main reception rooms at 3.9 m (13 ft.) could match the best Adelaide houses. However, for economic reasons, this dimension was subsequently reduced to 3.6 metres.

On the ground floor, elevated 1.5 m above the footpath, the two principal rooms are the drawing room (6.0 m x 4.5 m) with a large bay window overlooking the street, and the formal dining room (5.8 m x 4.2 m) behind. They are united by a five-leaf folding door—a device used previously in high-class houses for the creation of large entertainment spaces. Sometimes sliding doors disappearing into a wall cavity were also used for this purpose, as, for example, in the Botanic Chambers terraces. The reception rooms are reached by a 'Hall', being double the width of the earlier 'passage', adorned by an archway and neo-classical pilasters. Beyond the staircase (with turned balusters) the service wing, extending right up to the back boundary, completes the ground plan.

As before, the lobby at ground level connects the house to the kitchen, to which have been added a room for washing called 'scullery', a pair of privies (one for the family, one for the servants), and sheds for storage of coals and ashes. The kitchen forms part of a two-storey structure with the remainder covered by attached lean-tos of diminishing heights. (See the Cross-Section on line C-D, fig. 70). This basic layout of the service wing which, as already mentioned, eminated from the earlier London terrace, also has a counterpart in the eastern capitals of Australia, for example the Sydney terraces of the mid-1860s.[15]

The first floor contains three bedrooms together with a bathroom and a servant's room in the annexe accessible from the half-landing. The two main bedrooms with fireplaces are provided with generous dressing rooms. The largest 'best' bedroom (4.6 m x 4.2 m) is at the rear (west side) rather than the front, so as to overlook the sea. French doors open on to the balconies. The wide staircase and upstairs

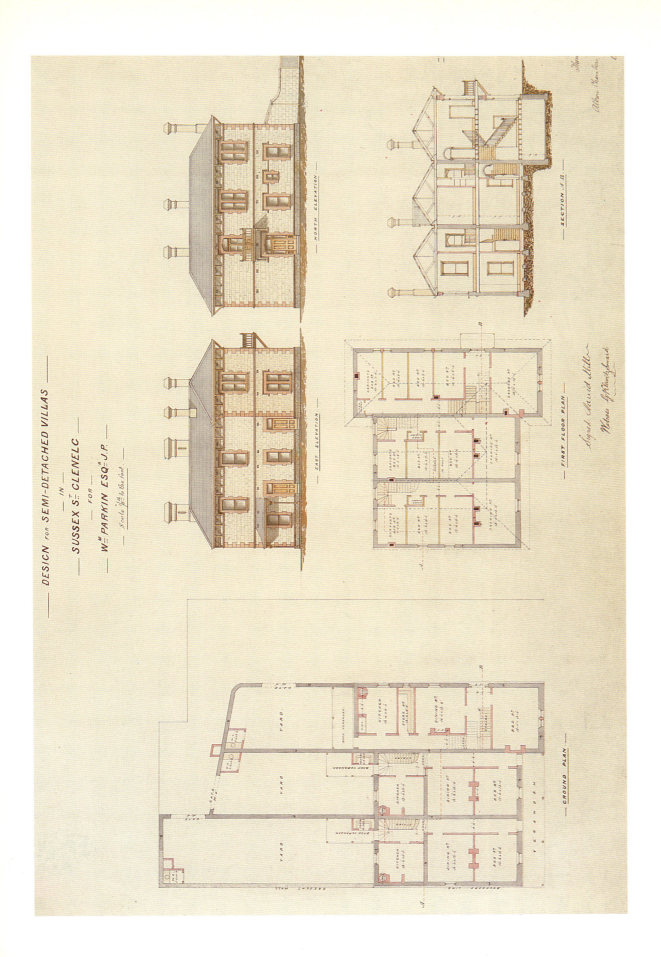

Plate 7: Terrace of three houses, Glenelg, c.1868. Thomas English, architect.

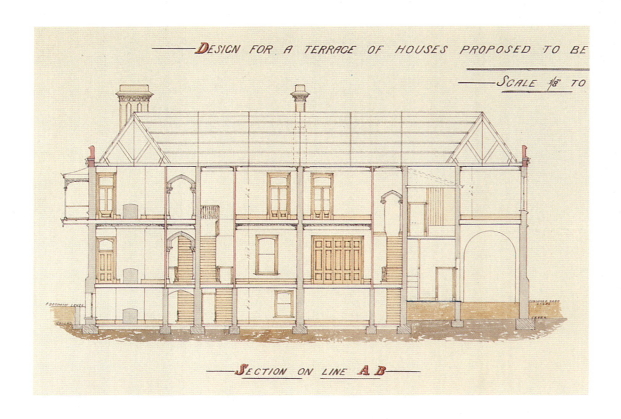

DESIGN FOR A TERRACE OF HOUSES PROPOSED TO BE

SCALE ⅛" TO

SECTION ON LINE A B

FRONT (EAST) ELEVATION

Plate 8: 'Alexandra Terrace', Glenelg, c.1876. Thomas English, architect.

ERECTED AT GLENELG FOR ALEXR CUNNINGHAM ESQ

THE FOOT

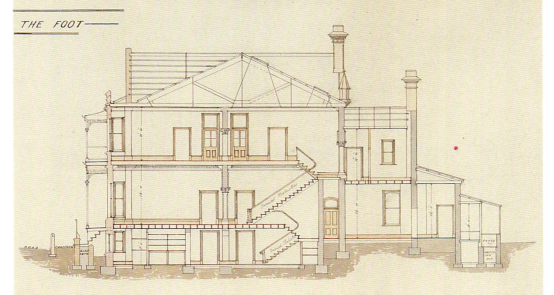

SECTION ON LINE C D

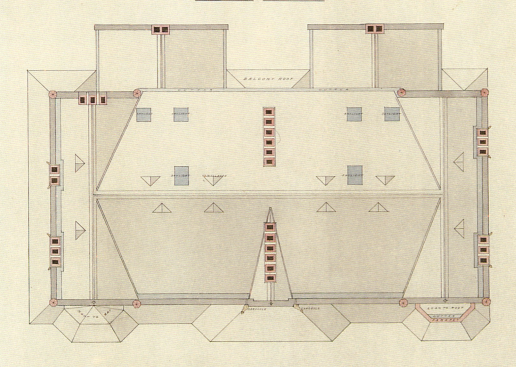

ROOF PLAN

ELEVATION TO SOUTH TERRACE

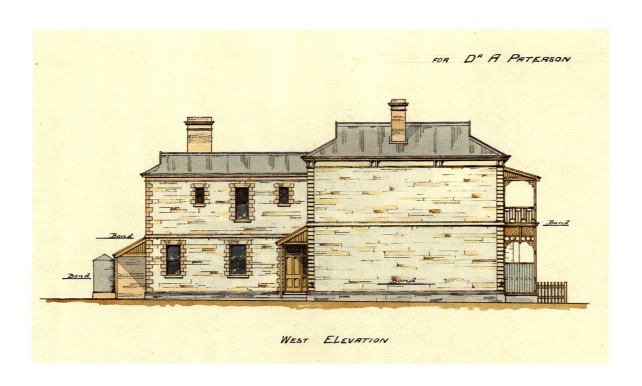

FOR Dʳ A PATERSON

WEST ELEVATION

Plate 9: Terrace of four houses, Adelaide, 1897. Edward J. Woods, architect.

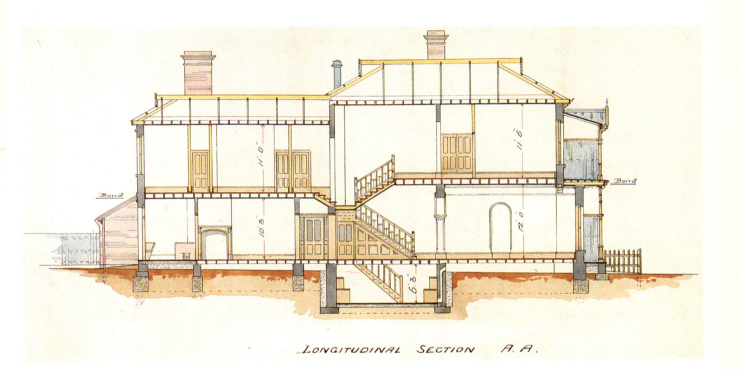

LONGITUDINAL SECTION A.A.

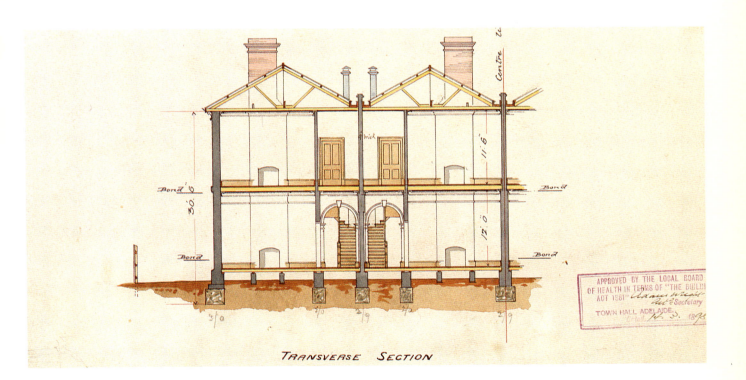

TRANSVERSE SECTION

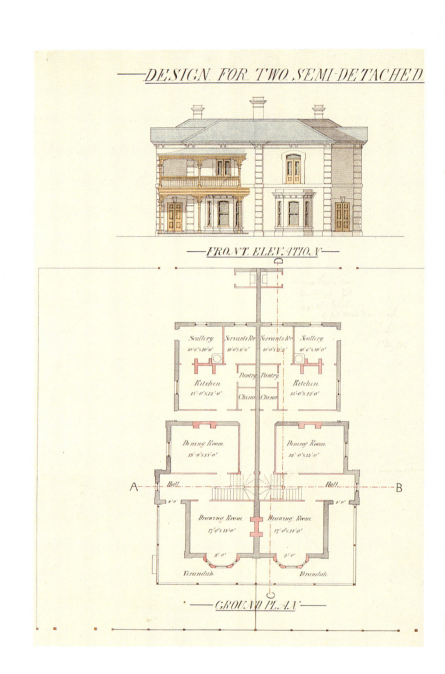

DESIGN FOR TWO SEMI-DETACHED

FRONT ELEVATION

GROUND PLAN

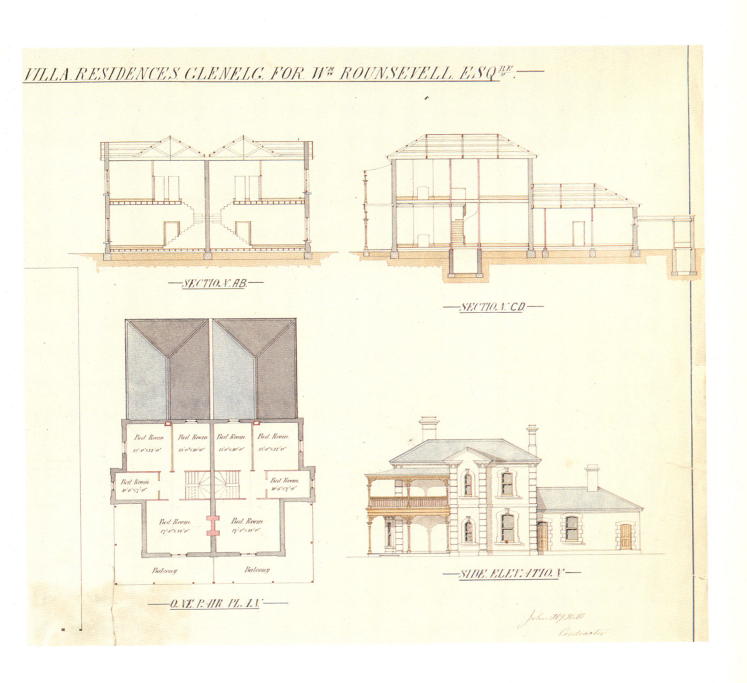

VILLA RESIDENCES GLENELG FOR Wᵐ ROUNSEVELL ESQᴿᴱ.

SECTION AB.

SECTION CD

ONE PAIR PLAN

SIDE ELEVATION

Plate 10: Pair of houses, Glenelg, 1883. George K. Soward, architect.

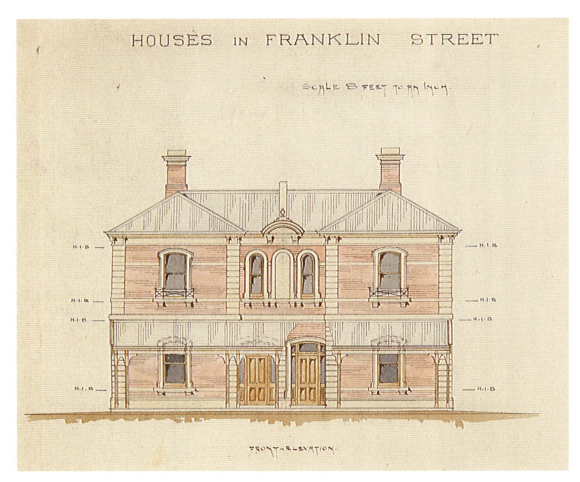

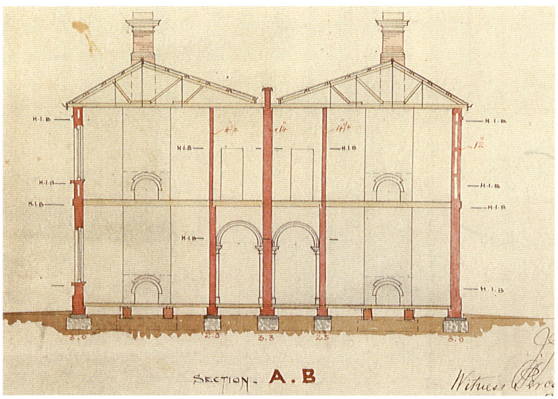

Plate 11: Pair of houses, Adelaide, 1891. Edward J. Woods, architect.

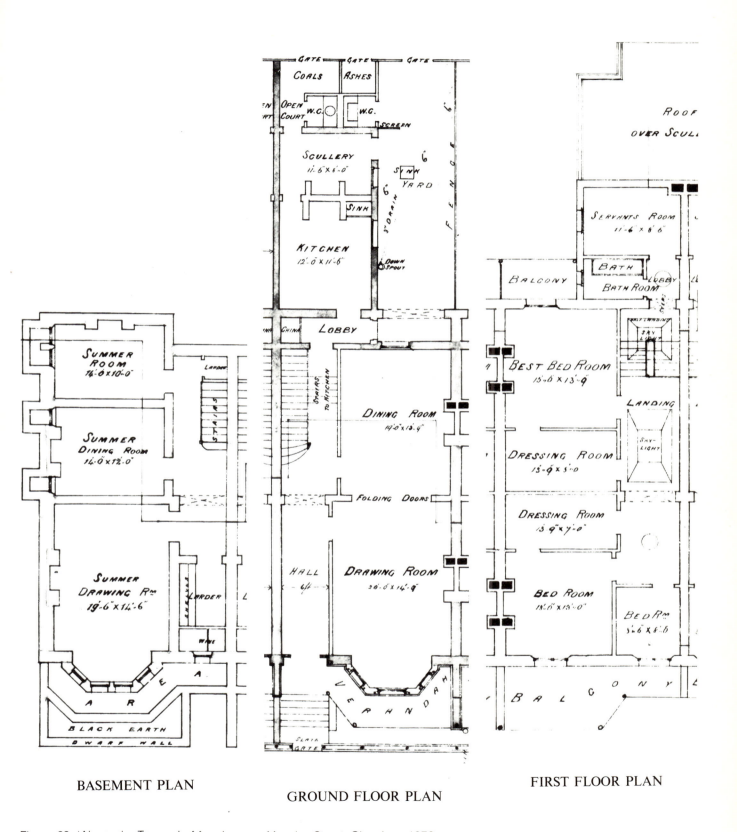

BASEMENT PLAN

GROUND FLOOR PLAN

FIRST FLOOR PLAN

Figure 69: 'Alexandra Terrace' of four houses, Moseley Street, Glenelg, c.1876.
Thomas English, architect. (See also Plate 8)

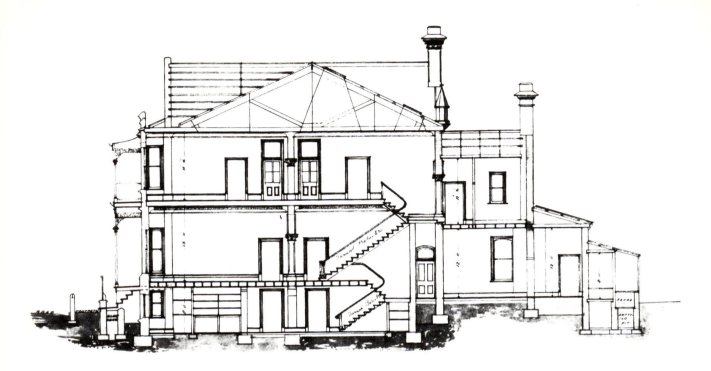

— SECTION ON LINE *C D* —

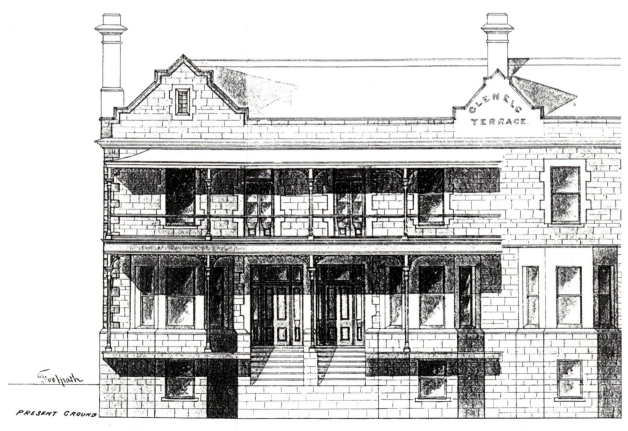

— FRONT (EAST) ELEVATION —

landing are lit through the roof by two large skylights. At this stage, the bathroom is only equipped with a plunge bath. The washstands in the bedrooms have yet to be replaced.

For the first time the W.C. compartment is physically linked to the house and could be reached without having to cross the open yard. It was not yet sewered and the drawings show a common piped drainage system for waste water from all four houses. The bath and the kitchen sink discharge into the yard sink and then along the private road a drain takes the waste into the 'drainage well'. It is likely that the houses had piped water supply with the only tap positioned in the yard. Cold and hot water for the bath and for the washstands in the bedrooms would have been carried upstairs by the maids, the hot being heated on the kitchen stove or scullery fireplace.

Figure 70: (opp.) 'Alexandra Terrace': Section C–D.

Figure 71: (opp. below) 'Alexandra Terrace': Half-Front Elevation to Moseley Street showing the much simplified architect's design as built in 1878. The originally proposed name, 'Glenelg Terrace' appears on the parapet.

Figure 72: (below) 'Alexandra Terrace': Half-Front (East) Elevation as originally designed by Thomas English. This drawing should be read with the plans and section shown in figs.69 and 70.

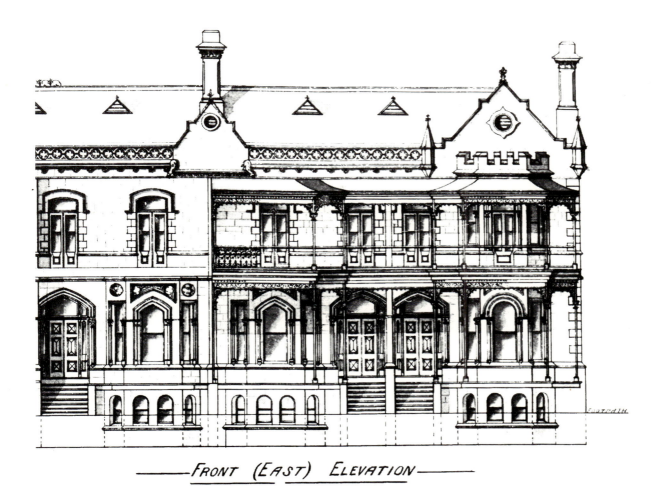

——FRONT (EAST) ELEVATION——

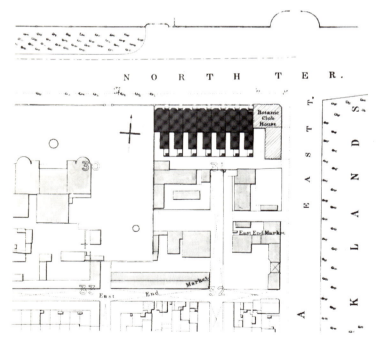

Figure 73: 'Botanic Chambers' North Terrace, Adelaide, 1877. Michael McMullen, architect. A terrace of nine houses with basements built in conjunction with the Botanic Club House, later the Botanic Hotel.
(Photograph: T. Fox, 1986. Site plan: Smith City Survey, 1880, Sheet no.75)

'Marine Residences', 1885

The close connection which existed between terrace building and a new railway is best illustrated by the early development of Grange—situated to the north of Holdfast Bay. The seaside subdivision at Grange commenced in 1878 with the formation of the Grange Land & Investment Co. The Company, which changed its name to the Grange Railway & Investment Co. opened in 1882 a branch railway line from Woodville to Grange, having completed the construction of jetties at Henley and Grange. 1881–82 were the land boom years in metropolitan Adelaide and hundreds of new allotments were offered for sale along the sea front at Grange and Henley Beach.

In order to entice the wealthier merchants who lived at Woodville Gardens, the Company built in 1885 near the Grange jetty '. . . the most magnificent seaside residences to be seen anywhere in Australia'.[16] Erected at a cost of £20,000 this imposing terrace of 8 houses (with provisions for future extension) stands on the Esplanade facing the sea (fig. 75). It still remains substantially unaltered with its walls of the same stone as the Company used for ballast in the construction of the new railway line. The identical houses—which became known as the 'Marine Residences'—rise to three floors above ground, which makes them unique in South Australia.

Each house has a frontage of about 7.0 m and originally contained some 10 rooms. The design, which was based on the orthodox plan, has been cleverly adapted to the site. The drawing room windows are specially designed to give access to the front verandah and the fenced-in front garden. The extra wide, 3.5 m, verandah offers not only greater protection from the setting sun and the winter weather, but also a useful entertainment area. Both upstairs balconies are roofed and decrease in width at each floor. Their slender cast iron supports and delicately patterned iron lace break down the vast bulk of the main facade, and contrast with the rich stucco decorations applied to the window dressings and parapets. Projecting arches, which identify the entrance to each house, introduce a strong sense of rhythm to the building which, for many years, remained a prominent landmark along the coast.

The project was not a commercial success. Arthur Harvey, the Secretary of the Grange Company, purchased the first house. The others remained empty for years as the overall development of Henley and Grange was not as rapid as the promoters had hoped. Today, some houses are being restored by private owners while others, previously converted to multiple flats, continue to be let as holiday accommodation.

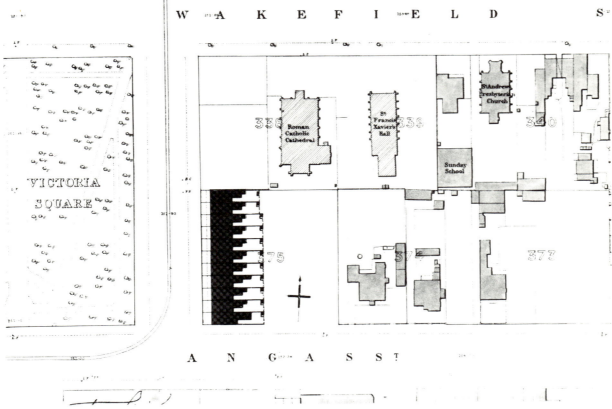

Figure 74: 'Landrowna Terrace', Victoria Square, Adelaide, 1875. This simple yet elegant terrace of 11 houses was Adelaide's longest. It overlooked the extensive gardens of the square until it was demolished in 1923 to make way for the offices of the Municipal Tramways Trust.
(Photograph taken in the early 1900s: Mortlock Library of South Australiana. Site plan: Smith City Survey, 1880, Sheet no.41)

Figure 75: 'Marine Residences': a three storey terrace of eight houses, The Esplanade, Grange, 1885.
(Photograph: T. Fox, 1986)

Terrace of four houses, 1897

This comprehensive turn-of-the-century project was designed by the architect Edward J. Woods[17] in 1897 as a speculative housing development for Dr. Alexander Paterson (fig. 77, Plate 9). In January, 1898, the builder R. & J. Couche signed the contract to erect the four terraced houses and an additional row of four cottages for £4,615.[18] This choice site, which occupied one half of Town Acre 675 (measuring 32 m x 67 m) was developed with two distinct dwelling types. A substantial terrace of four identical two-storey 'houses' along the street boundary overlooked the parklands, while a row of single-storey three-roomed 'cottages', designed for much cheaper rental, filled in the rear of the site accessed by private road. For site plan and details of the row houses—see Chapter 3 (fig. 33).

At the turn of the century the south-east corner of the city was an established high-class residential area, as indeed it is again today. The city's population exceeded the forty thousand mark and was at its historical peak. While Woods designed the terraces with restraint and some economies in mind, they did offer spacious and comfortable accommodation for those affluent enough to live in style and afford domestic help. They are superior in size and quality of building when compared, for example, with a nearby terrace of 9 houses at 355–371 Carrington Street, built about ten years earlier (fig. 76). These houses of only six rooms, had frontages 4.6 m wide and a floor area under 120 m².

Each of the South Terrace houses (fig. 77) has an above average 7.0 m frontage and contains eight well-proportioned rooms which in total give 237 m² of built space. These figures compare closely with the biggest of the pre-1890 terraces—for example, the 'Glenelg Terrace' and 'The Botanic Chambers' (their basements being discounted). While the Carrington Street terrace reflects a depressed economic period and different rental market, the South Terrace project is indicative of the steady rise in floor areas towards the end of the century.

The design shows practically no change in the general layout of the house or the disposition of its rooms. However, there are evident important improvements in sanitation and ablution arrangements made possible by the sewers laid in the city during the previous decade. The most notable is the second W.C. brought inside the house and located, for economy of plumbing, upstairs next to the servant's room. The earlier outside privy at the bottom of the yard is now seen attached to the scullery wall as a W.C. mainly for the servants' use. The scullery adjacent to the kitchen is now better equipped as a 'wet' room used for washing up and laundry; a wooden draining board has been added to the sink, now placed under the window; a double trough and a built-in copper are the laundry equipment (see fig. 62).

The apparent lack of a hand-basin in the upstairs bathroom suggests that the reticulated water supply was limited to the scullery area only. While the kitchen (4.7 m x 3.6 m) has grown larger, the formal

Figure 76: Terrace of nine houses, Carrington Street, Adelaide, c.1887.
(Photograph taken in 1937: Mortlock Library of South Australiana)

dining room (4.9 m x 4.4 m) is scaled down for family use. Traditionally placed fireplaces separate the dining room from the drawing room, which has an interesting off-centre bay window built with square corners. The window divided by a pier and the square bay are both typical of the period.

The effect of the Building Act of 1881 is visible in the elevation to South Terrace. Parapet walls, providing protection against the spread of fire, separate individual houses—see Transverse Section (fig. 77). Each house has a roof independently pitched from the party walls with the ridge running at right angle to the facade. Their hipped ends, ventilated at the ridge, are exposed to the street. The rhythm of the roof line is reinforced by decorative gablets attached to the balcony roof. Painted timber is used in the construction and decoration of the verandah/balcony structure. The six-panel front doors are recessed in arched openings, adorned by coloured glass incorporated in the glazing of fanlights and sidelights.

The semi-detached, double-storey house

Like the smaller, single-storey maisonette, discussed in Chapter 3, the double-storey semi-detached house shares only one party wall with its twin neighbour. Typically, the Adelaide house was intended for large families with the living rooms arranged on the ground floor and the bedrooms upstairs. In many instances its plan resembles a terrace house of just two dwellings jointed together along the common boundary.

The common party wall provided economy of cost in the construction and in the use of land. As the pair of houses was erected simultaneously—which was not necessarily the case with the single-storey maisonette, especially prior to the introduction of the mandatory parapet wall in 1881—the common party wall provided support for the roof and the first floor of both dwellings. The simple mirrored plan for the two houses made efficient use of space, allowing a relatively narrow allotment to be sub-divided lengthways into two. This, of course, became an important consideration where high-priced land was concerned.

In Australia, the semi-detached house, also known as 'duplex' in the eastern capitals, was the forerunner of the terrace. An example of this is Sydney's first duplex built in 1823 by a young mason named Glover, which originally overlooked Darling Harbour at Millers Point. The original stone building, now restored and extended for offices, had upstairs bedrooms set partly into the roof space, each with a small dormer window. Glover's traditional design set a pattern for Sydney's early terraced houses.

In Adelaide, the development of semi-detached houses runs parallel with the terraces, dating from the early fifties. One of the earliest examples is the pair of two-storey brick houses, or a 'short' terrace, still standing in North Adelaide. Built in 1851 for William Johnston,[19] the pair has a simple facade with slate roofs concealed behind a parapet, a traditional English detail dating from the Georgian era at the beginning of the nineteenth century. Each house occupied the full width of the 4.8 m frontage and had an area of about 120 m². While additions have been made at the rear, the street facade remains in its original state without a verandah (fig. 79).

109

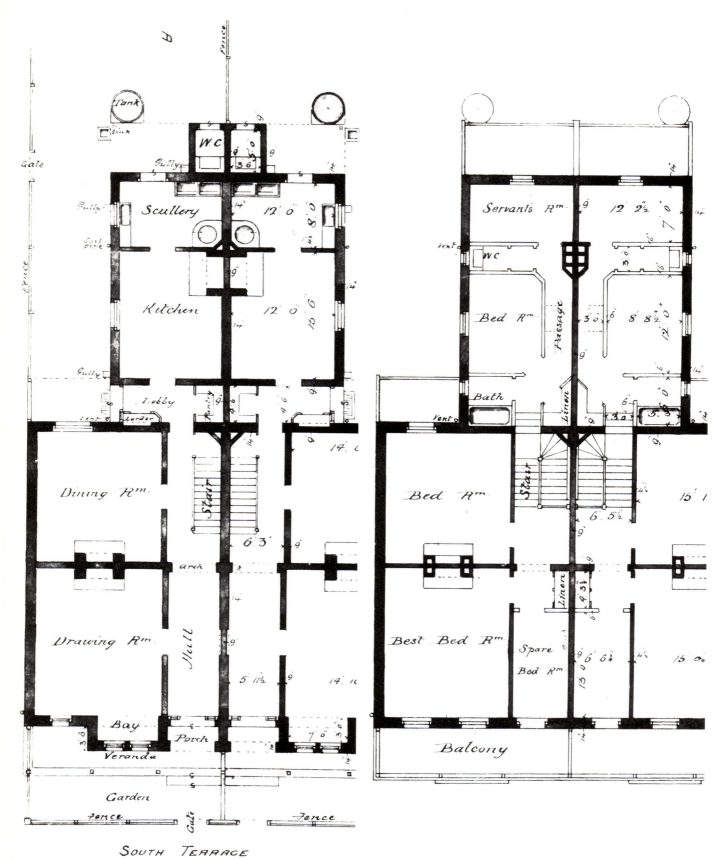

SOUTH TERRACE

HALF PLAN OF GROUND FLOOR

HALF PLAN OF FIRST FLOOR.

ELEVATION TO SOUTH TERRACE

Figure 77: Terrace of four houses, South Terrace,
Adelaide, 1897. Edward J. Woods, architect. (See also
Plate 9)

However, the main building period for large semi-detached houses extended from the mid-1860s until about the turn of the century. In the city of Adelaide the peak was reached during the building boom of the seventies and early eighties. Their locations were confined to the more densely built-up parts of the city and those suburbs highly regarded as residential areas. After 1880 the west end of the city was no longer favoured as a residential area, putting an end to large house developments there and consolidating further the growing popularity of the south-eastern section.

It is evident from the examples which follow that speculative builders had in mind the more prosperous clients at the upper end of the residential market. As a respectable residence, the semi-detached house fell half-way between the large terraced house and a mansion of ten rooms or more standing in large grounds. While the latter is beyond the scope of this book, it pegged the upper limits for house design, and on a social scale reflected the pinnacle of achievement for a colonist or a family clan. For example, in the period 1880–89, one architectural practice in Adelaide produced not less than 17 two-storey residences, containing from 10 to 24 rooms each, for the colonial gentry who chose to live in the suburbs of Glenelg, Somerton, Medindie, Glen Osmond and in North Adelaide. About 13 rooms was the average number for this sample, with at least 11 houses containing 10–12 rooms each.[20] This is about 50 per cent up on the average semi-detached house.

There were two variants of the semi-detached house, depending on the location and width of the block, both complying with the general definition given at the beginning of this section. The first occupied the entire width of a narrow block, 7.0 m to 8.0 m in width and utilized the terraced plan, discussed earlier. Sometimes there was the intention of building on additional houses that seldom, if ever, materialised, resulting in the external party walls being exposed for many years as a blight on the townscape.

The second variant was designed for a block of land 9.0 m and wider, which left a strip of land to separate the adjacent pairs of houses and allowed side access and opening in the side wall facing the neighbour. This design fell half-way between a detached and a terraced house and was based on a new concept which originated in England during the 1840s. In England, J.C. Loudon[21] was the first to promote the concept of a detached house as a feature of more spacious suburban development. In his book *The Suburban Gardener and Villa Companion*, published in 1838, he illustrated a pair of semi-detached houses at London's Bayswater, one of which was his own residence. Built during the previous year, the houses had a square plan with entrance porches at the sides leading to a central staircase hall around which the main rooms were arranged. A number of Adelaide's so-called 'semi-detached villa residences' of the eighties follow this design. In England by 1850, the semi-detached house became a common feature of suburban speculative

111

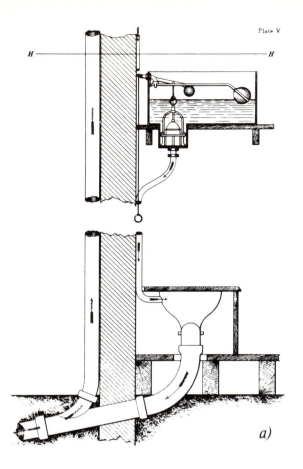

Plate V

a)

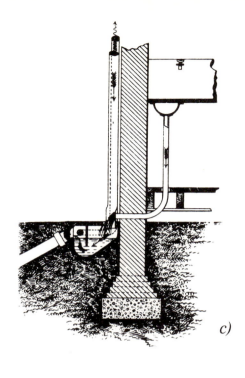

c)

Figure 78: The first house connections regulated under the Adelaide Sewers Act, 1878. These drawings, showing the 'best method of making house connections' were prepared by the Hydraulic Engineer, Oswald Brown, and passed by the Central Board of Health in 1882.

a) Out-of-doors 'cottage' water closet (WC), with the pan inside the traditional timber box seat. The overhead water supply cistern is fitted with a 'waste preventing valve' worked by a bell pull.

b) Scullery or Kitchen sink. The waste discharges into a 'disconnector trap' placed against the wall of the house with a ventilating pipe above. The disconnector trap was the forerunner of the square yard gulley with a tap over, its early version appearing in the 1904 Regulations.

c) Bath fixed on an upper floor. A waste pipe carried through the outside wall discharges into the open head of a vertical pipe that passes down to the disconnector trap at ground level. The waste pipe is fitted with a light brass flap valve to prevent back draught. As an alternative, an S-trap could be provided in place of the flap.

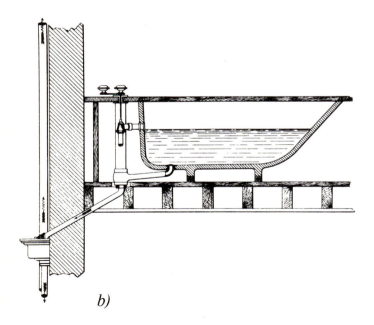

b)

Figure 79: An early pair of semi-detached brick houses, North Adelaide, 1851.
(Photograph: Stephen Gilbert, late 1960s)

development—and a likely model for William Johnston's North Adelaide paired houses, mentioned above. Designs, dated 1856, for five pairs of large semi-detached houses called 'Oakley Villas' survive in Adelaide Road, North London.[22] A basic three-storey plan above a semi-basement, with main entrance facing the street was used in this scheme. Each dwelling occupied a block, 9.2 m wide by 45 m deep, with the street elevations of the free-standing pairs being treated differently.

Pair of houses, Adelaide, 1891

This late example of semi-detached 'Houses in Franklin Street' Adelaide (now demolished) was built exactly forty years after Johnston's houses at North Adelaide. The architect, Edward J. Woods designed this pair of speculative houses which he labelled simply as 'House A' and 'House B'. The signature of J.J. Tealey (?) appears on the drawings as the builder, dated 24th April, 1891 (fig. 80, Plate 11). The contract price is recorded on the drawings at £2,300. Woods' layout, which follows his terraced house plans, has remained basically unchanged. Only the larger size of the house and the new domestic services distinguish this pair from its North Adelaide predecessor.

The Franklin Street houses were built on a corner allotment, (part of Town Acre 243) giving a 7.5 m frontage to each house. A narrow street alongside House A and common ownership of land alongside House B allowed the side walls placed on the boundaries to have windows. Service access was provided at the rear, and the houses enjoyed an above-average set-back for the city of 4.5 metres, thus allowing a sizeable garden area between the 1.8 m wide front verandah and the footpath.

'House B' (on the right hand side) contains eight habitable rooms, including two double and three single bedrooms on the first floor, and covers a gross area of 205 m². The corner 'House A' has an additional bedroom. Although the floor area is slightly smaller than that of the largest contemporary terrace, the main rooms (un-named on the drawings) are of good size. Each house has an internal cellar (5.1 m x 2.1 m) located under the stairs with access provided under the half-landing. On the ground floor the scullery attached to the kitchen combines the functions of the laundry and kitchen dishwashing area. The sink is now moved from the kitchen to the scullery, which also houses a built-in copper with a small fire underneath for heating water. (Note the flue from the copper connecting to the kitchen chimney shown in Section C-D.)

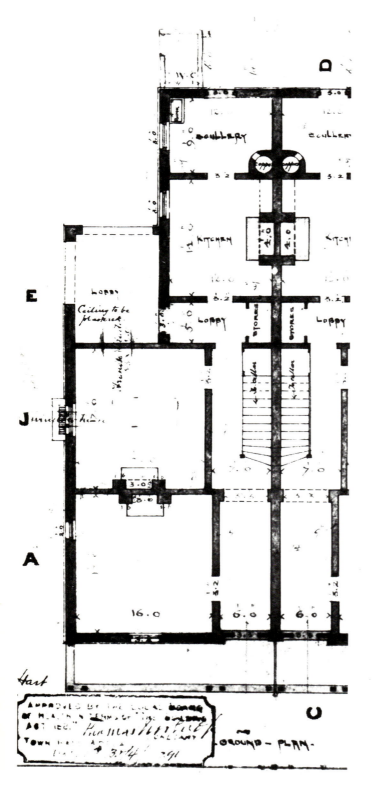

GROUND FLOOR PLAN

HOUSE A

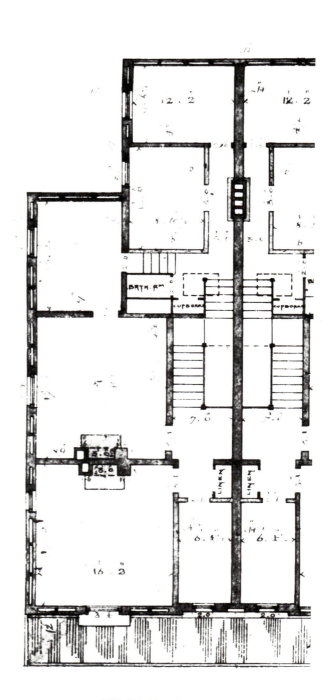

FIRST FLOOR PLAN

Figure 80: Pair of houses, Franklin Street, Adelaide, 1891.
Edward J. Woods, architect. (See also Plate 11)

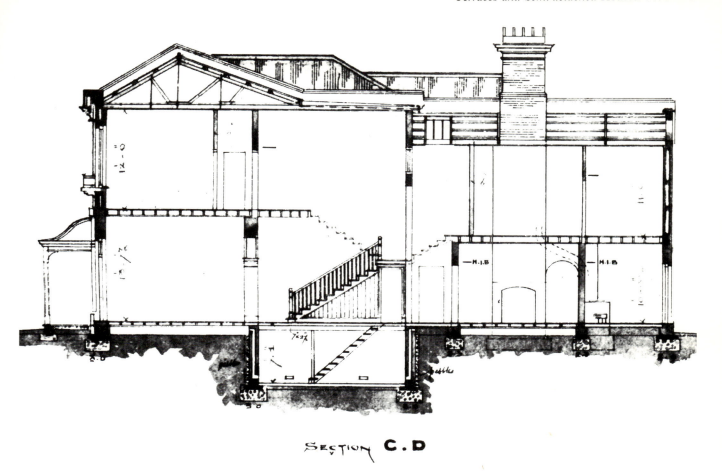

SECTION **C.D**

The uncertainty as to the appropriate position for the W.C. is typical of this period. The W.C. serving each house was originally shown on the drawing in the traditional position, back to back near the rear lane, in order to economize on connections to the sewer. However, for considerations of convenience and privacy the W.C.s were separated and attached to the back of each scullery, as shown amended on the ground plan. This became the standard position for a W.C. around the turn of the century—see Woods' design for South Terrace houses (1897), discussed earlier in this Chapter.

On the first floor, the wing extended at the rear, contains the small bathroom, with a bath only, adjacent to the stairs. Included in this area are two small bedrooms, one of which is probably the servant's room. Typically, for reasons of economy, the extension has reduced ceiling heights with a one metre difference in the levels of the first floor between the front and back of the house. The Section C-D running through the building reveals interesting changes in the ceiling heights, dimensioned to vary according to the perceived importance of the rooms. The front parlour and dining room command 4.1 m high ceilings; the two main bedrooms, 3.6 m; the two rear bedrooms, 3.4 m; while the kitchen/scullery area—the hottest rooms in the house and with windows facing east and west—has the lowest, 3.3 m high ceilings.

The brick building, with coursed stucco quoins, is an early example of the new cavity wall construction used, with caution, in the external walls of the first floor. Above the ground floor's traditional 35 cm walls of solid brick, the walls narrow in thickness to 30 cm and comprise two separate skins with strengthening internal piers. It is interesting to compare this application of an Australian invention with contemporary examples of brick cavity construction in single-storey houses, discussed in the two preceding Chapters.

The dominant features of the front (south) elevation are the well-proportioned arched openings and restrained detailing. Echoing the curved element is the S-shaped profile of the verandah iron roof and the small semi-circular pediment concealing the end of the mandatory parapet wall which separates the galvanised iron roofs covering each house. The continuous verandah and the pediment act as unifying elements in the design. Stuccoed piers flanking the double entrance follow the hipped ends of the roofs and add emphasis to the central elements designed to unify the two houses.

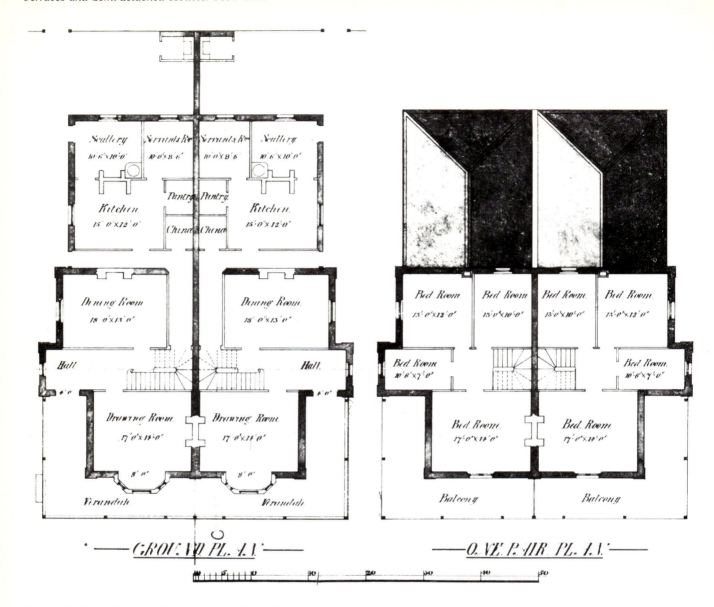

Figure 81: Pair of houses, Glenelg, 1883: Plans. George K. Soward, architect. (See also Plate 10)

Pair of houses, Glenelg, 1883

Dated initials, pencilled on the drawing, suggest that George K. Soward[23] was involved in the project entitled 'Design for two semi-detached villa residences' at Glenelg for William Rounsevell, Esq., and that the residences were built during 1883 by the 'contractor', John H.J. Hill. This identical pair of two-storey, semi-detached houses are typical of suburban speculative development, and demonstrate an Australian application of the English concept first promoted by J.C. Loudon in 1838, discussed above. They represent the up-market version of the contemporary single-storey maisonette, discussed in Chapter 3.

Each residence has a frontage of 8.2 m, and occupies a sub-divided block, 18.0 m wide and 31.0 m deep, with rear access. On this large block, the set-back is 6.0 m from the street boundary. The plans (fig. 81, Plate 10) are mirrored about the common party wall, each comprising eight rooms with the front section being double-storeyed. The main entrance hall containing the staircase is situated to one side and is reached via the returned verandah. On either side of the hall are the 'drawing' room (5.2 m x 4.3 m) with a 2.4 m wide bay window overlooking the street, and a 'dining' room (5.5 m x 3.9 m), each with its own fireplace. A total of four bedrooms on the first floor are arranged around the central staircase. The front bedroom (5.2 m x 4.3 m) has an open fireplace built into the party wall and French doors opening on to the balcony. As the house could not yet be sewered, there is no bathroom.

—FRONT ELEVATION—

—SIDE ELEVATION—

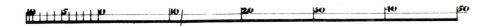

The rather compact planning of the main house is carried into the single-storey service wing attached at the rear containing the kitchen (4.6 m x 3.6 m), with an adjoining small 'scullery' and 'servants' room. A walk-in 'pantry' and a 'china' store complete the plan which covers a gross floor area of 220m². The privy, arranged back to back on the common boundary, is reached from outdoors; a common emptying cess-pit is provided under the private road serving the houses. The lack of a separate room for bathing and no sink in the scullery or kitchen suggests that there was no running water and that it was carried into the house in pails. The scullery, so inevitable in the planning of larger Victorian houses, was used here for all wet operations, including bathing in a portable tub in front of the open fireplace where water was heated. A built-in copper stands next to the fireplace.

Displaying a good sense of harmony, the imposing front elevation combines stone wall surfaces trimmed with stucco quoins with an intricate structure of cast iron and wood used in the 2.0 m wide verandah and balcony. The broad extent of the returned verandah and balcony, embracing the fronts of the two houses and all the projections, strongly unites the whole design, and also makes the building appear larger without increasing its bulk. Despite the date of construction, after 1881, the design did not provide the mandatory parapet on top of the party wall. Instead, the front section of the roof is pitched across the two houses, as we have seen in the earlier terraces. The common roofline and the ridge running parallel to the front wall create an impression of a single house with a broad frontage to the street.

Notes and Sources

CHAPTER 1: EARLY SHELTERS: 1836–1842.

1. John Stephen, *The Royal South Australian Almanack and General Directory for 1847* (J. Stephen, 1847) p. 49.

2. Edwin Hodder (Ed.) *The Founding of South Australia; as recorded in the Journals of Mr. Robert Gouger, First Colonial Secretary*, (Sampson Low, London, 1898), Vol. I, p. 35.

3. A. Grenfell Price, *The Foundation and Settlement of South Australia 1829–1845: A study of the colonization movement, based on the records of the South Australian government and on other authoritative documents* (F.W. Preece, Adelaide, 1924), p. 105.

4. 'The Second Annual Report of the Commissioners', *The Southern Australian*, 30/6/1838.

5. *The Southern Australian*, 21/7/1838. The article refers to an important instruction from the Colonizing Commissioners to Colonel Light concerning the security of investment in Adelaide's town acres. The choice of site and the general layout of the 'first town' of the new province were to ensure that the investment made by the initial purchasers did not diminish in future.

6. *The Southern Australian*. 25/8/1838.

7. *ibid.*, 25/8/1838.

8. *ibid.*, 4/8/1838.

9. William Light, watercolour drawing 1836/1837, *A view of the Country and of the Temporary Erections Near the Site of the Proposed Town of Adelaide in South Australia*. National Library of Australia, Canberra.

10. Price, p. 106. (See note 3, above.)

11. *Recollections of Pastor William Finlayson*, unpublished manuscript 1878, Public Record Office of South Australia, Adelaide.

12. Pisé construction, first described in a series of French articles in the late 18th century, became popular in Adelaide because it was cheap and very easily erected. The technique, as used in the first phase of building, is described as follows:

Into a wooden-frame about 6ft. long, by 3ft. in height [1.8 m x 0.9 m], a composition of good loam mixed with grass chopped very small, was put in small quantities at a time, and then rammed as hard as possible. The mixture having been previously slightly damped, the walls could be made any width, according to the height of the building, and the weight of the roof it had to support. The frame being bolted together was easily taken to pieces and readjusted until the necessary height and thickness of the walls was obtained. Spaces for the doors and windows could either be left, or easily cut out later.—James C. Hawker, p. 12 (see note 25, below).

While it was not uncommon for unprotected pisé walls to be demolished by the first winter rains, they proved quite durable when protected by roof overhangs and a coat of render. Sections of original pisé walls survive to this day beneath cement render, which was often neatly ruled to simulate stone, and covered by protective coats of paint.

13. J.J. Pascoe (Ed.), *History of Adelaide and Vicinity; with a general sketch of the province of South Australia and biographies of representative men* (Hussey and Gillingham, Adelaide, 1901), Appendix B.

14. Robert Gouger Esq., *South Australia in 1837; in A Series of Letters: with a Postscript as to 1838* (Harvey and Darton, London, 1838), p. 72. Gouger's account covers the period when he was the first Colonial Secretary.

15. Australian Bureau of Statistics, *Census of S.A. 1841*.

16. One who lived there nearly four years [anonymous], *South Australia, in 1842. Illustrated by drawings* (J.C. Hailes, London, 1843), p. 24. In May, 1841, the number of 'houses, shops, stores and other buildings, in Adelaide' was estimated at 1,960 in the above 'according to the return of the Town Surveyor'—presumably, G.S. Kingston.

17. *George Strickland Kingston* (1807–1880) was born in County Cork, Ireland, where he was trained as an architect and civil engineer. After moving to England he actively promoted the South Australian Act and was subsequently appointed Deputy Surveyor General, arriving in South Australia in September, 1836. As Colonel Light's deputy, he played a major role in the laying out of Adelaide. Following unsuccessful attempts to succeed Light after his death, Kingston established himself as an architect, civil engineer and surveyor. From 1839 to 1841 he held the position of

Inspector of Public Works and Buildings and, late in 1840, was appointed City Engineer by the first Adelaide Municipal Council. Notable buildings, which he designed during this period, included Government House and the Adelaide Gaol.

However, Kingston's professional work and other interests were not confined to the capital. His close association with the new mining town of Burra started when he became the original shareholder of the South Australian Mining Association in 1845. As the Association's surveyor and architect, with William Jacob, Kingston surveyed the mining township of Kooringa in 1846. Two years later he was elected a director of the Association and served as its chairman from 1857 until his death in 1880. At Burra, the Paxton Square scheme of attached miners' cottages was one of his early architectural commissions (see Chapter 3), where Kingston Terrace commemorates his name.

Kingston also devoted himself to the new Parliament of the province, initially representing Burra and Clare and then the electorate of Stanley. He became the first speaker in the House of Assembly and, with one break, remained in the chair from 1857 until his death. Source: Douglas Pike (General Ed.), *Australian Dictionary of Biography, 1788–1850*, Vol. 2. (Melbourne University Press, 1967).

18. Kingston, G.S., *Map of Adelaide, South Australia, Shewing the Nature and Extent of Every Building in the City* (J.C. Hailes, London, 1842) drawn to scale one inch to each acre, (1 inch representing 209 feet or 63.6 metres—being one side of the standard square allotment). Sheet size: 162 cm x 120 cm.

19. Thomas Worsnop, *History of the City of Adelaide: From the Foundation of the Province of South Australia in 1836, to the end of the municipal year 1877*. (J. Williams, Adelaide, 1878), p. 35.

20. Marginal sketches depicted: the Trinity Church, Government offices (present Treasury building), Government House, Congregational Chapel, South Australian School and Bank of South Australia. Although these were 'less perfect than professional drawings', they completed the usual format of contemporary city maps. For example, *The plan of London from Actual Survey 1832* represents a small-scale map of the central city area surrounded by 33 marginal illustrations of selected buildings and monuments.

21. A front-page advertisement in *The Adelaide Observer*, 8/7/1843, proclaimed Kingston's map of Adelaide as a 'handsome and valuable record for any person interested in the Colony'. Platt's Library in Hindley Street sold the map at £1/5/- per copy.

22. Illustrated in *South Australia in 1842* (see note 16, above).

23. *South Australian Gazette and Colonial Register*, 28/7/1838.

24. *ibid.*, 10/3/1838.

25. James C. Hawker, *Early Experiences in South Australia*, period 1838 to 1841 (E.S. Wigg & Son, Adelaide) (1899), p. 69. Hawker came to South Australia as Assistant Surveyor to Colonel Light.

26. *ibid.*, p. 69.

27. For a detailed description of Watson's cottage, see Gavin Walkley, *St. Mark's College, the buildings and grounds*, (St. Mark's College, Adelaide, 1985), pp. 6–28.

J.M. Freeland in *Architecture in Australia—a History* (Penguin Books, 1972) p. 105, incorrectly repeats the claim that the *Tyntyndyer* homestead in N.S.W., near Swan Hill, was the first building to be veneered with brickwork, around 1850.

For explanatory notes on 'portable' timber houses see note 33, following.

28. The 32 Town Acres contained within the sample area are numbered: 321–328, 385–400 and 461–468.

29. *Smith City Survey (1880)*, Sheet Nos. 34, 35, 38 and 39. (See Chap. 3, note 4.)

30. Surveyor General's Office, *Plan of the City of Adelaide*, (undated), State Library of South Australia.

31. *ibid*. Town Acre nos. 388–391 and 462–468 were bought originally on behalf of 'absentee' persons.

32. Anonymous (1843), p. 24 (see note 16, above).

33. Up to about 1842 some of the settlers brought with them timber prefabricated dwellings made by H. Manning, a London firm of carpenters and builders. Since 1830, the firm had exported 'portable' cottages to the far-off British colonies, particularly Australia and New Zealand, as an expedient housing solution to the immediate dwelling needs of emigants. Varying in size, they sold in England from £15 to £125, plus £30 freight to Port Adelaide.

In 1837, Manning began advertising in the *South Australian Record*, a newspaper published in London for prospective migrants:

> Portable Colonial Cottages. H. Manning, 251 High Holborn, London, manufactured on the most simple and approved principles, to pack in a small compass, may be erected with windows, doors and locks, painted inside and outside, floors etc. complete for habitation in a few hours after landing. Price 15 pounds and upwards. They may be taken to pieces and removed as often as the Settler may require.

A preliminary study carried out in 1979 at the Department of Architecture, University of Adelaide, suggests that there were only 75 possible locations of Manning houses in Adelaide. They included Kingston's own house shown in the sample area—the long timber wing probably comprised two houses put together.

There were also locally made 'movable wooden houses'—for example, John Crawford and Company, Architects, Builders and Contractors of Rundle Street, made complete portable dwellings of 'well seasoned Stringy Bark' (the Oak of South Australia), claimed to be more resistant to 'the influence of a powerful sun's rays' and 'against heavy rains' than the imported product (*The Southern Australian*. 15/12/1838.) A Crawford house of two rooms (about 45 m²) sold for £60, including delivery to 'any part of the town'.

34. Australian Bureau of Statistics, *Census of S.A. 1861*.

35. *Smith City Survey* (1880), Sheet no. 38 (see Chap. 3, note 4).

36. Gouger, p. 74 (see note 14, above). The fencing which was 'put up generally in Adelaide, is a close paling-fence of stringy bark, about five feet in height'. According to Gouger it was 'rather costly' at 18 shillings per rod (5 metres in length), but it was 'very substantial' and of 'neat appearance'.

37. The Building Act of 1923 prescribed that no dwelling house shall be erected on an allotment of land less than 3,960 square feet (368 m²) in area; and that no dwelling shall occupy more than ⅔ of the allotment

and leave open an area for private use of no less than 500 sq. ft. (46m ^{2}). Although not enforced until the turn of the century, the Municipal Corporations Act of 1880 stipulated the minimum widths for public and private streets to be 40 ft. (12 m) and 30 ft. (9 m), respectively. It was the combined effect of these two Acts that outlawed colonial row and terrace housing of the kind shown in this book.

CHAPTER 2: SMALL DETACHED COTTAGES: 1836–1860.

1. Robin Boyd, Preface to the paperback edition, *Australia's Home, its Origins, Builders and Occupiers* (Melbourne University Press 1961), first published 1952.
2. *The Housing Handbook*, Second Edition, (The National Housing Reform Council, London 1903). In Ireland, the original cost of building was £150 sterling, and the rent ranged between 1/3 and 1/6 per week.
3. The Censuses of South Australia lack information concerning the different dwelling types. In the colonial period dwellings were classified collectively, according to the number of rooms they contained.
4. For comparisons with recent characteristics of Australian housing, see Stefan Pikusa, *Homes Before Houses: let users influence design*, Urban Family Housing Research (Department of Architecture, University of Adelaide, 1975) pp. 41–52.
5. Municipality of Unley, South Australia, *Notices under Building Act*. During 1892, not less than 5 per cent of building approvals were two roomed dwellings.
6. The boundaries of the *County of Adelaide* extended from the Barossa Valley in the north to Willunga in the south, and as far as Echunga in the Adelaide Hills. In 1861, 16 'counties' surrounded the capital with the remote parts of the Province being divided into 6 'pastoral districts'. (Census of S.A., 1861, p. 145).
7. The Census of 1861 provided the first comprehensive return of the 'Dwellings of the People' to the Parliament of South Australia, following the proclamation of responsible government in 1856.
8. Report from the Select Committee of the Legislative Council of S.A. on the *Waterworks Bill*, 1851. Appendix, p. 9.
9. Australian Bureau of Statistics, *Census of S.A., 1861*.
10. *ibid*.
11. Gouger, p. 106 (see Chapter 1, note 14).
12. John Alexander Gilfillan (1793–c. 1866), oilpainting of *Adelaide in 1851*—a typical streetscape, presumed location to the east of Light Square. Art Gallery of South Australia.
13. George Blakiston Wilkinson, *South Australia; its Advantages and its Resources. Being a description of that Colony and a manual of information for emigrants* (John Murray, London 1848), pp. 74–75.
14. *Muelleria*, Vol 4, No. 1 (1978), p. 8. Not finding a farmer's life to his liking, Dr. Ferdinand von Mueller (1825–1896) returned briefly to Adelaide and late in 1852 joined the rush to the Victorian goldfields where

he intended to open a chemist shop. It was in the next year that von Mueller became the first Government Botanist for Victoria and later the Director of Melbourne Botanic Gardens. For his scientific work as a botanist and explorer he was made a Baron by the King of Wurtenburg and was also knighted by Queen Victoria.
15. *The South Australian Advertiser*, 12/10/1869. The Provincial Gas Company was formed in 1869 to produce gas for lighting of Adelaide and the near suburbs in competition with the South Australian Gas Company, established earlier at Brompton. However, the anticipated success from the new undertaking was not realized and the two companies amalgamated in 1878.
16. The traditional London stock brick was approximately 21.5 cm long x 10.5 cm wide x 6.5 cm high. For locally made bricks refer to Chapter 4.
17. Gouger, p. 68 (see Chap. 1, note 14).
18. *ibid*, p. 69.
19. *Historical Research; Township of Hampton*. Department of Environment and Planning. Unpublished report, 1982.
20. Land Titles Office, Certificate of Title, Vol. 542, Fol. 115.
21. The original contract drawings are dated '5.12.65'.
22. *George Thomas Light* (1838–1911) was a Civil Servant from 1857 to 1883. He does not appear to have ever practised as a private architect, and the role he played in the design of government buildings during his long period of employment at the Colonial Architect's Office remains 'a matter of conjecture', according to E.R.J. Morgan and S.H. Gilbert, *Early Adelaide Architecture, 1836–1886* (Oxford University Press, Melbourne, 1969), pp. 150–51.

CHAPTER 3: ROW COTTAGES AND MAISONETTES: 1836–1901

1. A *row cottage* is one of three or more small single-storey dwellings of similar design, joined together by a series of dividing walls—called 'party walls' along the common boundaries. In South Australia, *maisonettes* denotes a pair of semi-detached cottages sharing a central party wall. As far as can be determined, this term came into general usage after Federation. Interstate, maisonettes are called 'duplexes'.
2. Kingston map (1842), (see Chap. 1, note 18).
3. Gouger, p. 81, (see Chap. 1, note 14).
4. Charles W. Smith, *Trigonometrical Survey of the City of Adelaide*, (1880), undertaken by the South Australian Surveyor General's Office under the direction of C.W. Smith, City Engineer, Adelaide. Drawn to scale of 1 inch to 80 feet (1:960). Published on 126 sheets, 42 cm x 30 cm. Priced at £10 per set.

A measured survey of all existing buildings, roads and so on was necessary for the design and construction of piped sewers in the city area, authorised by the Adelaide Sewers Act of 1878. It was carried out between November, 1878, and August, 1880. After Kingston's map of 1842, the Smith City Survey provides an invaluable record of the built environment of late colonial Adelaide. Of particular importance are the external dimensions of buildings and their principal wall materials which are contained in the surveyors' field books.

5. The dimensions are scaled off the Kingston map (1842).

6. *Smith City Survey*, field book, pp. 61 and 62 (see note 4, above).

7. *ibid*, field book p. 41.

8. Ian Auhl and Dennis Marfleet, *Australia's Earliest Mining Era, South Australia, 1841–1851* (Rigby, Adelaide, 1975), p. 37.

9. Ian Auhl, *Paxton Square, Burra, S.A.* A booklet of the District Council of Burra (Investigator Press, Adelaide, undated, 1982?), p. 6.

10. See Chapter 1, note 17.

11. Auhl (1982?), p. 3 (see note 9, above). Kingston's plan of Kooringa, 1849, shows the site and the first row of cottages facing Bridge Terrace completed during that year.

12. *ibid*, p. 13.

13. *ibid*, p. 7.

14. *ibid*, p. 8.

15. William Cormack Calder (1825–1905), *Journal of a Trip from Edinburgh to Adelaide, South Australia, with a few weeks' residence there*, Adelaide, 1858. The annotated sketch plan, facing the last page of the journal, shows the layout of the end cottage with its back yard. Although the dimensions of the rooms are not shown, the inclusion of the main pieces of furniture in each room is of special interest.

16. *Smith City Survey 1880*, field book, p. 49, shows the row of three cottages located behind the Jewish Synagogue, accessible from Rundle Street. The outline of Calder's cottage appears to remain unaltered.

17. Calder (see note 15, above).

18. *Smith City Survey 1880*, field book, p. 52.

19. *Edward James Woods, F.R.I.B.A.* (1839–1916) was born in London where he was articled to the architect, C.J. Richardson. After arriving in Adelaide in 1860, he worked briefly on a cattle and sheep property in the south-east. Woods returned to Adelaide to take up a position as draftsman in the office of E.W. Wright, and subsequently became Wright's partner for about four years. In 1869, Woods commenced a sole architectural practice, with the new Anglican cathedral as his main commission. Four years later he joined government service as architect to the Council of Education, while still retaining the right to private practice. He was afterwards appointed Architect-in-Chief of South Australia and, in 1892, elected a Fellow of the Royal Insitute of British Architects. Woods left the government in about 1884 to resume private practice and took his former pupil, Walter H. Bagot, as a partner in 1905. After eighty years the names of Woods and Bagot still identify the firm of Adelaide architects that he founded. (Source: *The Observer*, 15/1/1916.)

20. Kingston Map (1842), (see Chap. 1, note 18).

21. *Daniel Garlick* (1818–1902) was the founder of the architectural firm of Garlick, Jackman & Garlick. Born in England, he arrived in Adelaide in 1837. With his father and brothers he set up a business in Kermode Street, North Adelaide, as builders and timber merchants. In the early 1850s, when the Garlick family moved to Munno Para and began farming, Daniel Garlick set up practice as an architect at Gawler. Here, he designed a large number of early churches and bank buildings in townships north of Adelaide. In the 1860s he transferred his practice to Adelaide where subsequent commissions included the original buildings of Prince Alfred College and St. Barnabas College. In 1882, Daniel Garlick took his son, Arthur, into partnership and in 1893 Herbert L. Jackman, who had been articled in the office for eight years, became the third partner. When the senior partner retired in 1899, the firm's name was shortened to Garlick & Jackman.

Daniel Garlick was a founding member of the South Australian Institute of Architects in 1886, and served as its second President from 1892 to 1900. In local government, he was Chairman of the District Council of Munno Para East from 1855–60 and represented Robe Ward on the Adelaide City Council from 1868–70. (Source: Douglas Pike (General Ed.) *Australian Dictionary of Biography, 1851–1890*, Vol. 4. (Melbourne University Press, 1972).

CHAPTER 4: DETACHED HOUSES: 1850–1901.

1. The extent of land subdivisions in the vicinity of Adelaide, circa 1901, shown shaded on the map, is based on the data compiled by Ann Marshall (1962), Department of Geography, University of Adelaide. Note that in the local government area of Unley, situated between Greenhill and Cross Roads, and Anzac Highway and Glen Osmond Road, the shaded areas conform with the 1903 sub-division shown in Corporation of the City of Unley, *City of Unley Heritage Survey* (National Estate Programme 1977/78, Project 32, 1978), p. 19.

2. Edwin Hodder, *The History of South Australia, from its foundation to the year of its jubilee* (Sampson Low, London, 1893), p. 40.

3. N.G. Butlin, *Investment in Australian Economic Development, 1861–1900* (Cambridge University Press, 1964), pp. 422–25.

4. Boyd, pp. 43–55 (see Chap. 2, note 1).

5. For further details, see L.S. Kingsborough, *The Horse Tramways of Adelaide and its Suburbs, 1875–1905* (Libraries Board of South Australia, Adelaide, 1967).

6. *South Australian Gazette & Colonial Register*, 24/3/1838. Advertisements of land for sale with own water supply from a well.

7. South Australian Parliamentary Papers, *Public Works Reports*.

8. The South Australian Gas Company, Extracts from *Records of Minutes, 1861–1919*.

9. For further details see Peter Cuffley, *Oil and Kerosene Lamps in Australia* (Pioneer Design Studio, Victoria, 1982).

10. Joseph Elliott, *Our Home in Australia: a description of cottage life in 1860*, original manuscript with introduction and architectural commentary by Stefan Pikusa (Flannel Flower Press, Sydney, 1984), p. 41.
11. *Telephone Exchanges, 100 years 1883–1983*, Telecommunications Museum, Adelaide (1983), p. 7.
12. Australian Bureau of Statistics, *Census of S.A. 1881*.
13. Australian Bureau of Statistics, *Census of S.A. 1861*.
14. Department of Mines, *The Building Stones of South Australia*, Bulletin No. 10 (Government Printer, Adelaide, 1923).
15. The term 'freestone' applies either to sandstone or limestone which, because of their properties, can be 'readily worked in any direction'. As well, the term has been loosely used to describe 'bluestone'.
16. For example, brick quoins and flint stone walling, dating to the twelfth century can be seen in Surrey, England. The use of brickwork to form the corners of a building and openings for doors and windows with irregular stonework such as flint, lime or bluestone, was a commonsense building practice. However, it was a complete reversal of the practice in the Georgian period which combined quoins of dressed stone with exposed brickwork as the main walling material.
17. *The South Australian Register*, 6/6/1840. According to an advertisement, Willunga roofing slate was 'selling in town at £10.10s. per thousand'.
18. For details of the manufacturing process and a description of colonial brickworks, see Anthony Moore, *Brickmakers in South Australia, 1836–1936*. A research project directed by Prof. David Saunders, Working Paper No. 8, Department of Architecture, University of Adelaide, 1981.
19. *The South Australian Advertiser*, 3/1/1860.
20. *The Adelaide Observer*, 24/12/1859.
21. Moore, p. 69 (see note 18, above).
22. South Australian Parliamentary Papers.
23. 'English' bond, which consists of courses of 'headers' (brick ends) alternating with courses of 'stretchers' (brick sides), has great interlocking strength.
24. 'Colonial' bond usually consists of three courses of stretchers, the fourth of headers.
25. In 1865, a pioneer Adelaide photographer, Townsend Duryea, produced a complete *Panorama of Adelaide* by displaying in the round fourteen photographs which he had taken from the top of the newly completed Town Hall tower in King William Street. (The Mortlock Library of South Australiana, Adelaide).
26. *The South Australian Advertiser*, 12/7/1858. G. Gray of 106 Rundle Street advertised for sale imported Morewood's plain and corrugated iron at 'cheapest prices' in town. Roofing 'in all its various forms' could be executed. He also made watertanks, half-round gutters and washtubs.
27. *An Act* [No. 17] *to regulate Buildings, and for preventing Mischiefs by Fire in the City of Adelaide*, was assented in January, 1858, with provision for extension to other 'Corporate Towns' in the Province.
28. Office records of the Adelaide architects, Garlick and Jackman, reveal that iron roofs were specified almost without exception for some 20 large houses designed between 1880 and 1901. They were built in prestigious suburbs, each house containing from 10 to 24 rooms, of single and double storey designs.
29. *The South Australian Advertiser*, 3/1/1860. Retail prices of building materials.
30. *ibid*, 24/1/1880.
31. Arnold Weindenhofer, 'Statistical record of sales, 1893–1945' (unpublished).
32. In 1860, Joseph Elliott wrote in the form of an extended letter a *Description of the house and its furniture, etc.* which he occupied with his wife and three young children in Jeffcott Street, North Adelaide. In 14,000 words and 18 pen and ink illustrations of the house and its contents, Elliott provides a unique insight into a standard of living of mid-Victorian Adelaide. (See note 10, above).
33. *Building Notices under Building Act 1881*. Municipality of Unley (1892).
34. Judith M. Brown, 'The Almonds, Adelaide' in Australian Council of National Trusts, *Historic Houses* (combined edition, 1982, Canberra, 1974), pp. 123–29.
35. Reproduced in Judith M. Brown, *The Almonds of Walkerville* (Griffin Press, Adelaide, 1970), p. 36.
36. Quoted in Brown, p. 123 (see note 34, above).
37. *ibid*, p. 124.
38. Australian Bureau of Statistics, *Census of S.A. 1861*.
39. Boyd, pp. 8–9 (see Chap. 2, note 1).
40. Elliott, p. 52 (see note 10, above). Writing in 1860, Elliott explains that 'great folk burn coal, but all houses built for letting have only wood fireplaces'.
41. *Thomas English* (1819–1884) arrived in South Australia in 1850 with his brother-in-law, Henry Brown. They set up the business of English & Brown, builders in Carrington Street, Adelaide, and opened up the Glen Ewin sandstone quarries at Tea Tree Gully from which they built the Town Hall, the National Bank and the Flinders Street Baptist Church. As a consequence of the Contractors' Act the partnership was dissolved; Brown remained a contractor and English commenced practice as an architect. At first he was a sole practitioner, from 1865 to 1870, then he formed a partnership with Rowland Rees, 1870–73. After Rees' death in 1873, English was again a sole practitioner until he took George K. Soward into the firm in 1877. From 1885 Thomas English's son, Joseph, took the place of his deceased father, thus continuing the firm of English & Soward until 1926. (See also Chap. 5, note 23).

Among the many buildings designed and executed solely by Thomas English are: Scots Church, North Terrace, 'Seafield Tower' at Glenelg and 'Benacre' at Glen Osmond. He also designed many large houses on Park Terrace (now Greenhill Road) including his own residence on the corner of George Street, Parkside.

Thomas English entered the City Council in the 1850s and was elected Mayor of Adelaide in 1862, and so was the holder of this office when the foundation stone of the Town Hall was laid in 1863. Two years later he was elected to the Legislative Council, serving in the Hart and Boucaut ministries

as Commissioner of Public Works from 1865–67. He remained a Member until 1878 and, after an extensive return visit to his native England, Thomas English served again in the Upper House from 1882 until just prior to his death.
Source: W.H. Bagot, *Some Nineteenth Century Adelaide Architects* (Pioneers' Association of S.A., 1958), p. 7.

42. Adelaide Botanic Garden, 'Minutes' of Board Meeting held on 4/6/1866.

43. See note 41, above.

44. *Henry Colls Richardson* (1837–1910) was born at Islington, London, and was brought to Adelaide by his parents in 1840. His father carried on the business of cabinetmaker in Adelaide. After finishing his schooling, Henry Richardson tried his fortunes in various Australian goldfields before taking up the occupation of builder and contractor. From the early 1870s, he also practised an as architect and, along with Daniel Garlick, became one of the foundation members of the South Australian Institute of Architects.

Henry Richardson was a member of the City Council from 1878 to 1886. During this time he was chairman of every permanent committee and so was involved in the inauguration of the sewerage system, the construction of the Torrens Weir and the Morphett Street Overway Bridge. As far as is known his architectural work was mostly of a domestic nature, the notable exceptions being his designs for the Blackwood Hotel and extensions to the East End Market in the early eighties. For most of his life Richardson lived in Sturt Street, Adelaide. (Source: *The Observer*. 8/10/1910.)

45. Municipality of Unley (see note 33, above).

46. *ibid*.

47. *Malcolm Reid—Furniture Manufacturer, General Furnishings, ironmonger*, of Franklin Street, Adelaide. The details quoted are extracted from the company's records, including sales catalogues and press advertisements for the period 1899–1908.

48. A. Simpson & Son Limited, *General Goods Catalogue, 1910 Edition*, lists a wide range of goods which had already become household names in colonial houses. Alfred Simpson arrived in Adelaide in 1849, and in 1855 started a tinsmith business in Topham Street, Adelaide. By the turn of the century, 'A. Simpson & Son—workers in various metals and vitreous enamellers'—had established factories and shops at four city locations.

49. *The South Australian Advertiser*, 6/1/1880.

50. *ibid*, 2/1/1880.

51. *ibid*, 8/1/1880.

52. *ibid*, 2/1/1880.

53. *ibid*, 2/1/1880.

CHAPTER 5: TERRACES AND SEMI-DETACHED HOUSES: 1850–1901.

1. As defined in this work a *terrace* is a row of contiguous dwellings of more than one-storey high, usually of repetitive design; a *terraced house* is one of the row joined together by fire-isolating party walls. The term 'town house', has also been used to describe a terraced house and indicates its urban nature and location. It appears that colonial architects avoided using the term 'terrace' on their drawings, and simply titled terraced houses, 'houses'.

2. *Smith City Survey*, field book, (1880), p. 43, and Burden, p. 71 (see note 3, below).

3. Michael Burden, *Lost Adelaide: a photographic record* (Oxford University Press, Melbourne, 1983), pp. 54, 71–74.

4. Quoted in Department of Environment and Planning, *Glenelg Heritage Survey, Stage 1*, Adelaide, (1983), p. 8.

5. *ibid*, p. 9.

6. Australian Bureau of Statistics, *Census of S.A. 1881*.

7. E.E. Morris, 'Adelaide' in *Cassell's Picturesque Australasia*, (1889), Facsimiled shortened edition (1978), *Australia's First Century* (Child & Henry, Australia), p. 167.

8. *Smith City Survey* (1880) (See Chap. 3, note 4) gives a detailed picture of the development along the parklands in the south-eastern corner of the city up to the end of the 1870s.

9. *ibid*, field book, p. 18.

10. Albert Hall Mansions, built in 1879 to a design by the architect Norman Shaw, was the first block of middle-class flats in London.

Adelaide's counterpart is the surviving 'Ruthven Mansions' built in Pulteney Street, 1911–1914, and refurbished in 1979.

11. Stefan Muthesius, *The English Terraced House* (Yale University Press, London, 1982), p. 79.

12. *ibid*, p. 84.

13. Thomas English (see Chap. 4, note 41).

14. Muthesius, p. 95 (see note 11, above).

15. Morton Herman, *The Blackets, An Era of Australian Architecture* (Angus and Robertson, Sydney, 1963), p. 100. This example shows the architect, Edmund Blacket's, design of 1865 for 3 terraced houses at Redfern (Sydney). Following the British precedent, an attic floor containing two small bedrooms is included. The use of roof space, common in Sydney houses, never gained general popularity in Adelaide.

16. Quoted in Susan Marsden, *A History of Woodville* (Corporation of the City of Woodville, South Australia, 1977), p. 90.

17. Edward J. Woods (see Chap. 3, note 19).

18. Woods Bagot Architects, Adelaide, 'Extract from Ledger of E.J. Woods of Principal Works executed by him'.

19. E.J.R. Morgan and S.H. Gilbert, *Early Adelaide Architecture, 1836–1886* (Oxford University Press, Melbourne, 1969), p. 88. Also, *Smith City Survey* (1880), field book, p. 45.

20. Jackman Gooden Architects, Adelaide, extract from the Ledger of Works executed by the partnership of *English & Soward* in the period 1880–89.

21. *J.C. Loudon* was a well-known English author of many handbooks on building and gardening.

22. Roger Dixon and Stefan Muthesius, *Victorian Architecture, with a short dictionary of architects* (Thames and Hudson, London, 1978), p. 60.

23. *George Klewitz Soward* (1857–1941) was born in the Adelaide suburb of Norwood and educated at St. Peters College, Adelaide. As a practising architect he was, from 1877 to 1884, the partner of Thomas English (see Chap. 4, note 41), and from 1885 the partner of Joseph English and, much later, of H.M. Jackman. In 1878 Thomas English returned to England for an extensive visit which, undoubtedly, had an influence on the designs produced by the partnership in the early eighties.

In a career that spanned more than half a century, George Soward was responsible for many large houses in and around Adelaide. Notable examples are 'Culver House' at Walkerville; 'St. Corantyn' on East Terrace, Adelaide; 'St. Margarets', Brougham Place, North Adelaide; and 'Dundrennan', Glenelg. From 1902 to 1904 George Soward was the member of the House of Assembly for the seat of Torrens. (Source: E.J.R. Morgan and S.H. Gilbert, *Early Adelaide Architecture, 1836–1886* (Oxford University Press, Melbourne, 1969), p. 153.

List of Colour Plates and Illustrations

Colour Plates

1   Rounsevell House, Glenelg, c.1875
2   Paterson's Row of four cottages, Adelaide, 1897
3   Para Para Lodge, south of Gawler, 1880
4   Lathlean House, College Town, 1877
5   Maesday House, Glenelg, 1906
6   Noltenius House, Glenelg, 1900
7   Terrace of three houses, Glenelg, c.1868
8   'Alexandra Terrace', Glenelg, c.1876
9   Terrace of four houses, Adelaide, 1897
10   Pair of houses, Glenelg, 1883
11   Pair of houses, Adelaide, 1891

Illustrations

1   Robert Gouger's tent and hut at Holdfast Bay, 1836
2   Finlayson's tea tree bower, Adelaide, 1837
3   Finlayson's shared hut, Adelaide, 1837
4   Typical early cottages, Adelaide, c.1839
5   Interior of settler's hut, early 1840s
6   Pioneer cottage near Adelaide, mid-1840s
7   NW corner of South Adelaide around 1842
8   East end of Rundle Street looking west, 1845
9   Map of Adelaide, 1839
10 and 11   Sample area, South Adelaide, 1842
12   Map of Adelaide district in the 1850s
13   Spital Cottage, Grampian region of Scotland, c.1850
14   Country cottages, near Cork, Ireland, c.1880
15   Adelaide streetscape, 1851
16   'Angmering House', Enfield. First section built in 1840
17   von Mueller Cottage, near Mount Barker, 1849
18   Thebarton Cottage, c.1869
19   Hampton Cottage, Burra North, c.1860
20   Griffin Cottage, South Adelaide, c.1855

21 and 22   Gatekeeper's Cottage, Adelaide, 1865

23   Development of minor streets and lanes in the sample area, 1837–1880

24   David Street Row of 17 dwellings, late 1870s

25   Gray's Row of four dwellings, pre-1841

26   The township of Kooringa (present Burra), c.1850

27 and 28   Paxton Square Rows, Kooringa, 1849–52

29   Tiver's Row, Redruth (present North Burra), 1856

30   Calder's Row, South Adelaide, pre-1858

31 and 32   Parker's Row, North Adelaide, 1878–79

33 and 34   Paterson Houses, Adelaide, 1897

35 and 36   City Maisonettes, 1894

37   Kent Town Maisonettes, 1892

38   A group of mid-century cottages, probably at Kent Town or Hackney

39   Map of Greater Adelaide, 1901

40   Richardson House, North Adelaide, 1851

41   Architectural details, 1857

42   Details of window, 1883

43   Details of solid brick construction, 1895

44–46   Elliott House, North Adelaide, 1856

47   Free-standing brick privy, 1857

48   'The Almonds', Walkerville, 1850–c.1865

49–51   'Heywood', Unley Park, c. 1858–1880

52   Para Para Lodge, south of Gawler, 1880

53   Botanic Garden Lodge, Adelaide, 1866

54   Rounsevell House, Glenelg, c.1875

55   Delano House, Norwood, c.1884

56   Lathlean House, College Town (present College Park), 1877

57   Rugless House, Glenelg, c.1895

58   Lucas House, Glenelg, 1897

59   Maesday House, Glenelg, 1906

60   Noltenius House, Glenelg, 1900

61   Stoves and ovens

62   Laundry equipment

63   A 'Simpson' bathroom, around 1900

64   Map of Adelaide, 1861

65   Terrace of six houses, Adelaide, 1851

66 and 67   Terrace of three houses, Glenelg, c.1868

68   Terrace of seven houses, Glenelg, c.1872

69–72   'Alexandra Terrace', Glenelg, c.1876

73   'Botanic Chambers', Adelaide, 1877

74   'Landrowna Terrace', Adelaide, 1875

75   'Marine Residences', Grange, 1885

76   Terrace of nine houses, Adelaide, c.1887

77   Terrace of four houses, Adelaide, 1897

78   The first house connections regulated under the Adelaide Sewers Act, 1878

79   Pair of houses, North Adelaide, 1851

80   Pair of houses, Adelaide, 1891

81   Pair of houses, Glenelg, 1883

Index

Page numbers in bold type refer to illustrations

Ablutions, 45, 67, 73, 108, 118
Absentee land owners, 4, 14, 16
Access lanes. See Streets, secondary
Adelaide and Suburban Tramway Co., 58
Adelaide Central telephone exchange, 59
Adelaide, Glenelg and Suburban Railway, 94
Adelaide, maps of. See Maps
Adelaide Municipal Council, 10; rates, 10, 37
Adelaide, Queen Dowager, 11
Adelaide Sewers Act (1878), 58; regulations under, **112**. See also Sewers Adelaide streetscapes, 8, 11, 23, 96, **10, 12, 24, 56**
Albert Hall Mansions, London, 124
Albert Houses, London, 96
Albert Terrace, 94
Alberton, 55
Aldgate, 58
Alexandra Terrace, 102, 105, **103-105**
Allotment size, 4, 12, 16, 31, 37, 39, 44, 47, 48, 50-51, 78, 82, 102, 111, 120-121
'The Almonds', 65, 68-70, 73, 102, **69**
Angas, John Howard, 22
Angas Street, 94
'Angmering House', **24**
Arch, 27, 60, 106
Archer Street, 96
Architects: Boyd, Robin, 19, 70, 96;
    English & Rees, 100, 123, **101**
    English & Soward, 73, 82, 83, 123, **74-75, 82-85**
    English, Joseph, 82, 123;
    English, Thomas, 73, 97, 100, 102, 123, **76, 98-100, 103-105**

Garlick, Daniel, 78, 122, **80-81**
Garlick, Jackman & Garlick, 50-51, **50, 52, 53**
Kingston, George, S., 10-17, 39-43, 119-120, **14-15, 41-42**
Light, George Thomas, 32, 121, **32-34**
McMullen, Michael, 102, **106**
Richardson, H.C., 78, 124, **77**
Soward, George K., 116, 123, **116-117**
Shaw, Norman, 124
Woods, Edward J., 47, 85, 108, 113, 115, 122, **48-49, 64, 86-87, 110-111, 114-115**
Wren, Christopher, 96
Archway in passage, 34, 47, 51, 73, 97, 102
Asphalte paving, 50, 51
Asymmetric design, 73, 78, 83, **74, 75**
Auction of town acres, 3, 4, 14
Australia's Home, 70, 121

'Back Houses', 50-51, **50**
Back yards, 16, 23, 40, 45, 67, **67**
Balconies, 51, 78, 79, 96, 102, 106, 109
Basements, 70, 96, 102, **103, 104, 106.** See also Summer rooms
Barge board, 79, 83, **34**
Barnard Buildings, 37
Bath, 47, 58, 78, 88, 90, 102, 115, **91, 112**
Bath, England, 96
Bath heater, 90, **91**
Bathroom, 47-48, 51, 78, 79, 82, 85, 88, 90, 102, 115, **91**
Bayswater, London, 111
Bedroom, 'best', 22, 23, 30, 66, 85, 88, 102
Belt, Edward, 70

Belt, William & Penelope, 68, 70, 102
Berkeley, Captain Charles, 4
Berkeley, Martha S. (artist), 8, **8**
Blackwood, 61
Boom style, 56
Bluestone. See stonework
Botanic Chambers, 102, 108, **106**
Botanic Garden Lodge, 73, **75**
Botanic Gardens, 32; map of (1874), 73
Bowden, 61
Bower, H.J., Benevolent Fund, 46
Bowers, 4, 6, **6**
Bower Street, 46
Box-seat W.C., **112**
Boyd, Robin (architect), 19, 70, 96
Bricks: Adelaide standard, 61; German, 61; Hoffmann kiln, 61; London, 27, 61; manufacture 60-61, 123
Brick/stone dwellings, early, 10, 14, 16, 23, 37, 50, 70
Brick-veneer construction, 12, 120
Brickwork, 25, 27, 59-63, 85, **64;** cavity walls, 63, 82, 115, **82, 114-115;** Colonial bond, 62, 123; stuccoed, 61; English bond, 62, 123; exposed, 60, 63, 85; Flemish bond, **64;** 'one brick thick' walls, 48
Brompton gas works, 58
Brownhill Creek, 8, 55, 70
Brown, Oswald (engineer), **112**
Brown Street, 12, 17
'Buffalo', HMS, 27
Buffalo Row, 6
Building Act (1858), 23, 35, 65, 123; (1881), 35, 48, 83, 109; (1923), 17, 47, 48, 120-121
Building boom, 56, 93, 111
Building costs, 56, 68, 73, 79, 83, 106, 108

Building distribution and density, 7, 10, 11, 14, 36, 47, 55-56, 93-94, 111
Building in stages, 50, 68
Building materials and methods, 59-66. See also Bricks, Brickwork, Concrete, Iron, Lath and plaster, Pisé, Pug, Slab, Stonework, Stucco, Thatch, Wood
Built-in cupboards, 27, 48, 51, **53**
Bungalow, 27, 70
Burnside, 55, 58
Burra, 30, 39, 55, 79, **40**
Byron Place, 14, 16

Calder, William, 122; row cottage, 44-46, 50, 68, **45**
Campbelltown, 55
Candles, 58, 88, 97
Carrington Street, 39, 94, 106
Cast iron. See Iron.
Cavity walls, early, 63, 82, 115, **82, 114-115**
Cawthorne, W.A. (artist), **40**
Ceiling, height, 25, 27, 35, 40, 44, 68, 73, 83, 97, 102, 115; cloth, 27, 31, 40
Cellar, 113
Cesspits, 58, 79, 97, 100, **67**
Central Board of Health, 100, **112**
Chalmers Church, 93
Chesser Street, 4
Chimneys, 7, 20, 23, 27, 46, 51, 71, 78, 97, 113, **24, 63**
City and Suburban Steam Brickmaking Co., 61
City Engineer, Charles W. Smith, 121
City Maisonettes, 50-51, **50, 52**
Climate, influence on building, 5, 26, 59, 73, 96
Closet. See Pantry
Clothes line, 67
Coal fires, 73, 123
College Town, 78
Collingrove, 22
Colonial Architect's Department, 32
Colonial oven, 89, **89**
Common ground space, 39, 43, **41**
Company housing, 39, **41, 42**
Concrete buildings, early, 23, 59
Conveyancing of land, 55
Cooke, Peter, 23
Coolgardie safe, 51, 88, 90
Coppers, washing; 48, 49, 68, 73, 78, 85, 88, 90, 97, 108, 113, **90**
Coromandel Place, 4
Corridor, 83
Corrugated iron. See Iron.

Cottage, British, 19-22, 27, 36, **20, 21**; Cornish influence, 43; cottage homes, 48; development of plan, 19, 22-23, 25, 30, 35-39, 44, 47, 48, 50, 51, 66, 70, 79, 97; double-fronted, 27, 30, 31, 36, 39, 43, 50; early, 8, 19-34, **9, 24**; row, 6, 14, 16, 30, 35-48, 93, 121, **37-49**; settler, 8, 19, 23, 25, 26, 34, **28-29**; single-fronted, 27, 30, 36, 37, 44, 47, 48, 50; space between, 37, 50, 51; 'starter', 22; three-room detached, 27, 30-34, **30-34**; two-room detached, 23, 25-26, 27, 32, **26, 28-29**; walkway between, 50. See also Maisonettes.
Cottages, detached, Elliott, 66-68, **66-67**; Finlayson, 8; Gatekeeper, 32-34, **32-34**; Griffin, 31-32, **31**; Hampton, 30-31, 40, **30**; Hindmarsh (Governor), 27; Municipal (Ireland), 20-22, **21**; Spital (Scotland), 19-20, 22, **20**; Swann, 68-70, **48**; Thebarton, 22, 23, 25, 26-27, 32, **28-29**; von Mueller, 16, 20, 23, 25-26, 27, **26**; Watson, 12, 120
Cottages, row, Barnard Buildings, 37, Calder, 44-46, 50, 68, 122, **45**; David Street, 37, 39, 46, **37**; Gray, 16, 35, 39, **28**; Parker, 46, 47, **46-47**; Paterson, 35, 47-48, 50, 51, **48-49**; Paxton Square, 31, 39-43, **41-42**; Tiver, 43-44, **44**
Couche, R. & J. (builders), 106
County of Adelaide, 22-23, 55-56, 59
Cox Brothers, 61
Cunningham, Alexander, 102
Currie Street, 6, 7, 11

Davenport, Robert (artist), 8, **9**
David Street Row cottages, 37, 39, 46
Decorations, 61, 71, 73, 76, 78, 79, 83
Delabole slate quarry, 61
Delano, William, 78; house, 78, 83, **77**
Delisser, C. & E.A., survey, **92**
Detached dwellings, 5, 14, 16, 19, 22, 30, 35, 37, 50, 55, 66-68, 94, 95, 111
Dickin, W. (builder), 73
Dining room, 51, 78, 79, 82, 85, 96, 102
Door, front, 23, 27, 76, 78, 82, 109; fan and side lights, 27, 76, 82, 109; side facing, 116
Doors, internal, 26, 31, 34, 40, 43, 67, 73; folding, 102; French, 70, 82, 96, 102, 116
Dorset House, 70-71, **72**
Dover Castle Public House, 96
Dover stove, 89, **89**

Downs, George, 68
Drainage of waste, 105
Drawing room, 51, 79, 85, 88, 97, 100, 102. See also Parlour and Living room
Dugout dwelling, 39, **40**
Duffield, Hon. Walter, 73
Duplex. See Houses, semi-detached
Dwelling characteristics, 14, 16, 22-23, 25, 47, 56-58, 59, 68, 78, 79, 94, 96, 97, 111; one room (single-cell), 6, 14, 22, 23; two room, 7, 8, 19, 20, 22, 23-27, 34, 39-43, 48, 56; three/four room, 19, 22, 27-34, 39-48, 50-51, 56, 58, 66-68, 73, 88; five or more rooms, 22, 51, 56, 68, 70, 73, 78, 79, 82, 83, 85, 88, 93-118
Dwelling occupancy rate, 7, 8, 10, 19, 22-23, 43, 58
Dwelling stock, city, 10, 14, 17; County of Adelaide, 22, 23, 55-56, 58

Eaves, 22, 78, 79; brackets, 97
Electricity, 58, 88-89
Elliott, Joseph, 66, 68, 123; house, 46, 59, 66-68, **66-67**
Encounter Bay, 59
Encroachments, 7, 17
English & Rees (architects), 100, 123, **101**
English & Soward (architects), 73, 82, 83, 123, **74-75, 82-85**
English, Joseph (architect), 82, 123, **82-85**
English terraced house, 96
English, Thomas (architect), 73, 97, 100, 102, 123, **76, 98-100, 103-105**
Entrance and hall, 30, 31, 51, 66, 67, 76, 82, 85, 96, 102; side, 85, 116, **86-87**
Equipment, household, 79, 88-91
Extensions, 70, 71

Fences, 10, 14, 16, 19, 22, 40, 51, 67-68, 120
Finials, 79, 83, **34, 63**
Finlayson, William & Helen, 5, 6-8, 10, 16, 23, 25, 50, 119, **6-7**
Fire-isolating wall, 35. See also Party wall
Fireplace, 5, 19, 20, 22, 23, 27, 34, 79, 83, 100; cooking in, 40, 48, 89, 97; corner, 30-31, 40, 51, 79, **42, 83, 84, 86**; in timber houses, 25; grate, 73, 79
Flats, 96, 124
Floors, mud, 7, 22, 27, 40; timber, 25, 27, 43; brick, 27, 43

Folding door, 102
Foundation Act, 3
Franklin Street, 11, 93, 113
Freestone. See Stonework
French doors/windows, 70, 82, 96, 102, 116
French Street, 4
Friends Meeting House, 12
Frome Street, 37, **12**
Functions of rooms, 6-8, 22, 23, 27, 30, 34, 40, 44-45, 66-67, 68, 79, 88, 96, 100, 102, **82**
Furniture, 22, 26, 44-45, 88, 124

Gablets, 82, 88, 109, **34**
Gable walls, 19, 20, 22, 23, 73, 79, 83, 85, **24, 56**
Gaol, 6, 12
Gardens, private, 16, 19, 23, 46, 68, 94, 113; public 94
Garlick, Daniel (architect), 78, 122, **80-81**
Garlick, Jackman & Garlick (architects), 50-51, **50, 52, 53**
Galvanised iron. See Iron
Gas, supply 47, 58, 79, 88; cost, 58; lighting, 51, **53**, 58-59
Gatekeeper's cottage, 32-34, **32-34**
Gawler, 55, 58, 73
Gawler, Governor George, 3, 12
Gentleman's residence, 78, 83, **77, 84-85**
Georgian design, 26, 27, 109, 123
Giffhorn stove, 89-90, **89**
Gilfillan, J.A. (artist), **24**
Gill, S.T. (artist), 8, 11, **8, 12**
Gilles Street, 11
Glass manufacture, 97
Glenelg, 55, 58, 73, 83, 85, 93-94, 97, 100, 102, 111, 116
Glenelg Terrace, 102, 108, **104**
Glen Osmond, 59, 111
Globe Timber Mills, 70
Glover,— (builder), 109
Goldfields, 30, 39, 65
Gouger, Robert, 27, 35-36, 119, 120, **5**
Gouger Street, 12, 14, 16, 17
Government House, 12, 27
Grange, 58, 106
Grange Land & Investment Co., 106
Grange Railway & Investment Co., 106
Gray Street, 39
Gray, W.H., 39; row cottages, 16, 35, 39, 40, **28**
Greater Adelaide, 22, 65, **18, 57**
Grenfell Street, 4, 11, 37, 59
Griffin, Martin, 31; cottage, 31-32, **31**
Grote Street, 11, 12, 14, 17, 39
Gutters, 65, 73, 97

Hall. See Entrance
Hamilton, Geo. E. (engineer), **62-63, 67**
Hampton cottage, 30-31, **30**
Hampton (North Burra), 30
Handbasins, 82, 88, 108
Harvey, Arthur, 106
Harvey, Simon, 70, **72**
Haslam, William, 70
Hawke, William, 70, **72**
Health Act (1873), 100
'Helenholme', 8
Henderson, William (builder), 39
Henley Beach, 55, 106
'Heywood', 70-73, 102, **71-72**
Hill, John, H.J., 116
Hindley Street, 11, 12, 14, 39
Hindmarsh, 55, 58, 61
Hindmarsh, Governor, 27
Hindmarsh Square, 37, 94
Hoffmann bricks, 61
Holdfast Bay, 4, 58, 93, 94, 106
Hollow wall. See Cavity wall
Homestead plan, 70-71
Hope Valley, 58
Hornsey Estate, North London, 102
Horse drawn cabs, 58
Horsetram, 58, 93, 122
Hot water, 48, 67, 73, 78, 89, 91, 97, 105, 113

Houses, detached, 'The Almonds', 65, 68-70, 73, 102, **69**; 'Angmering', **24**; Botanic Garden, 73, **75**; Delano, 78, 83, **77**; Dorset, 70-71, **72**; Elliott, 46, 59, 66-68, **66-67**; 'Helenholme', 8; 'Heywood', 70-73, 102, **71-72**; Lathlean, 78, **80-81**; Lucas, 79, 83, **83**; Maesday, 83-85, **84-85**; Manning, 12, 120; Noltenius, 85, **86-87**; Para Para, 73, **74-75**; Richardson, **60**; Richman, **64**; Rounsevell, 73, 76, 78, **76**; Rugless, 79, 82-83, **82**. See also Bungalow, Dwelling, Homestead, Prefabricated and Villa.

Houses, semi-detached, multi-story, 111-118; Adelaide, 113, 115, **114-115**; Glenelg, 116, 118, **116**; London, 111, 113; North Adelaide, 109, 113, **113**; Sydney 109

Houses, semi-detached, singe-storey. See Maisonettes

Housing demand, 3
Hurtle Square, 94
Huts, 6-8, 23, **7, 8**
Hutt Street, 11

Ice chests, 90
Ice manufacture, 90
Immigration Depot, 48
India, British in, 17
Intercolonial railway, 58
Iron, black, 65; cast, 71, 73, 79, 83, 106; flat, 23
Iron, corrugated galvanised sheeting, 23, 59, 63, 65, 123; cost, 65; curved verandahs, 46, 71, 73, 79, 97; fences, 51; roofs, 59, 65, 123; tanks, 34, 65, 123
Iron dwellings, early, 23, 59
Islington treatment works, 58

Jetties, Henley and Grange, 102
'John Renwick', 6
Johnston, William, 109, 113

Kensington, 58
Kent Town, 55
Kent Town Maisonettes, 51, **53**
Kermode Street, 11
Kerosene lamps, 58-59, 88, 97
'Key' house, 94, 96, 97, 102
Kingston, George Strickland (architect & surveyor), 10, 11, 12, 39-43, 119-120, **41-42**; own residence 14, 16, 17
Kingston Map (1842), 5, 8, 10-17, 120. Sample area of South Adelaide, 4, 12-17, 22, 35, 48, **14, 15**
King William Street, 11, 50
Kitchen, detached, 22, 27, 30, 31, 68, 70; early, 8, 22; furnishings, 88; integrated with house plan, 34, 51, 66-67, 68, 70, 79; multi-purpose, 22, 23, 25, 26, 34, 66; in terrace houses, 96, 97, 100, 102
Kitchen sink. See Sink
Kitcher, W., 50
Klemzig, 55
Kooringa (Burra), 30, 39, **40-42**

Land, allocation and sale, 3, 4, 12, 14; subdivision, 4, 16, 17, 36, 44, 47, 50-51. See also Speculation
Landrowna Terrace, 94, **107**
Land Titles Office, 55
Lanes. See Streets, secondary
Largs Bay, 58
Lath and plaster dwellings, 8, 10, 16, 25, 35
Lathlean, D., 78; house, 78, **80-81**
Laundry, 48, 67, 68, 73, 79, 85, 90-91, 108, **90**
Lean-to, timber framed, 83
Lewis Trust, 43

Light, Colonel William, 4, 11, 59, 94, 96, 119, **9**
Light, George Thomas (architect), 32, 121, **32-34**
Lighting, candles, 58, 88, 97; electricity, 59; gas, 51, 59, **53**; kerosene lamps, 58-59, 88, 97; oil lamps, 58
Light-well, 96, 97, 100
Lime kiln, 25
Lime mortar, 59
Limestone, 59
Living room, early all-purpose, 22, 23, 25, 26, 34, 66; post 1860 sitting room, 67, 73, 82. See also Parlour and Drawing room
Lobby, at rear of house, 76, 82, 100, 102
London bricks, 27, 61
London squares, 94
London terraces, 94, 96, 100
Loudon, J.C., 111, 116
Lucas house, 79, 83, **83**
Lunatic asylum, 32
Lysaght, John, Ltd., 65-66

McMullen, Michael (architect), 102, **106**
Maesday house, 83-85, **84-85**
Magill, 55
Maisonettes, 14, 16, 35, 48-51, 109, 116, 121; City, 50-51, **50-52**; Kent Town, 51, **53**
Malcolm Reid, 88, 124
Manning, H., prefabricated houses, 12, 120
Mansions, 56, 70, 94, 96, 111
'Marine Residences', 93, 106, **108**
Maps: City of Adelaide, Light (1839), **13**; Kingston (1842), 5, 8, 10-18, **14-15, 36**; Delisser (1861), **36, 92**; Smith (1880), 121, **36**; Greater Adelaide (1850s), **18**; (1901), **57**
Marion, village, 4
Meat safe, 90
Medindie, 111
Melbourne Street, 46
Miller, David (builder), 97, 100
Millers Point, Sydney, 109
Minor Streets. See Streets, secondary
Mintaro flagstone, 61
Mitcham, 8, 55, 59
Mixed housing development, 47, 50-51, **48, 50**
Morris, E.E., 94
Moss & Watts (builders), 51
Mount Barker, 25, 55
Mount Lofty Ranges, 55, 59
M-roof. See Roof

Mueller, Dr. Ferdinand J.H. von. See von Meuller
Multi-storey buildings, early, 12, 27; houses, 63, 78, 93-118
Municipal Corporations Act (1880), 35, 47, 65
Municipal cottages for Irish labourers, Ireland, 20-22, **21**
Municipal Tramways Trust, 96
Murray Bridge, 60
Murray, George (builder), 46
Murray River, 55
Music Saloon, 14

National Trust of S.A., 25
Nimmo & McGee (builders), 73
Noltenius, E., house, 85, **86-87**
North Adelaide, 4, 11, 12, 58, 59, 93, 96, 109, 113
North Terrace, 4, 6, 8, 11, 16, 32, 39, 93, 94, 102, **10**
Norwood, 55, 58, 61, 78

Oakley Villas, London, 113
The Observer, 61
O'Connel Street, 96
Oil lamps, 58-59
Oliver, Charles & Son (builders), 83
Omnibuses, 58, 93
Orientation of houses, 20, 26, 102, 106
Outbuildings (wash house, sheds, etc.), 10, 14, 20, 22, 23, 48, 67, 68, 79, 82
Overcrowding, 22, 27, 35, 40, 43

Paired houses. See Houses, semi-detached and Maisonettes.
Panorama of Adelaide (1865), 65, 123
Pantry, 34, 73, 78, 82, 97, 100
'parafine', 58-59
Para Para Lodge, 73, **74-75**
Parapet wall, 46, 48, 51, 109, 115
Parker Street row cottages, 46, 47, **46, 47**
Parken, William, 97, 100
Parklands, 36, 48, 55, 59, 93, 94, 108
Parlour, 30, 34, 43, 46, 66, 73, 78, 79, 82, 96, 100, 102; furniture, 88. See also Drawing room and Living room
Party wall, 35, 37, 51, 97, 109
Passage, full-length, 27, 34, 68, 70, 73, 79, 82; half-length, 30, 32, 34, 47, 66-67; L-shaped, 85; width of, 51, 76, 79, 82, 100, 102

Paterson, Dr. Alexander, 47, 108; row cottages, 35, 47-48, 50, 51, **48-49**
Paxton Square row cottages, 31, 39-43, **40-42**
Paxton, William, 39
Pennington Terrace, 12
Penola, slab houses, 25
Philanthropic housing schemes, 48
Pikusa, Stefan, 121, 123
Pirie Street, 11
Pisé, 7, 10, 14, 16, 35, 37, 59, 119
Plaster, 31
Plumbing regulations, 51, **112**. See also Sewers
Population, 10, 37, 39, 55, 94, 106
Porch, rear, 78, 88
Portable buildings. See Prefabricated
Port Adelaide, 6, 11, 55, 58, 59, 93, 94; Port Misery, 6
Powell, Thomas William, 30
Prefabricated buildings, 12, 16, 22, 120
Preliminary land orders, 4, 12
Pressed metal panels, 60
Privacy, 34, 40, 43, 46, 82, 85, 115
Private roads, 47, 50, 97, 108. See also Streets, secondary
Privy, 22, 23, 46, 67, 79, 97, 100, 102, 118, **67**
Provincial Gas Co., 26, 34, 121
'Pug', 25, 59
Public buildings, early, 11, **92**
Public transport, 58, 93-94
Public utilities, 58-59, 88-91

Quarries, 59-61
Queen Adelaide, 11
Quoins, 22, 27, 60, 73, 76, 115, 123, **62**

Railways, 58, 93-94, 106
Range, cooking, 48, 89, **89**
Real Property Act (1858), 55
Redruth (North Burra), 43
Rees, Rowland (architect), 100, 123, **101**
Regent Street, 35
Rental accommodation, 16, 30, 35, 37, 39, 48, 68, 94, 97, 123, 108, **45**
Richardson H.C. (architect), 78, 124, **77**
Richardson House, **60**
Richman House, **64**
Right of way, 47, 50
Ritchie, Mary, 31
River Torrens. See Torrens
Roads. See Streets

Roof coverings, corrugated iron, 23, 43, 59, 65, 70, 88; cost, 65; flat iron, 23; slate, 20, 23, 61, 65, 70, 73; thatch, 5, 6, 7, 23, 65, **24**; wooden shingles, 23, 31, 40, 43, 65

Roof types, gable (saddle-back), 19, 22, 23, 51; hipped, 23, 70, 109; lean-to (skillion), 23, 40, 68, 102; low profile, 23, 70, 73, 88; massive, 85-88, **87**; M-shaped, 73, 82, 97

Room numbers. See Dwelling characteristics

Rosetta Place, 93

Roughcast panels, 85

Rounsevell, William, 73; house, 73, 76, 78, 116, **76**

Row cottages. See Cottages

Rubble walls, 40, 59

Rugless, Charles, 82; house, 79, 82-83, **82**

Rundle Street, 6, 7, 10, 11, **12**

Saddle-back roof. See Roof

Sample area of Kingston Map (1842), 4, 12-18, 22, 35, 48, **14, 15, 18**. See also Kingston Map

Sandstone. See Stonework

Scandrett, Mrs., 44

Scots Church, North Terrace, 93

Scullery, 48, 58, 73-76, 78, 102, 108, 113, 118

Self-sufficiency in building, 4, 5

Semaphore, 55

Semi-basement, 96, 102, **103, 104, 106**

Semi-detached dwellings, 14, 16, 35, 48, 50, 51, 109-118. See also Houses, semi-detached and Maisonettes

Servants, 68, 70, 85, 97, 102; rooms, 27, 78, 97, 102, 108

Set-back from street, 17, 23, 32, 46, 51, 113, 116

Sewers, 11, 47, 50, 51, 58, 79, 88, 108; Act (1878), **112**

Shaw, James (artist), **56, 60**

Shaw, Norman (architect), 124

Shops, attached to dwelling, 94, 100

Shower, 78, 90, **91**

Shutters, 73

Simpson, A. & Son, 89-91, 124, **89-91**

Skylight, 37, 45, 105

Sink, kitchen and scullery, 48, 51, 58, 73, 78, 82, 97, 108, 113, **112**

Slab (wood pailing) houses, 8, 11, 23, 25, 27, **26**; construction method, 25

Slate, 61, 63, 78; cost, 65, 123; roofs, 20, 65, 73

Smith City Survey, 11, 16, 36, 121-122, **36**

Solid construction, trends towards, 16, 23, 59

Somerton, 111

Sorel, M., 65

South Adelaide, 4, 11; early development, 12, 22, 36, 47

South Australian Company, 8, 61

South Australian Gas Co., 58-59

South Australian Housing Trust, 48

South Australian Mining Association, 39

The Southern Australian, 4

South Terrace, 4, 11, 47, 50, 108

Soward, George K. (architect), 73, 82, 83, 116, 123, **116-117**

Speculation, land and building, 3, 4, 35-36, 37, 46, 47, 56, 93, 94, 96, 111, 116

Spital cottage, Scotland, 19-20, 22, **20**

Squares, Adelaide, 94, 96, **92**; London, 94, 96; Bath, 96

Staircase, 78, 96, 97, 102, 113, 116

Stamford Court, 50

'Starter' house, 22

Stephens, Edward, 11

Stepney, 61

Stone/brick dwellings, early, 10, 14, 16, 23, 37, 48, 50, 70

Stonework, 19, 20, 25, 27, 31, 79; bluestone, 59-60, 73, 123; cost, 61; freestone, 51, 60, 63, 85, 123; limestone, 59-60, 85; sandstone, 60; tuck pointing, 60

Stoves, 48, 59, 89-90, 97, **89**

Streets, poor condition, 11, 58; secondary, 4, 11, 14, 16, 35-36, 39, 46, 47, 50, **36**; terraces, 94; wide, 17, 96

Street lighting, electricity, 59; gas, 58

Stucco, 61, 71, 79, 115, **64**

Suburban development, 36, 47, 55, 56, 58, 93-94, 111, 122

The Suburban Gardener and Villa Companion, 111

Summer room in basement, 70, 102, **71, 103-104**

Swann, James, cottage, 68, **69**

Symmetry in design, 27, 32, 40, 66-68, 70, 73, 79, 82, **60, 66, 69, 76, 82**

Synagogue Place, 44

Tapleys Hill, 59

Tapson, Thomas, 94

Taylor & Forgie (builders), 73

Tealey, J.J. (builder), 113

Teatree Gully, 60

Telephone service, 59, 88

Temporary shelters, 10, 11, 14, 23

Tents, 4, 6, 8

Terraced house, 35, 47, 48, 93-109, 111, 113, 124; Adelaide's longest, 94, **107**; English plan, 94, 96, 100, 102; key house, 94, 96, 97, 102; Sydney, 109; three storey, 106, **108**

Terraces (houses), Albert Houses, London, 96; Albert Terrace, 94, **109**; Alexandra Terrace, 102, 105, **103-105**; Botanic Chambers, 102, 108, **106**; four houses, South Tce., 108-109, 115, **110-111**; Glenelg Terrace, 102, **104**; Landrowna Terrace, 94, **107**; Marine Residences, 106, **108**; nine houses, Adelaide, 108, **109**; seven houses, Glenelg, 100, 102, **101**; six houses, North Tce., **95**; three houses, Glenelg, 100, 102, **98-100**

Terraces (streets), 94

Thatch roofs, 5, 6, 7, 23, **24**

Thebarton, 55, 58

Timber-framed houses, 60, 83

Thebarton cottage, 22, 23, 25, 26-27, 32, **28-29**

Thorndon Park reservoir, 58

Tiled verandah, 61, 78

Timber dwellings, early, 10, 14, 16, 23, 35, 59

Tims, William (builder), 32

Tiver's row cottages, 43-44, **44**

Torrens River, 4, 6, 11, 39, 55, 58, 67, 96

Torrens system of land registration, 55

Torrens Valley, 60

Tradesmen, 5, 22, 25

Trinity Church, North Terrace, 11

Triple-fronted houses, 78, 83

Tuck-pointed stonework, 60

Unley, 58, 70; Municipality of, 79

Urban development, 47, 55, 56, 58, 96

Ventilators in roof, 48, 109

Venting pipe, 79, **67, 112**

Verandahs, 11, 14, 17, 35, 46, 51, 65, 68, 70, 71, 73, 79, 96, 97, 106, **63**; at rear, 47-48, 51, 78, 85, 97; returned, 78, 83, 85, 118, **77, 84**; tile and slate paved, 61, 78

Vernacular design, 97

Victoria Square, 4, 14, 94, **95**

Victorian era, 36, 63, 70, 79, 88, 102, 118
Villa, 19, 48, 51, 73, 78, 79, 83, 97, **74-75, 83, 84-85**; two-storey, 78, **80-81**
Villages, 55, 68, 70
von Mueller, Dr. Ferdinand J.H., 25, 121; cottage, 16, 20, 23, 25-26, 27, **26**

Wakefield, Edward Gibbon, 3
Walkerville, 55, 68
Walking, 58, 93, 96
Walkway between cottages, 50
Wark G.J. (builder), 50
Wash house, integrated, 88. See also Outbuildings and Laundry
Washing machines, 91

Washing troughs, 88, 91, 108, **90**
Water, cost, 45, 58; early supplies, 7, 11, 43, 45, 58, 67, 73; first reservoirs, 58; reticulated, 58, 79, 88, 105, 108
Waterhouse, G.M., 93
Watertanks, 34, 45, 65, 73, 82, 100, 123
Watson, Henry, prefabricated cottage, 12, 120
W.C., attached to house, 47-48, 51, 85, 105, 108, 115; outhouse, 79, 82, 115
Weindenhofer, J.H., 65
Wellington Square, 96
Wells, 11, 58, 100
West Terrace, 12
White, John, 16
Whitmore Square, 4, 94
Willunga, 55; slate, 23, 61, 123
Wilson, George Blakiston, 25

Windows, bay, 73, 78, 83, 109; casement sashes, 7, 8, 27, 31, 32, 43; dormer, 97, 109; double-hung sashes, 22, 27, 32, 97, **62, 64**; facing side boundary, 37, 50, 51; French, 70, 82, 96, 102, 116; paired, 79, 83; size, 44, 79; skylight, 37, 45, 105; unglazed, 7, 8, 22
Wood dwellings, early, 10, 14, 16, 23, 35, 59
Wood, solid fuel, 50, 78, 89, 123; storage, 16, 45, 67
Woods, Edward J. (architect), 47, 85, 108, 112, 115, 122, **48-49, 64, 86-87, 110-111, 114-115**
Woodville, 55, 106
Wren, Christopher (architect), 96
Wright Street, 12, 17, 50, 51
Wringers, 91